The Untold History of the United States

Young Readers Edition, Volume 1, 1898–1945

Also written by Oliver Stone

On History: Tariq Ali and Oliver Stone in Conversation

A Child's Night Dream

Also written by Peter Kuznick

Rethinking the Atomic Bombings of Hiroshima and Nagasaki:
Japanese and American Perspectives (in Japanese, with Akira Kimura)

Nuclear Power and Hiroshima:
The Truth Behind the Peaceful Use of Nuclear Power
(in Japanese, with Yuki Tanaka)

Beyond the Laboratory: Scientists as Political Activists in 1930s America

Rethinking Cold War Culture (with James Gilbert)

Also written by Oliver Stone and Peter Kuznick

The Untold History of the United States

Let's Talk About War: Let's Talk About What War Really Is
(in Japanese, with Satoko Oka Norimatsu)

Also by Susan Campbell Bartoletti

They Called Themselves the K.K.K.:
The Birth of an American Terrorist Group

Hitler Youth: Growing Up in Hitler's Shadow

Black Potatoes: The Story of the Great Irish Famine, 1845–1850

The Untold History of the United States

Young Readers Edition, Volume 1, 1898–1945

Written by
OLIVER STONE and PETER KUZNICK

Adapted by
SUSAN CAMPBELL BARTOLETTI

ATHENEUM BOOKS FOR YOUNG READERS

New York London Toronto Sydney New Delhi

ATHENEUM BOOKS FOR YOUNG READERS

An imprint of Simon & Schuster Children's Publishing Division

1230 Avenue of the Americas, New York, New York 10020

Text copyright © 2014 by Secret History, LLC, and Susan Campbell
Bartoletti

Adapted from Gallery Books' *The Untold History of the United States* copyright
© 2012 by Secret History, LLC

Jacket illustration of Uncle Sam copyright © 2012 by Showtime Networks,
Inc.

ATHENEUM BOOKS FOR YOUNG READERS is a registered trademark of
Simon & Schuster, Inc.

Atheneum logo is a trademark of Simon & Schuster, Inc.

For information about special discounts for bulk purchases, please contact
Simon & Schuster Special Sales at 1-866-506-1949 or
business@simonandschuster.com.

The Simon & Schuster Speakers Bureau can bring authors to your live event.
For more information or to book an event, contact the Simon & Schuster
Speakers Bureau at 1-866-248-3049 or visit our website at
www.simonspeakers.com.

Jacket design by Sonia Chaghatzbanian, interior design by Vikki Sheatsley

Vetted by Eric Singer

The text for this book is set in Bembo.

Manufactured in the United States of America

1114 FFG

First Edition

10 9 8 7 6 5 4 3 2 1

CIP data for this book is available from the Library of Congress.

ISBN 978-1-4814-2173-7

ISBN 978-1-4814-2175-1 (eBook)

To our children—Tara, Michael, Sean, Lexie, Sara, and Asmara—
and the better world that they and all children deserve
—O. S. and P. K.

To my eighth-grade students,
all grown up now and making the world a better place
—S. C. B.

Contents

Foreword

I was pleased and excited when I was approached to adapt Oliver Stone and Peter Kuznick's *The Untold History of the United States* for younger readers. I knew I would have to fasten my seat belt in order to complete a project of this scope.

I did not research and write this book in the usual sense. In this edition, you'll see that the words, opinions, facts, conclusions, and themes of the adult version are shared as well. You'll also see where I've added context, exploring some areas in greater detail and incorporating additional anecdotes while retaining the verve of the adult edition. You'll see additional images.

As I worked through the text, I was reminded with great pleasure of how similar and how fluid the rhythms of history and memory are, how they dip in and out and fold back on themselves, gathering energy and then pressing forward. History is quite a thrill ride! I tried to retain as much of that energy as possible, too.

I've long been drawn to the dark side of history. In my own work, I often look for the untold stories from history that have been marginalized, at best, or absent altogether. I especially look for stories where our actions don't match the words of our US Constitution and those times when we have strayed from our country's mission. These are the stories that have often fallen into the gaps. By shining a light on these dark moments, we dispel the darkness and, with great hope, we expose the truth.

History inspires me. It helps me find role models. It helps me see the sort of person I'd like to be—as well as the sort of person I don't want to be. As I adapted this text, I found myself thinking about something our former National Ambassador for Young People's Literature Katherine Paterson once said, "Though truth is seldom comfortable, it is, finally, the strongest comfort."

—*Susan Campbell Bartoletti*

The United States' run as the most powerful and dominant nation the world has ever seen has been marked by proud achievements and terrible disappointments. It is the latter story—the darker, untold story of US history—that we explore in the following pages.

We didn't try to tell all of US history. That would be an impossible task. We didn't focus extensively on many of the things the United States has done right. There are libraries full of books dedicated to that purpose and school curricula that trumpet US achievements.

Instead, we focus a spotlight on the ways we believe the United States has betrayed its mission and the ideals of its own Constitution. We do so with great faith that there is still time to correct those errors as we move forward into the twenty-first century, and beyond.

Have you ever wondered why our country has military bases in every region of the globe, totaling nearly 1,000 by some counts? Why does the United States spend almost as much on its military as the rest of the world combined? Why does America still possess thousands of nuclear weapons, many on hair-trigger alert, even though no nation poses an imminent threat? Why is the gap between the rich and the poor greater in the United States than in any other developed country? Why is the United States the only advanced nation without a universal health care program?

Why, according to recent studies, do eighty-five people in the world control more wealth than the poorest 3.5 billion? Why is a tiny minority of wealthy Americans allowed to exert so much control over US domestic politics, foreign policy, and media while the great masses see a diminution of their real power and standards of living? Why do the richest 1 percent of Americans have more wealth than the poorest 90 percent?

Why have Americans submitted to levels of surveillance, government intrusion, abuse of civil liberties, and loss of privacy that would have appalled the Founding Fathers and earlier generations?

Why does the United States have a lower percentage of unionized workers than any other advanced industrial democracy? Why do African Americans and Latinos still face discrimination?

Why, in our country, are those who are driven by personal greed and self-interest empowered over those who extol social values like kindness, generosity, compassion, sharing, empathy, and community building?

And why has it become so hard for the great majority of Americans to imagine a world that is substantially different from, and better than, what exists today?

Do you ever wish someone would put the country back on the right track? As you read this book, you will meet some of the individuals who have tried to do just that—sometimes heroically. You will learn about the social movements they participated in. You'll also meet the individuals who fought against change, often with tragic results. And you'll discover the social forces and conditions that make progressive reform so difficult to achieve.

These are only a few of the questions that we will address in this series. Although we can't hope to answer all of them, we hope to present the historical background that will enable you to explore these topics more deeply on your own.

—*Oliver Stone and Peter Kuznick*

INTRODUCTION

Rebirth of a Nation

1

Writing History with Lightning

The Birth of a Nation

It was 1915, and chairs lined the long Central Hall on the second floor of the White House. The drapes were drawn, the gaslights turned down. A film projector clicked and whirred, its beam of light focused on the far wall like the great eye of a cyclops.

President Woodrow Wilson, the twenty-eighth president of the United States, and his cabinet members and their families had gathered together to watch the first movie ever shown in the White House. The movie was called *The Birth of a Nation*. It was directed by D. W. Griffith.

The three-hour-long movie was a black-and-white silent film; it had no spoken dialogue. Actors used gestures and pantomime to convey what they wanted to say. During key moments, title cards summarized the action. In short, *The Birth of a Nation* was a story told without words.

Woodrow Wilson and the rest of the moviegoers that night didn't

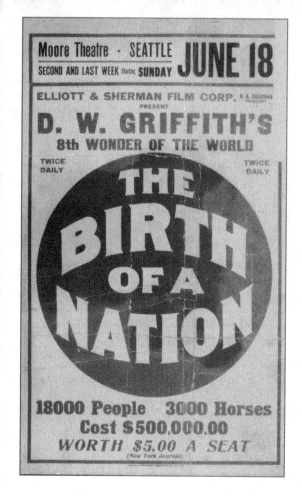

Moore Theatre · SEATTLE **JUNE 18**
SECOND AND LAST WEEK Starting SUNDAY

ELLIOTT & SHERMAN FILM CORP.

PRESENT

D. W. GRIFFITH'S

8th WONDER OF THE WORLD

TWICE DAILY

TWICE DAILY

THE BIRTH OF A NATION

18000 People   3000 Horses
Cost $500,000.00
WORTH $5.00 A SEAT
(New York Journal)

Movie poster for *The Birth of a Nation.*

need words. They knew the setting, the characters, and the plot. They knew the good guys—and the villains. The movie was based on a popular book called *The Clansman: An Historical Romance of the Ku Klux Klan*, a novel written by a Southern white Baptist minister named Thomas Dixon Jr.

Using the worst racial stereotypes, Dixon tells a story that encompasses the antebellum South, the Civil War, Lincoln's assassination, Reconstruction, and the rise of the Ku Klux Klan. The heroic Klansmen gallop in to rescue helpless white Southern women from the clutches of lustful black men.

Dixon claimed that his novel was the "true story of the Ku Klux Klan conspiracy that overturned the Reconstruction government." But it was the exact opposite of the truth, and the president of the United States was screening it in the nation's capital.

The Facts of Reconstruction and the Ku Klux Klan

The actual record of Reconstruction and the Ku Klux Klan reveals a different story: The Ku Klux Klan formed in Tennessee in 1866, one year after the Civil War ended. Soon Klan groups spread across the South. Its members committed themselves to the use of physical violence in order to maintain white supremacy and violate the civil rights of others.

The Klan attacked—and killed—black Americans who dared to speak out and who exercised their right to earn a living, buy land, attend school, worship as they pleased, and vote (a right granted to black men nation-wide in 1870 by the Fifteenth Amendment). They attacked and killed white Americans who supported the rights of black Americans and who didn't vote the way the Klan wanted.

The Klan's first wave of violence swept over the South from 1866 through 1871. That year, the federal government sent troops to arrest Klansmen and restore peace. For eight months, a joint committee of US senators and representatives investigated. They gathered testimonies, held trials, and handed down sentences.

Two members of the Ku Klux Klan in their disguises.

But it was too little too late. Most of the arrested Klansmen paid small fines and received minimal sentences. Many received suspended sentences and a warning. Often charges were simply dropped. Some Klansmen went into hiding or fled to avoid punishment. Many were pardoned.

By 1872, the federal government succeeded in breaking up the Klan, but it couldn't dissolve white supremacists' commitment to control elections and the lives of African Americans. That commitment led to the resurgence of the Klan in the 1920s in reaction to foreign immigration, and again in 1960 as a reaction to the civil rights movement.

Dixon's novel and D. W. Griffith's movie adaptation of it ignored the brutal realities of the Ku Klux Klan. Instead, the Klansmen were portrayed as noble white-robed knights who reluctantly took the law into their own hands in order to rescue white Southerners, especially "helpless" white women, from racial violence and what whites termed "Negro rule."

This view of history is false. Southern white women were not helpless. They showed physical and emotional strength as they worked and managed businesses and farms while their husbands, fathers, and sons fought in the war.

"Negro rule," or the notion that the newly freed and enfranchised black Americans would dominate and rule over white Americans, was true only in the wild imaginations of fearful whites—and perhaps in the wistful imaginations of black Americans who yearned to more fundamentally upset American racial hierarchy.

The Birth of a Nation premiered in Los Angeles and opened to a packed house at New York's Liberty Theater on March 3, 1915. Soon the popular film opened in theaters across the country. African Americans who attended the movie deplored the ugly portrayal of the freed people—those who could have very well been their parents or grandparents—as lawless, ignorant, amoral, lecherous, and violent characters.

The National Association for the Advancement of Colored People (NAACP) protested the movie vociferously. It cataloged the film's numerous falsehoods and attempted to educate the public about the dire circumstance blacks faced in the post–Civil War South.

Despite the protests and educational campaigns—and despite the blatant disregard for the historical record—the film became a phenomenal box-office hit.

In 1915, the film inspired a group of white Southern men to climb to the top of Stone Mountain in Georgia and burn a cross. With this cross burning, the Ku Klux Klan, disbanded since 1872, rose again. The Klan used the movie to launch a recruiting campaign. Soon the group spread throughout the United States, and membership exploded to more than five million.

The second wave of Klansmen renewed the fight to maintain white supremacy throughout the United States. They portrayed themselves as a pro-Christian, pro-American brotherhood. They added Catholics, Jews, immigrants, liberals, welfare recipients, and labor unions to their list of hated targets.

That same year, 1915, fifty-six blacks and thirteen whites were lynched. Five were women.

The Embellished History

Woodrow Wilson sat in the darkened Central Hall, watching the closing scenes of *The Birth of a Nation*. In these scenes, Ku Klux Klan members ride in on their horses to rescue a poor white family from corrupt federal soldiers. The Klansmen take guns away from the freedmen and intimidate black voters at the polls. In this way, the Klansmen believe they have restored peace to South Carolina. The movie's final title card appears: *Liberty and union, one and inseparable, now and forever.*

After the final credits, the film projector whirred and clicked to the end of the reel. Someone must have asked the president what he thought about the movie, because an enthusiastic Wilson reportedly said, "It is like writing history with Lightning and my only regret is that it is all so terribly true."

Except it wasn't.

It was all so terribly untrue.

How did such a movie, one filled with so much misinformation disguised as fact, make its way to the White House? And, perhaps more disturbing, why did the president of the United States, a man with a PhD from Johns Hopkins University who went on to become president of Princeton University, accept the film's version of history so easily?

President Wilson screened *The Birth of a Nation* as a personal favor to his close friend Thomas Dixon Jr. The president was also a historian who wrote many works, including the five-volume *A History of the American People*, published in 1902, and *The New Freedom: A Call for the Emancipation of the Generous Energies of a People*, published in 1913. This latter work, *The New Freedom*, served as a cornerstone to his presidential campaign.

There is little doubt that the story told in *The Birth of a Nation* appealed to Woodrow Wilson, given his strong Southern heritage. The son of a Presbyterian minister, Wilson was born in Virginia in 1856 and was raised in Georgia and South Carolina. He was old enough to appreciate the horrors of a war that left at least 750,000 soldiers dead on both sides and one million wounded.

Like his Southern forebears, Wilson grew up to regret the war's outcome and the radical changes it brought—namely, the freedmen's right to vote and receive equal protections under the law.

During his presidential campaign, Wilson pledged to support justice for black Americans. "Should I become President of the United States they may count upon me for absolute fair dealing for everything by which I could assist in advancing the interests of their race."

To many African Americans, Wilson betrayed that promise after his inauguration when, in line with Jim Crow laws that had separated blacks from whites since 1876, he too encouraged the separation of races. Although federal agencies were not segregated and black and white employees had worked side by side in the same offices for more than fifty years, Wilson permitted the offices of the Postmaster General, the Treasury, and the US Navy to separate black workers from white workers. The cafeterias and restrooms were segregated too. All federal job applicants had to submit photographs so that it would be easier to tell each applicant's race.

Angry at the obvious discrimination, African-American leaders pressed Wilson to end discrimination based on a person's color. Wilson responded,

"It is as far as possible from being a movement against the negroes. I sincerely believe it to be in their interest. [S]egregation is not humiliating but a benefit, and ought to be regarded so by you gentlemen."

Both the novel *The Clansman* and the movie *The Birth of a Nation* distorted the history of race relations and reshaped it into a story that many people, including Wilson, believed. Ultimately, Wilson's belief in white supremacy may have influenced his domestic policies.

Wilson, his supporters, and many other white Americans believed *The Birth of a Nation* because it *felt* true to them. History is storytelling. Usually, it's the winners who get to write it. In this case, even though the South lost the Civil War, Southerners had a big say in the history that was taught in the United States over the past 150 years. And that history has so often served to empower whites and disenfranchise black Americans.

2

The Rumblings of Revolution

Woodrow Wilson's views were also shaped by his hatred of revolution. He opposed radical change—change that transformed the basic structure of society—in any form. In 1889, he wrote: "In politics nothing radically novel may safely be attempted. No result of value can ever be reached . . . except through slow and gradual development." He liked the American Revolution because he believed it wasn't revolutionary at all. But he despised the French Revolution. It had turned society upside down. He believed change should come slowly and in small steps. For that same reason he disapproved of workers' strikes and farmers' rebellions. His sympathies instead lay with businessmen and moderate reformers.

But workers and farmers knew that strikes and uprisings had often helped them achieve higher pay and better working conditions. This was especially true in the last three turbulent decades of the nineteenth century.

The Paris Commune:
An Example for American Workers

No uprising during those years was more radical than the one that swept Paris in 1871. The previous year, France had declared war on Prussia. But the French army proved no match for the Prussians, who soon surrounded Paris. Fearing for their lives, French officials fled from the city and set up shop in nearby Versailles. With the old government gone, the citizens of Paris took matters into their own hands. They elected a new government called "the Paris Commune." It would be an experiment the likes of which the world had never seen.

Governments had almost always acted on behalf of the wealthy and powerful. Their highest priority was to safeguard private property rights and maintain order. But the commune was a government run by working people, in the interests of the workers and the poor. It made reforms that most governments would never consider—the kind that Wilson would denounce as revolutionary and improper.

The Paris Commune established free schools for the children of working people. And even more extraordinary for the time, the schools were open to girls as well as boys.

The new government cut the high salaries of government workers down to the level of average workers. It took empty homes and apartments and gave them to homeless people. It seized unused workshops and factories and gave them to trade unions—groups of workers who united to bargain for higher pay and better working conditions—to run together and share the profits. It prevented employers from punishing workers like they used to do by cutting their pay. And it demanded a complete separation between church and state.

The former government bided its time while waiting for its chance to return to Paris. It couldn't allow such a radical government, one so disrespectful of private property, to succeed. Workers everywhere might follow the Parisians' example. The Versailles army invaded Paris in late May.

The workers of Paris, known as Communards, fought bravely, but they were outgunned. The Commune fell after seventy-three days. Almost 900 Versailles soldiers lay dead alongside between 20,000 to 25,000 Parisian citizens. But the uprising would live on in the memory and imagination of workers everywhere, including those in the United States.

Karl Marx, the brilliant German-Jewish revolutionary thinker and author of the famous 1848 *Communist Manifesto*, later praised the Communards for "storming heaven." But for others, the Paris Commune represented not the stuff of dreams, but the stuff of nightmares. When American capitalists—the rich people who owned the factories, banks, and big farms—thought about what the Parisian workers had done, it sent shivers down their spines. They went to bed at night praying that something like that would never happen in the United States. But they knew that if American workers and farmers were hungry and miserable and mistreated, the same thing would happen here too. It was just a matter of time.

The Rumblings of Protest

The end of the civil war in 1865 cleared the way for an era of rapid growth and change. New factories opened. Cities swelled with recently arrived people, some of whom came from the farms. Others pulled up stakes in their old countries, said good-bye to friends and relatives, and moved to America in hopes of a better life. Recently freed black slaves tried to build new lives. They savored the taste of freedom, but faced new obstacles everywhere they turned.

In 1873, conditions abruptly worsened in the United States. An economic depression hit the country. Depressions always brought hard times, especially for working people. The number of workers who couldn't find work increased sharply. Those who had jobs saw their pay cut. Many went hungry. Others lost their homes and farms. The year 1873 wasn't America's first depression, and it wouldn't be its last. Depressions occurred with unfortunate regularity— in 1819, 1837, 1857, 1873, 1883, 1893, 1920, and 1929. Some lasted many years.

The 1873 depression sent the economy into a tailspin. Railroads, which had spurred the post–Civil War economic growth, were not immune to the effects of the depression. Railroad owners decided to cut workers' pay in order to make sure that their own profits remained strong.

By the summer of 1877, workers had had enough. Their pay was low, their hours long—some were forced to work as many as eighteen hours a day—and the paltry pay they did receive was sometimes delayed for months. When the B&O Railroad announced on July 11 that workers' wages would be cut another 10 percent, crews stopped their trains in the middle of the tracks in West Virginia, shutting down much of the freight traffic between Baltimore and the Midwest.

The Great Railroad Strike of 1877 had begun. Railroad workers simply walked off their jobs and refused to work until employers restored their stolen wages.

"The American Commune"

As the strike spread along the railroad line to other parts of the country, mothers and wives of workers joined the protests. Local authorities called out the police and militias to restore order. But there was little they could do. The community backed the strikers, knowing they had good reason to refuse to work. Some of the militiamen stood with the strikers, too. "Many of us have reason to know what long hours and low pay mean," said one officer, "and any movement that aims at one or the other will have our sympathy and support. We may be militiamen, but we are workmen first."

Workers in other industries, equally frustrated, came out in large numbers to show their solidarity. Some were armed. They had fought in the Civil War, and they would fight again if they had to. Many workers in other trades also went on strike against their own bosses.

Fearing a greater rebellion, the governor of West Virginia and the president of B&O both asked President Rutherford B. Hayes to send federal troops to break the strike. Hayes was deeply indebted to the railroad owners for helping put him in the White House during the hotly contested 1876 election. He granted the owners' request.

For the second time in US history, federal troops were called out in peacetime, and they were being called out against law-abiding American citizens.

And the fight didn't end there. Maryland's governor ordered the state's National Guard's troops to provide support for the federal troops in West Virginia. When workers heard what was about to happen, thousands rushed to Baltimore's Camden Station to prevent the troops from boarding trains. The city became a battle zone, with more federal

In this August 11, 1877 engraving from Frank Leslie's *Illustrated Newspaper*, various scenes from the Great Railroad Strike are shown.

troops sent at the president's order. By the time a tentative peace was reached on July 23, thirteen people had been killed and fifty wounded.

The *National Republican* newspaper of Washington, DC, carried an editorial titled "The American Commune," which stated, "The fact is clearly manifest that communistic ideas are very widely entertained in America by the workmen employed in mines and factories and by the railroads."

There was much truth to this claim. Why, workers were beginning to wonder, should some people have so much more wealth and power than others? The widening gap between rich and poor seemed to undermine America's core republican beliefs.

The enormous and growing gulf

Poet Walt Whitman celebrated American progress, but he described the excesses of capitalism as "a sort of anti-democratic disease and monstrosity."

between wealthy capitalists and impoverished workers and farmers shook the foundations of Americans' democratic ideals. Most farmers and workers hated that a handful of bankers and industrialists, along with their stable of rubber-stamp legislators and judges, should run the country. Poet Walt Whitman captured that feeling when he described the excesses of capitalism as "a sort of anti-democratic disease and monstrosity." Depressions, like the one the country was enduring in the 1870s, only made the injustices more obvious.

Similar battles occurred all over the country. In Pittsburgh, after troops fired into a crowd killing between ten to twenty people, angry citizens destroyed eleven and a half miles of railroad cars.

In St. Louis, millworkers, miners, steamship crews, steelworkers, iron smelters, and other factory workers walked off their jobs and joined railroad workers in a general strike. The St. Louis newspaper, *The St. Louis Republican*, newspaper exclaimed, "It is wrong to call this a strike; it is a labor revolution."

The uprisings struck fear in the hearts of business owners and government officials. They worried that American workers were following in the path of the Parisian revolutionaries.

3

"Workingmen, to Arms!"

In 1888, Edward Bellamy's novel *Looking Backward* captured the imagination of Americans young and old, rich and poor. It gave them an idea of how the world could be better. The book struck a chord with readers, especially in a country that had undergone more than a decade of what seemed like warfare between the rich and the poor.

In the novel, Julian West, a wealthy thirty-year-old Bostonian, is hypnotized in 1887 in order to fall asleep but then wake up in the year 2000. He is slowly introduced into a new world. And what a world it is!

Unlike the world of 1887—in which a handful of people gobbled up more and more of the wealth, and strikes by angry workers caused chaos and disruption—the new world is one in which everyone gets along. Instead of people competing with one another for the necessities of life, they instead cooperate in solving problems and share equally what the workers and farmers produce. Everyone receives the same pay, regardless of who they are and what kind of work they perform. Money does not motivate them, but the appreciation of their fellow citizens, and the personal satisfaction that comes from doing well and contributing to society, does. Poverty has been eliminated once and for all.

Julian happily adapts to his new world, and he even falls in love with the great-granddaughter of the woman he was engaged to marry in 1887. But one day he wakes up back in the world of 1887. Everything seems wrong to him. He tried to explain to others that the hunger and poverty and suffering that surrounds them are unnecessary. There is a better way to do things that will make everyone's life happier and more fulfilling. But no one will listen. Thankfully, Julian awakes back in 2000. The return to 1887 had been a nightmare.

Bellamy's book was known as a utopian socialist novel. It imagined a world that did not yet exist, but its goal was to show readers that a different world was possible. It challenged them to dream about the way the world should really be. And what was most remarkable about it was that it was enormously popular. In fact, no novel in the nineteenth century sold more copies, except for *Uncle Tom's Cabin*. People were desperate for change, and Bellamy offered a vision.

"The Concern of All"

Looking back on the period, the reformer Ida Tarbell recalled that "the eighties dripped with blood." Though the decade did not literally drip with blood, workers questioned the fairness of a society that favored the wealthy—the new corporate and banking elite—over the overwhelming majority of workers and farmers.

They searched for a way to change things. In the 1880s, a new labor union—the Knights of Labor—exploded onto the scene. The Knights tried to unite all the working people in a region into one big union. Everyone was invited to join regardless of race, gender, or place of birth. Only bankers, speculators, lawyers, gamblers, and liquor salesmen were excluded. Businessmen were judged on a case-by-case basis.

The Knights' motto was "an injury to one is the concern of all." They mistrusted the capitalist system and called for peaceful reform.

The Knights captured the nation's attention when they went on strike against Jay Gould's 15,000-mile railroad network in 1885. Gould was no ordinary robber baron. He had once bragged that he could "hire one half of the working class to kill the other half" and was perhaps the most hated man in the country.

Jay Gould, railroad tycoon. He was one of the ten wealthiest men in the country in 1892.

Gould's acceptance of the Knights' demands, in what the business newspaper *Bradstreet's* called a "complete surrender," shocked the nation. Nothing like this had ever happened before. Knights' membership skyrocketed around the country, jumping from 103,000 on July 1, 1885 to more than 700,000 a year later. There seemed to be no limits to its potential for growth. Workers believed they had discovered a way to fight. And win.

Haymarket Massacre

Events in Chicago in May 1886 dealt a crushing blow to the reform movement. On May 1, workers around the country went on strike in hopes of achieving an eight-hour workday. Workers had long been demanding shorter working hours. Now they were doing something about it.

Chicago workers were perhaps the most radical in the country. Their movement contained many anarchists, who believed that workers needed to defend themselves, with guns if necessary, against the army and the police. In Chicago, tens of thousands demonstrated for the eight-hour day. On May 3, Chicago police fired into a crowd of striking workers, killing several people.

News about the killings spread like wildfire across the city. Labor leaders rushed to printing presses and made flyers urging workers to unite against their employers and the police. One read:

> WORKINGMEN, TO ARMS!!! The masters sent out their
> bloodhounds—the police; they killed . . . your brothers at [the
> factory] this afternoon. They killed the poor wretches because
> they, like you, had the courage to disobey the supreme will of
> your bosses . . . To arms we call you, to arms!

The next evening, May 4, protesters gathered in Chicago's Haymarket Square at the center of the city's lumber and meatpacking district. The rally of less than 3,000 was peaceful as speakers condemned the murders from the previous day and demanded the eight-hour day. Chicago's mayor was in the audience. He saw that there was no threat of violence and instructed the police chief to dismiss his men. A thunderstorm sent most people home early. When only a few hundred protesters remained and the last speaker was finishing up, 180 policemen suddenly entered the square and demanded everyone leave. At that moment, a bomb exploded, killing 7 police officers and wounding 66. Nobody knew who threw it. The police panicked and started to fire blindly into the crowd, killing three and wounding dozens.

One police official told the *Chicago Tribune* "a very large number of the police were wounded by each other's revolvers. . . . It was every man for

Haymarket Riot, May 1886. Authorities used the death of
policemen in Haymarket Square to crush organized labor. Soon
workers, reformers, and immigrants across the nation were
being targeted.

himself, and while some got two or three squares away, the rest emptied their
revolvers, mainly into each other."

A national panic ensued. Newspapers around the country sounded the
alarm. The *Chicago Tribune* called on Congress to deport troublemakers and
restrict immigration to keep out "foreign savages, with their dynamite bombs
and anarchic purposes." In the eyes of Mother Jones, one of the country's
most famous labor leaders, "The city went insane."

Thereafter, workers, unions, immigrants, and reformers everywhere were
targeted and persecuted in what became America's first "Red Scare"—a
widespread campaign to smear all reformers with the brush of disloyalty and
sedition. The greatest casualty was the Knights of Labor. Even though the
Knights had always rejected violence and sought peaceful change, society's

leaders saw them as the greatest threat. Knights' meetings were broken up. Their members were fired from jobs and put on blacklists. Their leaders were threatened and sometimes jailed.

The capitalists had won—for now.

Private Greed versus Greater Good

Discontent was rife among farmers too, especially the ones who organized the farmers' alliances in the 1880s and the People's Party, or Populists, in the 1890s. The People's Party adopted a platform at its first convention in Omaha, Nebraska, in 1892 that declared, "The fruits of the toil of millions are boldly stolen to build up colossal fortunes for a few."

Populists, like the Knights, always differentiated between the productive classes—the farmers and workers—and the parasites—the bankers and speculators who lived off the labor of others.

Although the Populists' appeal was limited to parts of the South, Midwest, and West, they won almost 9 percent of the presidential vote in 1892. The People's Party carried five midwestern and western states and elected more than 1,500 candidates, including three governors, five senators, and ten congressmen. The Populists doubled their vote in 1894. Farmers, like workers, were looking for change.

And it was largely the middle class who devoured Bellamy's *Looking Backward*. Even they questioned whether individuals motivated by private greed could somehow produce a better society. Middle-class Americans had often sided with the railroad workers in the Great Railroad Strike of 1877.

Americans from all walks—workers, farmers, and middle class—clamored for change, and the future looked bright as the new century approached.

PART ONE

Roots of an Empire

All That Glitters

After the Civil War, the United States enjoyed economic growth and expansion during a time that became known as the Gilded Age. Industrialists amassed great fortunes: John D. Rockefeller in oil; Andrew Carnegie in steel; and bankers such as J. P. Morgan, who controlled many industries. Robber barons such as Jay Fisk and Jay Gould became rich through ruthless and unscrupulous business deals.

These wealthy capitalists were a minority of the population. In 1890, the United States had 12 million families. The majority of these families—11 million—earned an average of only $380 per year. Many were immigrants who lived in tenements and worked in the factories, mills, mines, and sweatshops.

Clouds of economic trouble, however, were gathering on the horizon, causing anxiety and unrest. The financial panic on Black Friday—May 5, 1893—triggered the nation's worst depression, which would last five long years. Within months, four million workers lost their jobs. Unemployment soon approached 20 percent.

In 1890, 91 percent of American families earned less than
$1,200 per year. The average income for this group was $380.
The lowest-paid workers were immigrants who lived in dire
housing conditions, shown here. To eke out a subsistence
living, many families required the wages of their children.

The nation debated the depression's causes. Some believed the 1893 depression resulted from overproduction. To fix the problem, these critics argued that the United States needed more overseas markets to absorb its growing surplus.

Socialists, trade unionists, and reformers believed the crisis of the 1890s resulted from *under*consumption. They proposed a different solution to fix the economy. They suggested that the industrialists should hire more workers and pay them a living wage so that the workers could afford to buy the goods produced by America's farms and factories.

But few capitalists endorsed that approach. They wanted cheap workers and foreign markets and natural resources. To ensure these things, they involved the United States in world affairs that would fundamentally transform the nation.

"A Splendid Little War"

American capitalists wanted to be able to buy raw materials from other countries. They also wanted to take advantage of the cheap labor in those countries. However, American capitalists needed the US government to build a modern steam-powered navy and bases around the world to supply that navy.

The US government granted their wish. In 1889, the United States annexed the harbor of the Pacific island of Pago Pago. Between 1890 and 1896, it built a new navy.

Mark Twain once quipped that the goal of every man was to get rich. "Dishonestly, if we can; honestly, if we must," he wrote in *The Revised Catechism* (1871).

Pago Pago was just the start. The United States then went after Hawaii. In 1893, American sugar planters toppled Hawaiian queen Liliuokalani. In her place, they installed an American named Sanford Dole, a cousin of pineapple magnate James Dole, as president. When the United States annexed Hawaii in 1898, President William McKinley enthusiastically justified it as "Manifest Destiny."

That same year, on April 25, 1898, the United States declared war against Spain, purportedly to deliver Cuba from Spanish tyranny.

The fighting began thousands of miles away in Manila, Philippines, one of Spain's few remaining colonies. There, on May 1, Commodore George Dewey destroyed the Spanish fleet.

Colonel Theodore Roosevelt led the Rough Riders unit during the 1898 Spanish-American War. He gained fame as a war hero.

One anti-imperialist noted, "Dewey took Manila with the loss of one man—and all our institutions."

This battle, which was later known as the Spanish-American War, was over in three months. It was, according to Secretary of State John Hay, "a splendid little war."

Not everyone thought the war was so splendid. On June 15, 1898, the Anti-Imperialist League tried to block the annexation of the Philippines and Puerto Rico, another of Spain's colonies. League members included such prominent individuals as Andrew Carnegie, Clarence Darrow, Mark Twain, Jane Addams, William James, William Dean Howells, and Samuel Gompers.

But the anti-imperialists' efforts were no match for a nation enthralled with the glory of war and the thrill of easy victory in the name of a righteous cause.

When the dust of the war settled, the United States had secured the beginnings of an overseas empire. It had annexed Hawaii and acquired Puerto Rico, Guam and the Philippines from Spain. The Philippines were the perfect refueling stop for American ships in Asia.

McKinley wavered about what to do with the Philippines after the war. The Treaty of Paris of 1898 ceded Puerto Rico to the United States, made Cuba a US protectorate, and stipulated that the United States would pay $20 million to Spain in exchange for the Philippines. The Spanish monarchy accepted the terms of the treaty on December 10, 1898, effectively ending the war. However, the treaty would not be ratified until four months later. As bitter debate about the meaning of the treaty raged in the US Senate, many Senators worried that expansion beyond American borders would turn the United States into an imperial power, just as Spain had been. The US Senate, painfully divided, ratified the treaty by only one vote more than the two thirds majority needed on April 11, 1899.

Walking the White House floor night after night and praying to "Almighty God" for guidance, McKinley opted to annex the islands, seizing upon the opportunity to civilize one of the world's "inferior" races, which Rudyard Kipling called the "white man's burden."

"To Rule, We Must Conquer"

Under the leadership of Emilio Aguinaldo, the Filipinos had been rebelling against Spanish rule for years. They naively believed the United States would help them gain independence. The Filipinos drafted a constitution and established a republic on January 23, 1899, with Aguinaldo as president.

On February 4, US forces opened fire in Manila. US newspapers reported that Filipinos had fired upon unarmed US soldiers in a completely unprovoked attack. Twenty-two soldiers were killed and 125–200 wounded. Filipino losses were estimated in the thousands.

Newspapers predicted that the attack would rally support for the imperial cause and 'ensure Senate approval of the Paris treaty that had ended the war. *The New York World* observed that the United States was "suddenly without warning, face to face with the actualities of empire. . . . To rule, we must conquer. To conquer, we must kill."

Pressure mounted on those who opposed the treaty to support the troops. General Charles Grosvenor, a congressman from Ohio, declared, "They have

In this January 1899 cartoon from *Puck* magazine, the blackboard reads, "The consent of the governed is a good thing in theory, but very rare in fact.—England has governed her colonies whether they consented or not. By not waiting for their consent, she has greatly advanced the world's civilization.—The US must govern its new territories with or without their consent until they can govern themselves."

fired on our flag. They have killed our soldiers. The blood of the slain cries from the ground for vengeance."

But Senator George Frisbie Hoar of Massachusetts warned that the United States would become a "vulgar, commonplace empire founded upon physical force, controlling subject races and vassal states, in which one class must forever rule and the other classes must forever obey."

Senator Hoar later observed that the United States "crushed the Republic that the Philippine people had set up for themselves, deprived them of their independence, and established there, by American power, a Government in which the people have no part, against their will."

Senator Richard Pettigrew called the betrayal of Filipino independence "the greatest international crime of the century."

Filipinos overwhelmingly supported the rebel forces. They provided them with food and shelter. The Americans responded with extraordinary brutality. Following one ambush, General Lloyd Wheaton ordered all towns within a twelve-mile radius destroyed and all their inhabitants killed.

In a surprise attack, Filipino rebels killed fifty-four of the seventy-four Americans stationed at Balangiga on the island of Samar. In retaliation, Colonel Jacob Smith ordered his troops to kill every Filipino over the age of ten and to turn the island into "a howling wilderness."

Some of the soldiers happily obliged. One soldier wrote home, saying, "Our fighting blood was up. . . . This shooting human beings beats rabbit hunting all to pieces." US officers herded hundreds of thousands of Filipinos into concentration camps.

One of the most vigorous backers of the US takeover of the Philippines was Senator Albert Beveridge of Indiana. He'd visited the Philippines to get a firsthand look at the situation.

In Washington, the Senate and others eagerly anticipated Beveridge's views. He addressed a crowded Senate chamber in early July 1900, offering one of the most colorful, blunt, and chauvinistic defenses on record of US imperial policy:

Soldiers riding down the street in Malolos, Philippines.

The bodies of murdered Filipinos.

The Philippines are ours forever. . . . This island empire is the last land left in all the oceans. . . . Our largest trade henceforth must be with Asia. The Pacific is our ocean. More and more Europe will manufacture the most of its needs, secure from its colonies the most it consumes. Where shall we turn for consumers of our surplus? Geography answers the question. China is our natural customer. . . . The Philippines give us a base at the door of all the East. . . .

Most future wars will be conflicts for commerce. The power that rules the Pacific, therefore, is the power that rules the world. And, with the Philippines, that power is and will forever be the American Republic. . . .

God . . . has marked the American people as His chosen nation to finally lead in the regeneration of the world. This is the divine mission of America, and it holds for us all the profit, all the glory, all the happiness possible to man. We are trustees of the world's progress, guardians of its righteous peace. The judgment of the Master is upon us: "Ye have been faithful over a few things; I will make you ruler over many things."

But for President McKinley, the real prize was the fabled China market. Japan and the European powers had been carving China into exclusive areas for investment. But the Chinese did not throw out the welcome mat for foreign nations that wanted to dominate them or for missionaries who wanted to Christianize them.

Chinese nationalists resented all foreign domination. In 1900, the nationalists, mostly peasants, sparked a massive uprising called the Boxer Rebellion. They attempted to drive all foreign occupiers and missionaries from China.

McKinley sent 5,000 US troops to join those from Europe and Japan in a joint effort to suppress these Chinese nationalists.

What Really Happened in the Philippines

It was a presidential election year in the United States. Once again, Republican president William McKinley found himself pitted against Democrat William Jennings Bryan. As the campaigning took place, US troops were tied down in three countries: China, Cuba, and the Philippines.

At the Democratic National Convention in July, Bryan defined the presidential contest as a fight between "democracy on the one hand and plutocracy [a government by the wealthy] on the other."

He launched into an impassioned attack on imperialism. In his booming baritone voice, he quoted Thomas Jefferson: "If there be one principle more deeply rooted than any other in the mind of every American, it is that we should have nothing to do with conquest."

Socialist Eugene Debs also ran for president that year as the Social Democratic Party's candidate. He called the Republican Party platform "a self-congratulation of the dominant capitalist class," the Democratic platform "the wail and cry of the perishing middle class," and the Social Democratic platform "an indictment of the capitalist system." Social Democrats, according to Debs, stood for "class consciousness and political action of the exploited working class" and advocated for "collective ownership of all the means of production and distribution."

The November election between McKinley and Bryan was close. By a narrow margin, William McKinley and his war hero vice president Theodore Roosevelt won. The voting public had chosen the imperial course laid out by McKinley and his advisers. Debs barely registered in the polls. Debs had said in a campaign speech, "It is definitely better to vote for freedom and fail than to vote for slavery and succeed."

Soon after the election, disturbing stories from the Philippines began to circulate. Newspapers carried lurid accounts of US soldiers who murdered, raped, and tortured.

The presidential election of 1900 pitted Republican William McKinley against Democrat William Jennings Bryan. McKinley was a proponent of American Empire whereas Bryan was an outspoken anti-imperialist who warned voters against conquest and a government led by the wealthy.

In November 1901, the *Philadelphia Public Ledger* reported that US soldiers had committed atrocities against the Philippine people:

> Our men have been relentless; have killed to exterminate men, women, children, prisoners and captives, active insurgents and suspected people, from lads of ten and up. . . . Our soldiers have pumped salt water into men to "make them talk," have taken prisoner people who held up their hands and peacefully surrendered, and an hour later, without an atom of evidence to show that they were even insurrectos, stood them on a bridge and shot them down one by one, to drop into the water below and float down as an example to those who found their bullet riddled corpses.

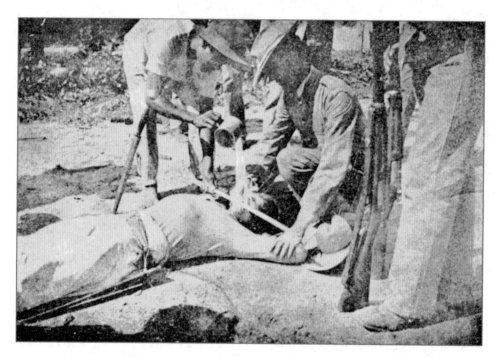

In the Philippines, US troops employed the torture we now call waterboarding.

One soldier described waterboarding in the following account to the *Omaha World-Herald*:

> Lay them on their backs, a man standing on each hand and each foot, then put a round stick in the mouth and pour a pail of water in the mouth and nose, and if they don't give up pour in another pail. They swell up like toads. I'll tell you it is a terrible torture.

On September 6, 1901, President McKinley was shot. He died eight days later. His vice president, Theodore Roosevelt, became the twenty-sixth president. The fighting in the Philippines continued for ten more months. In July 1902, President Roosevelt declared the islands pacified.

The United States had deployed a total of 126,000 troops. Of these troops, 4,374 died. The toll among the Filipinos was much higher. As many as 20,000 guerrillas and more than 200,000 civilians had lost their lives. Many died from cholera.

Americans comforted themselves with the thought that they had spread civilization to a backward people. Such civilization came at a hefty price—$400 million. The only senator to have visited the Philippines, Senator Beveridge, considered it money well spent.

But Beveridge underestimated the real cost to the republic that had been created by George Washington and Thomas Jefferson—a republic that inspired democratic and revolutionary movements around the world.

The United States had started down a new road that would soon make it the enemy of meaningful change. Instead of spreading democracy, the United States would defend the status quo—all in the name of empire.

5

I Pledge Allegiance to Big Business

For Cubans, the Spanish-American War was a war for Cuban independence. Despite gaining their freedom from Spain, Cubans didn't find much to celebrate.

In February 1901, the United States further dispelled any notion that Cuba might truly have independence. The US Congress passed the Platt Amendment. This amendment asserted the United States' right to intervene in future Cuban affairs.

The amendment limited the amount of debt Cuba could accumulate, restricted Cuba's power to sign treaties, and granted the United States a naval base at Guantánamo Bay.

The United States made it clear that the US Army would not withdraw from Cuba until the amendment was incorporated into the Cuban Constitution.

American businessmen swooped in, grabbing all the assets they could seize. The United Fruit Company gobbled up 1.9 million acres, at 20 cents per acre, of Cuban land for sugar

Plowing on a Cuban sugar plantation. The Spanish-American War proved profitable for American businessmen.

production. Chocolatier Milton Hershey and other American businesses also bought land cheaply for sugar factories. Soon Cuba became a one-crop economy.

American companies owned much of Cuba's valuable minerals beneath the land too. By 1901, Bethlehem Steel and other US businesses may have owned more than 80 percent of Cuban minerals.

Presidential Assassination

A twenty-eight-year-old anarchist, Leon Czolgosz, was angry over the "outrages committed by the American government in the Philippine islands." He

At forty-three, Theodore Roosevelt became the youngest president to date in 1901.

shot President McKinley at the Pan-American Exposition in Buffalo, New York, in 1901. Ironically, the assassination brought to office a much more committed imperialist, Teddy Roosevelt.

Roosevelt liked the thought of building a canal through the Isthmus of Panama. Such a canal would connect the Atlantic and Pacific Oceans, reducing the need for ships to navigate the treacherous Cape Horn in South America. It would also increase profits.

But Panama was a province of Colombia, a small country in northwest South America. The United States offered $10 million, but the Colombian government officials in the capital city of Bogotá refused. The financial terms were unacceptable.

Losing patience, Roosevelt took matters into his own hands. He hatched plans to seize the canal route from those "cut-throats of Bogotá." The United States orchestrated a conflict between the Panamanians and Colombians, supporting the Panamanians.

Eventually, the Panamanians revolted. As fighting broke out between the two sides, Roosevelt ordered warships to Panama City on the Pacific side and to Colón on the Atlantic side to neutralize the Colombians.

The battle for Panama ended nearly as soon as it started. The Panamanians prevailed and set up their own government. On November 3, 1903, the United States quickly recognized it.

"South Americans Now Hate Us"

In addition to gaining rights to the Canal Zone, the United States extorted the right to intervene in Panamanian affairs, just as it had done in Cuba. Secretary of War Elihu Root warned that building a canal would force the United States to police the region for the foreseeable future.

And police it would, as American investments in South American countries grew by leaps and bounds in the late nineteenth and early twentieth centuries.

Americans took over banana and coffee plantations, mines, railroads, and similar enterprises. So much land was devoted to export crops that the countries became dependent on food imports to feed their citizens.

The United Fruit Company and other US corporations insisted on stable, compliant governments in South America that would protect their interests. American businessmen—the owners and stockholders of these companies—looked to the US military to defend their investments. The military propped up corrupt and dictatorial governments and suppressed revolutionary movements.

In 1905, Root wrote candidly, "The South Americans now hate us, largely because they think we despise them and try to bully them."

Was the United States a bully? The number of times that the United States intervened with military force in Latin America in order to support a dictatorial government or to suppress a rebellion is telling. During a twenty-five year period, from 1900 to 1925, the United States sent troops twenty-four times: to Honduras in 1903, 1907, 1911, 1912, 1919, 1924, and 1925; to Cuba in 1906, 1912, and 1917; to Nicaragua in 1907, 1910, and 1912; to the Dominican Republic in 1903, 1914, and 1916; to Haiti in 1914; to Panama in 1908, 1912, 1918, 1921, and 1925; to Mexico in 1914; and to Guatemala in 1920.

In five instances, US troops occupied countries for extended periods of time: Nicaragua from 1912 to 1933, Haiti from 1914 to 1933, the Dominican Republic from 1916 to 1924, Cuba from 1917 to 1922, and Panama from 1918 to 1920.

Wars South of the Border

In impoverished countries in Central America, bananas were big business for American fruit companies and banks. The American-owned businesses required the help of the US government to protect American investments.

In 1776, the United States overthrew the domination of a "foreign" government that controlled its markets. Yet just over a century later, it did not support other countries that attempted the same rebellion—especially when the investments of American companies were at stake. Then the United States sent troops to intervene and to install US-friendly governments.

These instances became known as the "banana wars."

For the Sake of Money

Between 1890 and 1910, foreign banana companies transformed Honduras, an impoverished country in Central America.

In 1907, Honduras had foreign debt of $124 million, with a

Having already received two Medals of Honor, Butler would command the Thirteenth Regiment in France during the First World War. For that service, he received the Army Distinguished Service Medal, the Navy Distinguished Service Medal, and the French Order of the Black Star.

national income of only $1.6 million. US bankers controlled Honduras's debt, and American-owned fruit peddlers, such as the Vaccaro brothers and later Sam "the Banana Man" Zemurray, controlled the bananas. Fruit peddlers bought up vast plantations. Soon the powerful United Fruit Company of Boston joined them.

The American fruit companies needed friendly governments in order to make sure the banana business ran smoothly. US bankers also needed friendly governments to protect their investments.

When the Nicaraguan army attempted to overthrow the government in neighboring Honduras in 1907, the United States sent in troops. As soon as the political climate improved, United Fruit bought up more land. It increased its holdings from 14,000 acres in 1918, to 61,000 in 1922, to 88,000 in 1924. In 1929, Zemurray sold out to United Fruit and became the company's top official. The people of Honduras have remained impoverished ever since.

The Nicaraguans fared no better. In 1910, seeing an opportunity to establish a government friendly to American interests, the United States deployed 400 marines under Smedley Darlington Butler's command.

The Nicaraguans rebelled against the growing US domination of their country. Once again, Butler's marines intervened to defeat the rebels, killing 2,000 Nicaraguans in the fighting.

Butler soon realized that the United States was using him and his marines to protect US commercial and banking interests. During the fighting, the thirty-year-old commander wrote to his wife: "It is terrible that we should be losing so many men fighting the battles of those d—d spigs—all because Brown Bros. have some money down here."

In 1907, President Roosevelt had established the Central American Court with much fanfare. Its purpose was to peacefully adjudicate conflicts in the region. The court condemned American intervention. But US authorities ignored the court's ruling, effectively destroying its authority. US troops would occupy Nicaragua for the next twenty years.

In 1922, *The Nation* ran a scathing editorial titled "The Republic of Brown Bros." The piece detailed how the bankers had systematically secured control over Nicaragua's customs, railroads,

General Butler, shown here pointing, fought in the Philippines, China, and Central America. He wrote that he was "a high class muscle-man for Big Business, for Wall Street and for the Bankers. . . . [A] gangster for capitalism."

national banks, and internal revenues. It accused "the State Department in Washington and the American Minister in Managua [of] acting as private agents for these bankers, using American marines when necessary to impose their will."

War Is a Racket

No one had more firsthand experience intervening in other countries than Major General Smedley Darlington Butler. Butler enlisted in the marines at age sixteen when the 1898 war against Spain began. He first fought against the Filipino insurgents and then helped put down the Boxer Rebellion in China. Before long, Butler was leading one Central American intervention after another.

A tiny bulldog of a man, Butler wrote a book titled *War Is a Racket*, a work still quoted and admired by many military men. At the end of his long and highly decorated service, Butler reflected upon his years in uniform:

> I spent thirty-three years and four months in active military service as a member of this country's most agile military force, the Marine Corps. I served in all commissioned ranks from Second Lieutenant to Major-General. And during that period, I spent most of my time being a high class muscleman for Big Business, for Wall Street and for the Bankers. In short, I was a racketeer, a gangster for capitalism.
>
> I helped make Mexico, especially Tampico, safe for American oil interests in 1914. I helped make Haiti and Cuba a decent place for the National City Bank boys to collect revenues in. I helped in the raping of half a dozen Central American republics for the benefits of Wall Street. The record of racketeering is long. I helped purify Nicaragua for the international

banking house of Brown Brothers in 1909–1912. I brought light to the Dominican Republic for American sugar interests in 1916. In China I helped to see to it that Standard Oil went its way unmolested. . . .

During those years, I had, as the boys in the back room would say, a swell racket. Looking back on it, I feel that I could have given Al Capone a few hints. The best he could do was to operate his racket in three districts. I operated on three continents.

Long after Butler's retirement, war would remain a "racket" as US troops and intelligence operatives fanned out across the globe to defend the wealth and political interests of American businesses and investors.

Occasionally, US troops improved the lives of those whose countries they had invaded and occupied and then left behind. But more often, as you'll read in the coming pages, the troops would leave behind misery and squalor. There have been times when American values and achievements have led the way to major advances in human history and social progress. But there have been just as many times, if not more, when the United States has undermined human progress in pursuing its policies.

The record of the American Empire is not a pretty one. But it is a record that must be faced honestly and forthrightly if the United States is ever to undertake the kind of fundamental structural reforms that will allow it to play a leading role in advancing the progress of humanity—and not hindering it.

Mexico, Inch by Inch

President Wilson had once promised that the United States would "never again seek one additional foot of territory by conquest." Instead, the United States would promote "human rights, national integrity, and opportunity" and not "material interests." However, it was the material interests of American bankers and businessmen that thrust the United States, under Wilson's leadership, into Mexico's domestic politics. Wilson's staunch defense of US trade and investment colored his presidency and influenced his politics both at home and abroad.

At home, Wilson had campaigned on a platform that promised Americans "New Freedom" from the growing corporate control over their lives. Once in office, he sided with businesses and corporations and showed his lack of sympathy for labor and farmer activism.

Abroad, American bankers and businessmen were taking over Mexico, inch by inch. They didn't use soldiers. They used money. The takeover had begun during the previous administration, under President Taft's watch, and continued in earnest during Wilson's tenure. Regardless of Wilson's feelings about revolution, one was brewing in Mexico.

By 1913, Americans owned approximately 43 percent of Mexican property. The millionaire publisher William Randolph Hearst owned a whopping 17 million acres himself, an area of land larger than the state of West Virginia. By contrast, Mexican nationals owned 33 percent of their country's property.

American investors also owned rich natural resources under the land. American and British corporations owned nearly all of Mexico's mineral and oil deposits. They

William Randolph Hearst owned 17 million acres in Mexico.

also owned nearly all of Mexico's railroads. Altogether, American bankers and businessmen owned investments worth nearly $2 billion in Mexico.

Wilson followed Mexican developments closely. He didn't like what he saw. He dismissed Victoriano Huerta's regime as a "government of butchers."

Wilson once said he wanted to teach Latin Americans "to elect good men." Now he was ready to intervene directly, overthrow Huerta, and teach the revolutionaries about the benefits of capitalism and democracy.

On April 9, 1914, a shore party of nine US sailors blundered their way into a prohibited zone in Tampico, a prosperous oil town on the Gulf of Mexico.

Victoriano Huerta *(center).*

Right away, Mexican officials arrested the sailors for entering a war zone without a permit. Some newspaper accounts say the sailors were humiliated and paraded through town on their way to jail.

Before they reached the jail, however, a superior officer ordered the arresting officer to release the prisoners. The sailors were released. The Mexican commanding officer apologized to the sailors and to their US commanding officer, Admiral Henry Mayo.

General Huerta even apologized to Mayo directly. He promised to punish the arresting officer and offered a reciprocal salute to the flags of both countries. This wasn't enough for Mayo, who demanded a twenty-one-gun salute to the American flag.

President Wilson stands before Congress, April 20, 1912.

President Wilson agreed: "Th[is] incident cannot be regarded as a trivial one," as two of the arrested sailors had been taken directly from an American boat, which Mayo and Wilson considered US territory.

"A series of incidents have recently occurred," Wilson told Congress, "which cannot but create the impression that the representatives of General Huerta were willing to go out of their way to show disregard for the dignity and rights of this government and felt perfectly safe in doing what they pleased, making free to show in many ways their irritation and contempt."

President Wilson asked Congress to authorize use of the US military "in such ways and to such an extent as may be necessary to obtain from General Huerta and his adherents the fullest recognition of the rights and dignity of the United States."

Congress eagerly complied. Wilson sent a force of seven battleships, four fully manned marine troop transports, and numerous destroyers to Mexico.

When Mexicans at Vera Cruz resisted US seizure of a custom house, more than 150 people were killed. Six thousand marines occupied Vera Cruz for seven months.

General Huerta stepped down in July 1914. He was soon replaced by Venustiano Carranza, whom the United States initially supported. Later that year, Wilson withdrew American troops from Veracruz.

Some view the United States' involvement in Mexico as a struggle to promote Wilson's "human rights, national integrity, and opportunity" and the dignity and moral obligations of the United States. Others view the involvement as a fight to protect the $2 billion worth of American-owned oil, minerals, railroads, and land in Mexico.

7

The "Great War" Begins

Despite the scars of war, the terror of white supremacy, and the ultimate failure of Reconstruction, the twentieth century opened with a rush of optimism. By the time Woodrow Wilson took office in 1913, the US population had grown to more than 97 million people living in forty-eight states. War seemed like a distant memory. Fifty-two years had passed since the first shot of the Civil War was fired over Fort Sumter.

An ocean away from emerging conflicts in Europe, Americans took comfort in the belief that what happened in Europe wouldn't involve them. Most paid little attention to the fact that since 1900, the United States had sent troops on twelve occasions to support dictatorial governments or suppress rebellions in Honduras, Cuba, Nicaragua, the Dominican Republic, Panama, and Colombia.

Meanwhile, European nations convinced themselves that by producing weapons of war and building strong armies, they would be able to maintain peace. Great Britain's powerful navy still ruled the seas, but Germany's merchant fleet was making rapid gains.

Additionally, the need for oil to fuel their armies, navies, and industries locked the two countries in competition for fossil fuel.

And that wasn't all. The European countries were forming vast standing armies. These nations had established alliances that needed only a single spark to turn Europe into one great conflagration.

In his 1910 book *The Great Illusion*, Norman Angell, future British Nobel Peace Prize winner, warned that an arms race would not guarantee peace but would only lead to increased insecurity and a greater likelihood of war.

Angell also warned that war between industrialized nations was futile. "It is an economic impossibility for one nation to destroy or seize the wealth of another nation or for one nation to enrich itself by subjugating another," he wrote.

In other words, war didn't pay for the winners or the losers. War was expensive and drained countries of human and natural resources.

But the imperial rivals in Europe paid no heed to Angell's words—and neither did most Americans. Each nation was destined to find out for itself that war doesn't pay. But for the banks and industries involved in arms production, war does pay—and it pays big.

A Single Spark

While US troops guarded American business interests in Mexico, far more troubling developments were unfolding across the

President Woodrow Wilson.

Atlantic. Just as Norman Angell had warned, the buildup of military power had not secured peace after all.

The assassination of Archduke Franz Ferdinand of Austria by a Serbian fanatic on June 28, 1914, triggered a chain of events that, in August, plunged the world into the most brutal bloodshed and destruction humanity had yet seen.

Europe was already awash in rivalries. Great Britain, with its powerful navy, had reigned supreme in the nineteenth century. But it had failed to invest in homegrown manufacturing. In 1914, only 1 percent of young Brits graduated from high school compared to 9 percent of their American counterparts. As a result, Great Britain was being eclipsed by the United States in terms of industrial production.

Germany, Great Britain's rival, was competing in the production of steel, electrical power, chemical energy, agriculture, iron, coal, and textiles. Germany's banks and railroads were growing too. In the battle for oil, the new fuel that was necessary to power modern navies, Germany was rapidly gaining on Great Britain. Britain was now 65 percent dependent on US oil and 20 percent on Russian. It coveted potential new reserves in the Middle East, part of the unstable Ottoman Empire.

These tensions launched a European arms race on land but especially at sea, where Great Britain and Germany battled for naval dominance. Great Britain's big-gun battleships gave it the upper hand—for now. And European nations drafted young men into enormous standing armies.

Entangling alliances threatened to turn local conflicts into global ones. And in August 1914, when Austria-Hungary declared war against Serbia, the war quickly spiraled out of control. The Central powers (Germany, Turkey, and Austria-Hungary) lined up against the Triple Entente (France, Great Britain, Italy, Japan, and Russia). Others would soon join. The battlefields and seas would run red with blood.

The "Great War" would only be the start of a century of unending

From left to right: Archduke Franz Ferdinand; Countess Baillet de Latour; and Sophie, Duchess of Hohenberg.

warfare and horrific violence, human and technological barbarism on an unimaginable scale, that would later come to be known as "the American Century."

Neutrality

In August 1914, as war erupted in Europe, Woodrow Wilson issued a "Declaration of Neutrality." In his speech before Congress, he implored Americans not to take sides. "The people of the United States are drawn from many nations, and chiefly from the nations now at war," he said.

By proclaiming neutrality, Wilson intended for the United States to avoid the financial and political burdens of warfare. In essence, neutrality permitted the United States to continue trading with the warring nations. It meant business as usual as long as Americans were not selling arms.

The *Lusitania*

In May 1915, just nine months after Wilson's "Declaration of Neutrality," Germany sank the British liner *Lusitania*, leaving 1,200 dead, including 128 Americans. Many Americans, including former president Teddy Roosevelt, called for war. Despite initial disclaimers, the ship was, in fact, carrying a large cargo of arms from the United States to Great Britain. As it turns out, the United States had not been as neutral as most Americans believed.

In 1916, Wilson won reelection on the slogan "He kept us out of war." But he increasingly came to believe that if the United States didn't join the war, it would be denied a role in shaping the postwar world.

On January 22, 1917, Wilson dramatically delivered the first formal presidential address to the Senate since the days of George Washington. He

The RMS *Lusitania* departs New York Harbor carrying 1,959 passengers and war munitions in its hold. Seven days later, a German U-20 commander would find the four-stacker in his sights.

This 1915 drawing shows the RMS *Lusitania* as a second torpedo
hits its hull. The drawing was published in the *New York
Herald* and the *London Sphere*.

This German U-20 submarine is said to be the one that sank the
Lusitania. Here, it is photographed on the Danish coast.

laid out his soaring vision for peace and the future. He called for "peace without victory" based on core American principles: self-determination, freedom of the seas, and an open world with no entangling alliances. The centerpiece of such a world would be a league of nations that could enforce the peace. This demand was initially advanced by groups within America's peace movement.

When he concluded, the Senate erupted in applause. Senator John Shafroth of Colorado called it "the greatest message of a century." *The Atlanta Constitution* wrote, "'Startling,' 'staggering,' 'astounding,' 'the noblest utterance that has fallen from human lips since the Declaration of Independence,' were among the expressions of senators. The president himself after his address said: 'I have said what everybody has been longing for, but has thought impossible. Now it appears to be possible.'" Wilson's peace message struck the right chord with most Americans. But Europeans, having suffered immense losses in two and a half years of fighting, were not as enthusiastic about it.

From Neutrality to War

American sympathy for Great Britain and other Allies translated into financial support. Between 1914 and 1917, US banks loaned the Allies $2.5 billion, almost a hundred times more than the $27 million they loaned Germany and other Central powers. In 1915 alone, US bankers loaned $500 million to France.

American investors profited from these loans, and the Allies benefited from borrowing money at low interest rates to fund the war and buy military weapons, ammunition, and equipment.

And buy they did; 84 percent of Allied munitions bought from American manufacturers passed through Britain's only purchasing agent, the American banking dynasty, the House of Morgan. Bethlehem Steel produced and sold armor plates, steel for shells, artillery ammunition rounds, and large-caliber guns throughout the war. American companies profited from the sales—and once America entered the war, they would profit even more.

Determined to break the British naval blockade and prevent munitions from reaching the Allies, Germany broke its promise to end unrestricted warfare in war-zone waters. It announced that it intended to once again wage unlimited submarine warfare, sinking all ships—military or civilian—that sailed in disputed waters. The announcement was made on January 31, 1917, just days after US troops withdrew from Mexico.

Germany's belligerence on the seas—and its unsuccessful attempt to forge an alliance with America's neighbor to the south, Mexico—angered US policymakers. But

This powerful war propaganda poster was created by artist Fred Spear, just one month after the sinking of the *Lusitania*. It calls out to men to enlist to save defenseless women and children from a hostile force.

Wilson's real motive for entering the war was his belief that by doing so, he could be guaranteed a voice in negotiations over the postwar order. On April 2, 1917, Wilson asked Congress for a declaration of war, saying that the "war to end all wars" would make the world safe "for democracy." Six opposed the declaration in the Senate and fifty voted against it in the House, including Jeannette Rankin of

Montana, the first woman elected to Congress. Despite their dissent, the declaration passed resoundingly, and the American government appealed for one million volunteers to enlist.

Only 73,000 men signed up in the first six weeks. Many Americans did not understand why the United States should risk blood and treasure for a war that was unfolding so far away. As a result of dismal enlistment numbers, the federal government instituted a draft. Called the Selective Service Act, it required men between the ages of twenty-one and thirty to register for military service, and it gave the president the power to draft soldiers.

Among those who volunteered for service was future historian William L. Langer, who later recounted:

> One would think that, after almost four years of war, after the most detailed and realistic accounts of murderous fighting . . . , it would have been all but impossible to get anyone to serve without duress. But it was not so. We and many thousands of others volunteered. . . . I can hardly remember a single instance of serious discussion of American policy or of larger war issues. We men, most of us young, were simply fascinated by the prospect of adventure and heroism. Most of us, I think, had the feeling that life, if we survived, would run in the familiar, routine channel. Here was our one great chance for excitement and risk. We could not afford to pass it up.

It would take more than a year to train the soldiers and transport them across the Atlantic. In the meantime, as they drilled and learned to handle weapons, a different kind of army was amassing on the home front.

Preaching to America

It was clear that Woodrow Wilson faced a dilemma. He could conscript young men into the army, but he still needed to convince the American public that the cause for war was righteous. After all, he had campaigned on the platform of keeping America *out* of the war.

For this, Wilson would need a different kind of army. He needed soldiers who would influence the public's thinking, shape the war's image, and solicit support for the war effort.

Some people call this "propaganda." President Wilson called it "patriotism." The army was named the Committee on Public Information (CPI). It was created on April 13, 1917, just one week after the United States declared war on Germany.

To run the committee, Wilson turned to a former campaign worker and journalist named George Creel, who had a great deal of energy and drive. "Democracy is a religion with me," Creel had once said. "Throughout my whole life, I have preached America as the hope of the world."

All Creel needed to do was figure out how to get the American people to believe that America was the hope and savior of the Allies, too. That America would make the world safe for democracy. That this war would be the war to end all wars.

It was a massive undertaking. It meant a national propaganda program. It meant controlling and spinning the news. It meant sustaining morale and public support for the war at home. It meant getting the press to voluntarily censor its reporting of the news. It meant developing a strong propaganda program abroad.

To accomplish these goals, Creel created thirty-seven divisions to help get out the war message. These included the Division of Pictorial Publicity, which helped to design patriotic posters; the News Division, which fed positive reports to newspapers; the Film Division, which produced three feature films; and an army of 75,000 volunteers called "Four Minute Men."

Four Minute Men

The name "Four Minute Men" harkened back to the patriotic minutemen of the American Revolution, who could be ready to fight at a minute's notice.

But the Four Minute Men did not carry guns. They carried words. Wherever they could find an audience, they gave rousing, patriotic speeches. They called on men, women, and even children to do their part to support the war. No speech lasted longer than four minutes.

"I hope that any man who has the ability to speak and is asked for that service as a Four Minute Man, will count it a great privilege and feel that in so doing he is helping in a very direct and important way toward winning the war," said Carl E. Milliken, governor of Maine.

The speakers were carefully recruited and screened. Most were American-born. Others were recent immigrants or the grown children or grandchildren of immigrants who could address immigrants in their own language and convince them that the war was necessary and important.

And so it went: Italians, Poles, Lithuanians, Russians, Armenians, Bohemians, Slovaks, and Yiddish-speaking Jews visited theaters, churches, synagogues, factories, labor halls, and lodges, and reached out to their communities.

The Four Minute Men's bulletin reported: "At the present time the Jewish section is operating in thirty theaters, sending speakers to each twice a week. Among these are all the large Jewish playhouses of the city, each one of which has an average attendance of 2,000 at a performance. In this way we are reaching about 25,000 people per week."

Some Four Minute Men were soldiers home from active duty. One was a full-blooded Sioux Indian who spoke to tribal members throughout South Dakota.

A CPI poster portrays the Four Minute Men as town criers.

It was tricky at times, since for some immigrants, it meant siding with America against their homeland. Afterward, speakers passed out naturalization papers to audience members.

These methods of controlling and shaping public opinion would become a central element in all future war planning. "Indeed, there is no question but that government management of opinion is the unescapable corollary of large-scale modern war," said Harold Lasswell in *Propaganda Technique in World War I.* "The only question is the degree to which the government should try to conduct its propaganda secretly, and the degree to which it should conduct it openly."

Liberty Bonds

For those who couldn't enlist—perhaps they were too old or couldn't pass the physical or were female—no problem! They could support America and the war financially. The Four Minute Men urged men, women, and children to purchase government-issued Liberty Bonds.

"Earn the right to say I helped to win the war," urged the Four Minute Men. "This is a Loyalty Bond as well as a Liberty Bond."

Children supported the war bond drive. "Stop and think, people, what it means to buy Liberty Bonds. It means much to the boys who are fighting

The US government sold Liberty Bonds to help finance the war effort. This poster shows that a bond purchase helped to buy a torpedo that could be shot at a German submarine.

for us over there," wrote Myrle Tageson, a seventh-grade student. "They are giving their lives for you and all you are asked to do is buy a Liberty Bond."

Patriotic duty turned some citizens into thugs. Late one night in Outagamie County, Wisconsin, a group of men who called themselves the Council of Defense banged on the door of German immigrant John Deml. They demanded that Deml sign up for $800 worth of bonds. When Deml refused—he had already purchased as many bonds as he could afford—the men tied a rope around his neck, dragged him outside, and struck him in the face.

The US government sold approximately $21 billion worth of Liberty Bonds to finance the war effort. Although some individuals bought the bonds out of a sense of patriotic duty, most bonds were purchased by banks and financial groups who considered them a good investment. The bonds paid 3.5 percent interest.

Propaganda and Discrimination

The Committee on Public Information was committed to disseminating positive reports about the war. It published a daily newsletter that was distributed to every newspaper, post office, and government office. Its news stories reinforced the message that the war was a noble crusade for democracy.

Some CPI stories falsified and exaggerated the news. For example, a CPI story that US escort ships sank several German submarines was discredited when the "dead" German submarine officers later appeared alive in England.

The CPI also encouraged newspapers to print horror stories about German soldiers bayoneting Belgian babies, mutilating young boys, and raping women.

CPI propaganda efforts infected the nation. Americans were asked to inform on fellow citizens who criticized the war effort. The CPI placed advertisements in popular magazines, urging readers to report "the man who spreads pessimistic stories . . . cries for peace, or belittles our efforts to win the war."

Robert "Fighting Bob" La Follette led congressional opposition to World War I and was condemned in Washington and in his home state of Wisconsin as a traitor. He was one of six senators who voted against US entry into the war.

It soon became patriotic to vilify all things German. German Americans—America's largest immigrant group—faced discrimination in all aspects of life. Schools banned German from their foreign language curricula. Libraries across the country discarded German books. Orchestras refused to play works by German composers. Hamburgers were renamed "liberty sandwiches" and sauerkraut was called "liberty cabbage." German measles were "liberty measles" and German shepherds were simply "police dogs." The states of Iowa and Nebraska banned the speaking of all foreign languages over the telephone.

Lola Gamble Clyde, the daughter of an Irish-born minister, was a teenager living in Idaho during the war. She recalled seeing the word "Kraut" painted on shop windows in town. Late one night, the windows on the marked shops were smashed. In another instance, a shop owner gathered up every German-made item and burned them in a bonfire in the middle of the street. Some Germans changed their names. "There was lots of that kind of hysteria going on," said Clyde.

What would happen if someone dared to act or speak out against the war? What if that person was a family member, a best friend, a neighbor, a teacher, or a fellow worker?

R.I.P. Freedom of Speech

Congress passed two new federal laws that stifled the American people. The Espionage Act of 1917 and the Sedition Act of 1918 were two of the most repressive pieces of legislation in the history of the United States. Under these acts, people who spoke out against the war, the US government, or the armed forces could be fired, fined as much as $10,000, or sent to jail. Individuals found guilty of conveying information to help the enemy could be sentenced to death.

These laws did more than curb speech. They created a climate of intolerance toward dissent. Professor Charles Beard was a leading historian who supported the war. But he didn't support the new laws. "If we have to suppress everything we don't like to hear, this country is resting on a pretty wobbly basis," warned Beard. "This country was founded on disrespect and the denial of authority, and it is not time to stop free discussion."

As a result of these two new laws, colleges, universities, high schools, and even elementary schools saw the end of academic freedom.

At Columbia University in New York City, the college president, Nicholas Murray Butler, issued a warning: "There is and will be no place in Columbia University, either on the rolls of its Faculties or on the rolls of its students, for any person who opposes or who counsels opposition to the effective enforcement of the laws of the United States, or who acts, speaks, or writes treason." Those who speak out against the war will be dismissed, Butler vowed, "as speed[ily] as the discovery of his offense."

This was no idle threat.

Among the first to be fired was Henry Wadsworth Longfellow Dana, grandson of the famous poet. An English professor, Dana was active in the antiwar People's Council. The organization opposed Wilson's decision to bring America into the war. It published antiwar pamphlets, conducted demonstrations, and held mass meetings in an effort to mobilize workers and intellectuals against the war.

The New York Times applauded the firing. "The fantasies of 'academic freedom' . . . cannot protect a professor who counsels resistance to the law and speaks, writes, disseminates treason," argued the newspaper. "That a teacher of youth should teach sedition and treason, that he should infect, or seek to infect, youthful minds with ideas fatal to their duty to the country is intolerable."

The War Department wanted to influence those youthful minds. It found that college campuses were ideal military training grounds. On more than 500 campuses across the country, students were inducted into the army as part of the Student Army Training Corps. They were given the rank of private and received privates' pay, tuition, housing, clothing, equipment, and meals. They drilled eleven hours each week and studied forty-two hours of "essential" and "allied" military-type subjects.

At the University of Virginia, for example, these subjects included mathematics as it related to field artillery; military geography for mapmaking purposes; and international military law. In English classes, students learned how to write "terse and unequivocal English," the sort that officers needed to issue and understand orders.

Across the country, college and university teachers as well as elementary and high school teachers who spoke out against the war were fired. Some were reported by their students and colleagues.

Professor Charles Beard would later charge that his university, Columbia, saw the war as an opportunity "to drive out or humiliate or terrorize every man who held progressive, liberal, unconventional views on political matters in no way connected with the war."

The Spread of Censorship

Censorship spread to the post office. Postmaster General Albert S. Burleson banned mail that advocated treason or insurrection, opposed the draft, or smacked of socialism. (One socialist leader, Norman Thomas, charged that the postmaster general didn't know "socialism from rheumatism.")

The Espionage and Sedition Acts encouraged patriotic thugs to take the law into their own hands. They broke into union halls and meeting places of socialist organizations and attacked—and even killed—labor organizers and antiwar activists. Local authorities jailed hundreds of people for criticizing the war or attending union and socialist gatherings.

Among those targeted were the Wobblies—members of the Industrial Workers of the World, or the IWW, a labor organization that formed in 1905. The IWW believed that the greatest conflict lay between capitalists and laborers, not between workers from different countries. IWW members pledged that if the capitalists went to war, they would refuse to follow. They knew that war lined the pockets of capitalists, not workers. Why should they die to make their employers rich?

One of the IWW founding members in America was Eugene Debs. He ridiculed the idea that a country that called itself a democracy jailed people

Labor organizer Eugene Debs, shown here in 1912, urged workers to oppose the war. After giving an antiwar speech in 1918, he was arrested, convicted, and sentenced to serve ten years in prison. He lost his voting rights for life.

for expressing their opinions. "They tell us that we live in a great free republic; that our institutions are democratic; that we are a free and self-governing people," said Debs. "That is too much, even for a joke."

Debs summed up the war in this way: "Wars throughout history have been waged for conquest and plunder. . . . And that is war in a nutshell. The master class has always declared the wars; the subject class has always fought the battles."

In June 1918, Debs addressed a large crowd outside the prison in Canton, Ohio, where three socialists were being held for opposing the draft. Local authorities arrested him. He was indicted on ten violations of the Espionage Act.

Debs pleaded guilty. The judge reprimanded him and others like him "who would strike the sword from the hand of this nation while she is engaged in defending herself from a foreign and brutal power." Debs was sentenced to ten years in prison.

Another IWW labor organizer named Frank Little wrote a letter to the anti-union governor of Arizona, saying, "I don't give a d— [*sic*] what your country is fighting for; I am fighting for the solidarity of labor."

In Butte, Montana, Little referred to the soldiers sent to break up the copper miners' strike as "Uncle Sam's scabs in uniform." That night, angry masked men broke into his rented room, seized Little, and hanged him from a railroad trestle outside of the town.

In an editorial, *The New York Times* called the lynching "a deplorable and detestable crime, whose perpetrators should be found, tried, and punished by the law." But the *Times* seemed more upset that Little was a member of the IWW and had denounced the government and the war. The editors called the IWW "agents of Germany" and said, "The Federal authorities should make short work of these treasonable conspirators against the United States."

In 1918, sixty-seven lynchings took place. Sixty-three of those victims were black; four were white. Thirteen were dragged from jail or from police custody, fifty-four taken from their homes or lodging houses.

The Washington Post assured its readers that occasional lynchings were a small price to pay for a healthy upsurge of patriotism. "In spite of excesses such as lynchings, it is a healthful and wholesome awakening in the interior part of our country. Enemy propaganda must be stopped, even if a few lynchings may occur."

Despite the new laws, the mass arrests, and the threat of violence, antiwar activists would not be silenced. Their rallies continued to draw thousands of supporters. Socialist Party candidates won increasing numbers at the ballot box throughout the country. In 1917, ten socialists won seats in the New York State legislature.

Chamberlain-Kahn Act of 1918

Just as war created an upsurge in patriotism, it also gave moral reformers an opportunity to police sexual behavior. Concerned about the health of soldiers,

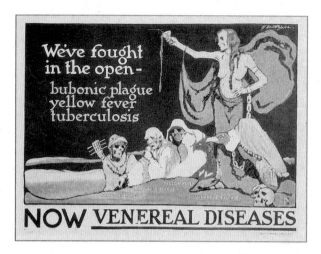

The Commission on Training Camp Activities tried to rein in male sexuality with an abstinence campaign, including anti-venereal disease posters such as these.

they waged an aggressive campaign against prostitution and venereal disease. This led Congress to pass a law that repressed the civil rights of women.

The 1918 Chamberlain-Kahn Act gave authorities the right to hold any woman who was suspected of having a sexually transmitted disease such as syphilis or gonorrhea. This was done for the "protection of the military and naval forces of the United States."

Women suspected of having such a disease were forced to endure a physical examination to determine their disease status. Ironically, in 1918, the year Congress passed the law, no medically approved test for sexually transmitted disease was available.

Although the Constitution protects the right of individuals from unreasonable search and seizure and arrest without probable cause, any woman walking alone on a city street, in a park, or near a military base could be arrested and examined for disease.

If found to have a venereal

disease, the women were sentenced to federal institutions. The average sentence was ten weeks, but some women were detained for a year or more.

The Commission on Training Camp Activities (CTCA) also tried to rein in the sexual behavior of its soldiers. Whereas women were subjected to arrest, medical exams, and sentencing, men were subjected only to CTCA posters that said, "A German Bullet Is Cleaner Than a Whore" and "A Soldier Who Gets a Dose [of Venereal Disease] Is a Traitor." One pamphlet asked, "How can you look the flag in the face if you [are] dirty with gonorrhea?"

The Cost of Control

It wasn't cheap to exercise control over the American people. The federal government needed to hire agents to enforce the crackdown on dissent. This expense contributed to a federal budget that ballooned from less than $1 billion in 1913 to more than $13 billion in 1918.

Hundreds of people went to jail for criticizing the war. But it wasn't enough to slow the war machine. US troops began to arrive in Europe, where they quickly boosted Allied morale and contributed significantly to the Allied victory.

10

Weapons of Mass Destruction

By November 1917, the war had been raging in Europe for more than three years. Americans had heard reports of the unrelenting agony of trench warfare, the misery of mud and disease, the suffering from poison gas attacks, and the bloody five-month-long Battle of the Somme in France.

Former president Theodore Roosevelt had been campaigning for the United States to enter the war since 1914 when it began. He detested Wilson's Declaration of Neutrality and criticized the Americans who supported Wilson. In a letter to a friend, Roosevelt wrote, "I am pretty well disgusted with our government and with the way our people acquiesce in and support it."

But on April 6, 1917, the United States at last declared war on Germany. Eight days later, Roosevelt paid Wilson a visit. He requested permission to lead a unit of volunteers into battle, just as he had led the "Rough Riders" in Cuba during the Spanish-American War in 1898. Roosevelt told Wilson that he was eager to serve. If Wilson agreed, Roosevelt promised to cease his attacks on Wilson.

Wilson refused the request.

Furious, Roosevelt accused Wilson of playing politics. Roosevelt reportedly vowed that his four sons would fight in his place—and they did, even Quentin, who at nineteen was too young to be drafted.

With his father's permission, Quentin left his studies at Harvard and enlisted. He served as a fighter pilot and became known for his sense of humor and daring.

Over the next twelve months, two million men like the four Roosevelt brothers voyaged across the Atlantic Ocean and landed in France. Some were volunteers like the Roosevelt brothers; most were draftees.

In France, the American soldiers

Quentin Roosevelt dropped out of Harvard University to join the First Reserve Aero Squadron. He became known as a daring fighter pilot.

would experience firsthand the horrors of modern warfare. An unprecedented mobilization of science and technology created new and improved machine guns, bullets, tanks, bombs, and deadly poisonous gases—with the promise of even more frightening weapons soon to come.

But still, America's young men like the Roosevelt brothers served. They arrived in time to help the French forces turn the tide of the war and repulse the Germans along the Marne in July 1918. In September, 600,000 Americans fought valiantly to break through the German lines.

The Germans surrendered on November 11, 1918. The United

States had mobilized more than 4.7 million troops, 116,000 of whom would not return alive. An additional 204,000 were wounded and 4,500 were taken prisoner or missing. The casualty rate was 7.1 percent.

By comparison, European casualty figures were staggering—as many as 8.5 million dead soldiers. It's harder to estimate civilian casualties, but some sources claim as many as 13 million. Many civilians died from disease and starvation. France lost half of its young men between the ages of fifteen and thirty.

Kermit Roosevelt would return home safely. Ted Roosevelt Jr. and his brother Archie would be wounded in action. Ted would also be gassed. But the youngest Roosevelt brother, Quentin, would die when his plane was shot down over France in July 1918. He was twenty years old.

To an Associated Press reporter, Roosevelt said this about his son's death: "Quentin's mother and I are very glad that he got to the front and had a chance to render some service to his country and show the stuff that was in him before his fate befell him."

Privately, Roosevelt never recovered from the loss of his youngest son, who was said to be most like him. Roosevelt's health deteriorated, and he died in his sleep six months later, at age sixty.

All Gloves Are Off

It may seem ironic that something as barbaric as war has rules. But it does. It's been said that rules of war are necessary in order to curb the beast in man. One of the earliest rules of warfare was a taboo against using chemical weapons and other poisons. This taboo was so long-standing, in fact, that one of the only reported uses of chemical agents prior to the twentieth century dates back to a Spartan attack on an Athenian city in the fifth century BC.

During the American Civil War, several people devised chemical-laced projectiles as a means to decide battles quickly. An 1862 *Scientific American* article informed readers that "several incendiary and asphyxiating shells have

Soldiers begin the gruesome job of removing the dead from the trenches.

been invented for the purpose of scattering liquid fire and noxious fumes around the space where they explode."

That year, a New York schoolteacher named John W. Doughty designed a projectile filled with explosives in one compartment and liquid chlorine in the other. He sent the design to Secretary of War Edwin Stanton and suggested that the projectile could be used to drive Confederate troops out of their fortifications.

Soon after, an agricultural chemistry professor proposed a weapon using hydrogen chloride gas. And later, William Tilden reportedly offered General Ulysses S. Grant a means of using chemicals to "[settle] wars quickly by making them terribly destructive."

The US War Department and General Grant rejected the idea of using chemical weapons. In 1905, *The Washington Evening Star* reported that Grant told Tilden: "Such a terrific agency for destroying human life should not be permitted to come into use by the civilized nations of the world."

Grant's was not a new sentiment. Since 1863, the US War Department's "Lieber Code" prohibited "the use of poison in any manner, be it to poison wells, or food, or arms."

During the Hague Peace Conferences held in 1899 and 1907, the attending countries resolved to ban the use of projectiles that spread certain poisonous gases. They also banned the use of aerial attacks from balloons and added a clause that banned the use of projectiles, weapons, and other materials that could cause unnecessary suffering.

Planes such as these British and German bombers first bombed targets, including civilians, during World War I.

Germany became the first country to bomb civilians from the air when an August 1914 attack on a Paris railway station missed its target and killed a woman. In September, during the First Battle of the Marne, German airmen bombed Paris on several occasions. The first Allied urban aerial bombing came in December, when French airmen bombed Freiburg. By spring of 1918, German bombing had injured more than 4,000 British civilians and left more than 1,000 dead.

"Should a nation . . . attain complete control of the air, it could more nearly master the earth than has ever been the case in the past," General William "Billy" Mitchell later wrote of these dangerous developments. Mitchell is considered the father of the US Air Force. Later, the American B-25 bomber would be named after him.

Though used on a limited scale, the potential of aerial bombing as a key to military victory was apparent. British forces began the war with 110 planes; by the war's end, Great Britain and France combined had produced 100,000 more. Germany produced 44,000.

During the first month of the war, the French also used tear gas grenades against the Germans. In a battle against the French shortly thereafter, the Germans retaliated, firing gas grenades that contained chemicals that caused sneezing fits. In using chemical irritants, both the French and the Germans violated the Hague Conventions. Within nine months, the use of chemicals would turn deadly.

On April 22, 1915, Germany broke the spirit, if not the letter, of the Hague Conventions when it successfully used poison gas at the second battle of Ypres. A yellowish-green plume of chlorine gas blanketed French troops along four miles of trenches, with catastrophic results. More than 600 soldiers soon lay dead. Many more were temporarily blinded, and a good number were taken prisoner.

The Washington Post headlined its front-page article with CRAZED BY GAS

BOMBS. The soldiers had died from "agonizing suffocation." The gas turned their bodies black, green, and yellow. The pain had driven many insane. The newspaper reported German threats, that more potent gas weapons were on the way. The newspaper opined, "The use of poison gases will doubtless go on record as the most striking and distinguishing novelty of the present war, just as every great war of the past has been marked by some peculiarly surprising method of destroying life."

A *New York Times* editorial condemned the use of poison gas, not because it killed more people than other weapons of war, but because the survivors' suffering was "unparalleled in the dreadful annals of conflict."

Furthermore, if one side used such weapons, the *Times* warned, "Others will be obliged in self-defense to imitate the deplorable example."

Armies developed fairly effective countermeasures against the gases. Initially, the British handed out cotton pads that soldiers dipped in bicarbonate of soda—baking soda—and held over their face. In an emergency, soldiers soaked cloth in urine.

By 1918, soldiers had an early form of a gas mask—a filter respirator that used charcoal or antidotal chemicals. Casualties still skyrocketed, but the number of fatalities dropped sharply.

American chemists were determined to raise the number of fatalities. As *The New York Times* said, "That, as everybody says, is war."

The Chemists' War

The United States established the Chemical Warfare Service on June 28, 1918. Scientists were eager to assist the war effort. Nearly 2,000 of the nation's leading chemists descended on the Experiment Station at American University in Washington, DC. By the war's end, 5,400 chemists would serve the military in what was called the "Chemist's Crusade."

"For the first time in the history of science, men who are devoting

US soldiers undergo anti-gas training at Camp Dix, New Jersey.

their lives to it have an immediate opportunity of proving their worth to their country," declared J. S. Ames, a physicist from Johns Hopkins University. "It is a wonderful moment; and the universities of the country are seizing it."

Another physicist, this one a Nobel Laureate from the University of Chicago, was equally excited. "The world has been waked up by the war to a new appreciation of what science can do," said Robert Millikan.

It became a race to create more terrible chemical weapons. The Chemical Warfare Service prioritized speed over safety. Working at such a furious pace meant that leaks and other accidents were common. In laboratories, canaries were kept in cages. If a canary dropped dead, it was time to evacuate the building.

Some men volunteered for dangerous experiments. At American University, an experiment with gas went horribly wrong. "Three men were burned by a deadly dose of gas," recalled George Temple, an electrical engineer. "The bodies were hauled away on a cart, the flesh jiggling off their bones." Still, Temple volunteered seven times.

At the end of the workday, the researchers and other employees left the laboratories and headed home on city trolleys, carrying the noxious gas fumes and chemical residue on their clothing. "As the trolley cars neared the downtown area, civilians began boarding them," said Temple. "Soon they were all sneezing or crying, depending upon the type of gas the soldiers had been working with."

One of the chemists at American University, James Conant, oversaw a project to mass-produce lewisite. This extremely toxic agent causes the skin and mucous membranes to blister on contact. Conant and his team produced artillery shells and aerial bombs packed with the deadly substance. Even the smallest amount was believed to cause "intolerable agony and death within hours." Its production, however, came too late to be used in the war.

Edgewood Arsenal was the largest production facility. Located near Aberdeen, Maryland, *The New York Times* described it as "the largest poison gas factory on earth." The size of a small town, the facility housed almost 300 buildings, twenty-eight miles of railway, and fifteen miles of roads.

Twelve hundred researchers and 700 assistants studied more than 4,000 potentially poisonous substances there. The facility produced 200,000 chemical bombs and shells daily—an estimated three to four times as much as the British, French, and Germans combined.

Such a large-scale operation meant large-scale accidents. "I went through the hospitals and saw the men who had been struck down by the fiendish gases while at work," said Richard Barry, a *New York Times* reporter who toured the facility. "Some with arms and legs and trunks shriveled and scarred as by a horrible fire, some with the deep suppurations still oozing after weeks of careful nursing." The reporter guessed that the casualty rate at Edgewood Arsenal might have exceeded that of any American division in France.

Two months before the war ended, the commanding officer of Edgewood Arsenal claimed that the United States had perfected a new deadly approach to using chemical weapons. It was prepared to have its planes drop one-ton mustard gas containers over fortified German cities. "Not one living thing, not even a rat, would live through it," said Colonel William H. Walker.

During the war, the Allies and the Central powers used a total of 124,000 metric tons of thirty-nine different toxic agents. For the most part, the gases were dispersed by 66 million artillery shells.

A young German lance corporal claimed to be among the victims of Allied gassing. The gas temporarily blinded him. "My eyes were transformed into glowing coals, and the world had grown dark around me," wrote Adolf

Soldiers wear gas masks during training at the Edgewood Arsenal, Maryland. The soldiers have just been sprayed with gas from a plane.

Hitler claimed he was gassed during World War I.

Hitler in his autobiography, *Mein Kampf.*

After the Germans surrendered on November 11, 1918, the machinery at the Edgewood plant was "carefully taken apart, oiled, and wrapped and stored away," wrote Richard Barry, "ready for the next war, should there ever be one."

Chemists took pride in their contribution to the war effort. *The New York Times* called the chemists "among the best soldiers of democracy" and the "most effective of our national defenders."

At the end of the war 2,500 tons of mustard gas sat on piers, ready to be shipped overseas. "Somehow we have been cheated of our prey," said Colonel Walker. But he took comfort in his belief that the gas had expedited Germany's surrender.

In 1925, seven years after the war's end, the Geneva Protocol—a protocol to the earlier Hague Conventions—would again forbid the use of chemical and bacteriological weapons in war. Over the next ten years, forty countries—including every great power except the United States and Japan—would ratify the treaty.

American veterans' groups, the American Chemical Society, and chemical manufacturers did not support such a ban. Chemists argued that chemical weapons were more humane than other weapons. They also argued that the United States needed to be prepared for their use in the next war.

11

Revolution in the Air

During the bitter winter of January 1917, revolution swirled in the cold Russian air. After a series of battlefield defeats, the dead, missing, and wounded Russian soldiers numbered six million.

The defeats left the Russian railroads unable to transport food and supplies. Soldiers mutinied, turning against their commanders. An estimated 34,000 soldiers deserted their posts each month.

On the home front, morale was no better. Russian workers went on strike. Tired of going hungry and struggling to feed their families, they protested the food shortages and staged demonstrations demanding bread. Students, white-collar workers, and teachers joined the strikes, holding public meetings and rioting in the streets.

Although most Russians had supported the war in 1914, many now considered it a war not worth fighting. One man who condemned the war was the driven leader of the Bolshevik movement—Vladimir Lenin.

Soon Lenin was joined by Leon Trotsky, a skilled orator who

gave rousing speeches. Together, they called for Russian workers to unite against the unpopular Czar Nicholas Romanov and his German-born wife, Alexandra.

On March 8, 1917, rioting and strikes over food shortages broke out in St. Petersburg. Shouts for bread filled the streets.

At first, the protests didn't appear to threaten the Russian monarchy. But in the coming days, the situation changed dramatically.

Czar Nicholas II ordered the army to end the rioting. The troops disobeyed his orders. Instead, the soldiers joined the strikers.

Realizing he had lost control over his people and was now in danger, Czar Nicholas left the throne on behalf of himself and his young son. He offered the crown to his brother, who declined.

The leaders of the Russian legislature formed a provisional government. Thirty-six-year-old Aleksandr Kerensky was appointed minister of justice. In July 1917, he became prime minister.

Kerensky was a moderate socialist and an intellectual who despised the Romanovs and all that they represented. He immediately introduced a series of reforms, granting freedoms, and abolishing capital punishment.

For a brief eight months, the Russian people enjoyed more civil liberties than Americans did. But Kerensky made two decisions that contributed to his downfall: He kept Russia in the war, and he didn't offer land to the peasants.

Lenin's Rise to Power

On November 7, 1917, the Bolsheviks, led by Vladimir Lenin and Leon Trotsky, seized power from the Kerensky government.

They were inspired by Karl Marx, a nineteenth-century German-Jewish intellectual. Marx believed that class struggle would eventually result in a more equal socialist society.

In 1917, Russia was ripe for change. On November 7, Vladimir
Lenin and the Bolsheviks seized power, dramatically altering
the course of world history.

In the weeks following the takeover, the Bolsheviks set out to transform
life in Russia. They nationalized banks. They took land owned by elites and
gave it to the peasants. They put workers in control of factories and seized
church property. Meanwhile, Kerensky escaped to Paris and, later, the United
States.

Lenin's newly formed Red Guard ransacked the old Foreign Office. They
found a web of secret understandings between the Allies from 1915 and 1916.
Those agreements showed the Allies' plan to divide up the colonies and other
territories of the Central powers.

One of those understandings, the Sykes-Picot Agreement, divided the
Ottoman Empire among Great Britain, France, and Russia. Sykes-Picot
created new nations with little regard for historical or cultural realities. This
would plant the seeds for future conflict within the oil-rich Middle East.

To the Allies' great embarrassment, the Red Guard published what it found. This proved that the war to make the world safe for democracy was really a war to colonize most of the globe, especially Asia and Africa. The plan to create new nations exposed the hollowness of Wilson's call for "self-determination" after the war. How could Middle Eastern countries govern themselves and determine their futures if they were divided and controlled by governments set up by the Triple Entente?

Not since the French Revolution some 125 years before had Europe been so profoundly shaken and changed. Lenin's vision of worldwide communist revolution captured the imagination of workers and peasants around the globe. It posed a direct challenge to Wilson's vision of liberal capitalist democracy.

Fourteen Points

Wilson decided to make his own bold move in an attempt to steal Lenin's thunder. On January 8, 1918, he announced his Fourteen Points.

This liberal, open, anti-imperialist peace plan promised no more secret agreements, freedom of the seas, free trade, and disarmament. Perhaps Wilson's fourteenth point was most significant: a league of nations to strengthen international cooperation.

To Wilson, only this vision would justify continuing "this tragical and appalling outpouring of blood and treasure." "The day of conquest and aggrandizement is gone by; so is also the day of secret covenants," he declared, in what later would turn out to be a bold-faced lie. But suddenly, two competing new visions for the postwar world were on the table.

The Aftermath in Russia

Lenin caught the world off guard. On March 3, eight months before the end of the war, he signed a peace treaty with Germany, pulling Russian troops from the war. Lenin so wanted peace that he agreed to the harsh terms of the Treaty of Brest-Litovsk. These terms called for giving up control over Poland, Finland, the Baltic states, Ukraine, Georgia, and more. Altogether, Lenin agreed to abandon more than 30,000 square miles of territory and 50 million people. Wilson and the Allies were furious. They reacted quickly.

Armies attacked the new Russia from all directions—native Russians and Cossacks, the Czech legion, Serbs, Greeks, Poles in the west, the French in Ukraine, and some 70,000 Japanese in the Far East. In reaction, Lenin's co-revolutionary leader Leon Trotsky ruthlessly put together a Red Army of approximately five million men. The outspoken Winston Churchill, who would go on to become British prime minister in 1940, spoke for capitalists everywhere when he said that Bolshevism should be strangled in its cradle.

Japan, France, Great Britain, and several other nations sent tens of thousands of troops to Russia, in part to assist conservative White Russians attempting to overthrow the Bolshevik regime. The United States initially hesitated to send troops. "Any attempt to check a revolutionary movement by means of deployed armies is merely trying to use a broom to sweep back a high tide," said Wilson.

Then Wilson changed his mind and finally sent over 15,000 troops. Wilson, however, rejected Churchill's and other Allied leaders' proposal for direct military intervention. Regardless, US troops remained in Russia until 1920, long after the original military rationale had ceased to exist.

Opposition at Home

US support for the White Russians poisoned its relations with the new Soviet government from the start. The support also stirred up opposition at home. Many Americans, including a group of progressive midwestern senators, protested.

These "Peace Progressives" hated the idea of US military intervention.

Hiram Johnson, a Republican senator from California, argued that the United States should deal with the issues that had led to Bolshevism in Russia—"oppression, and poverty, and hunger"—rather than overthrow the new Russian government. He regarded that undertaking as part of Wilson's war against revolution in all countries.

Mississippi senator James Vardaman charged that the military intervention had been conducted on behalf of international corporations that wanted to collect the $10 billion the imperial Russian government owed them.

Wisconsin senator Robert La Follette called it "a mockery" of the Fourteen Points: "the crime of all crimes against democracy, 'self determination,' and the 'consent of the governed.'"

Idaho senator William Borah accused the Wilson administration of presenting misinformation. He noted that people who returned to the United States after spending months in Russia told a very different story about conditions there. "The Russian people very largely support the Russian government," claimed Borah. "If the Soviet Government represents the Russian people, I take the position that the Russian people have the same right to establish a socialistic state as we have to establish a republic."

US support of the White Russians' cause ultimately deepened national and global mistrust of the United States and its motives. This mistrust would have devastating consequences throughout the rest of the twentieth century.

12

The War to End All Wars?

Workers' uprisings were not confined to Russia. They became a global phenomenon by 1919. Years of widening income inequality and poor working conditions spurred workers to action.

American workers joined their compatriots in other countries. More than five million workers went on strike in 1919 alone— 365,000 striking steelworkers led the way, followed by 450,000 miners and 120,000 textile workers. A general strike in Seattle was led by a branch of the Soldiers', Sailors', and Workmen's Council, modeled on the workers' councils of the Russian Revolution. In Boston, police voted 1,134–2 to strike, leading *The Wall Street Journal* to warn, "Lenin and Trotsky are on their way." Wilson called the strike "a crime against civilization."

Determined to put down the strikes and break up the unions, industrialists brought in strikebreakers to cross the picket lines. To protect the strikebreakers, the industrialists hired armed guards, and they also turned to the local police and newly sworn-in deputies. When this wasn't sufficient, state militias and federal troops were sent in to finish the job.

In 1877, the use of federal troops on behalf of capitalists had been extremely controversial. But by 1919, striking workers had learned that the police, courts, and troops could be used against them.

Government actions had badly weakened the Left during the war. Now government officials tried to finish it off.

In November 1919 and January 1920, a spate of anarchist bombings took place. The bombings caused little damage, but Attorney General A. Mitchell Palmer used them as an excuse to unleash federal agents. The agents raided radical groups and labor organizations around the country.

Called the "Palmer Raids," the operation was headed by twenty-four-year-old J. Edgar Hoover, director of the Justice Department's Radical Division.

Hoover had an elaborate index-card system cataloging all potentially threatening individuals, groups, and publications.

By 1920, more than 5,000 alleged radicals had been arrested, many imprisoned without charges for months. This flagrant abuse of civil liberties not only wreaked havoc on the progressive movement, it deliberately equated dissent with un-Americanism. But for Hoover, it was just the beginning. By 1921, his index-card system would contain 450,000 entries.

"Extremely Serious Problems"

Wilson still offered a beacon of hope for war-weary Europeans. Adoring crowds mobbed him when he arrived in Europe on December 18, 1918, for the Paris Peace Conference. Author H. G. Wells recalled, "For a brief interval Wilson stood alone for mankind. Or at least he seemed to stand for mankind. And in that brief interval there was a very extraordinary and significant wave of response to him throughout the earth. . . . He ceased to be a common statesman; he became a Messiah."

The Germans had surrendered on the basis of Wilson's Fourteen Points, believing that they would be treated fairly. One German town greeted returning troops with a banner reading: WELCOME, BRAVE SOLDIERS, YOUR WORK HAS BEEN DONE; GOD AND WILSON WILL CARRY IT ON. The Germans even got rid of the kaiser and adopted a republican form of government as a sign of good faith. But the vagueness of the Fourteen Points proved a weak foundation upon which to base negotiations.

Wilson had mistakenly failed to get Allies to concur on the Fourteen Points during the war, when he had leverage. Naively, he hadn't anticipated the impact that human nature, global imperialism, and the desire for revenge would have. Among the victorious Allies, there was scarcely a family who wasn't mourning a dead son, father, brother, or other loved one. Some families had lost every male member, leaving behind only widows and orphans. Many who survived the war had lost an arm or a leg, or had suffered disfiguring battle wounds, or endured the lifelong effects from the chemical gases.

The British made it clear that they had no intention of accepting Wilson's "freedom of the seas" concept. They didn't want to limit their navy's abilities to defend British trade routes. The French also remembered their defeat by Germany in the Franco-Prussian War of 1870–1871. This bitter loss fueled their desire to seek revenge on Germany.

Allied leaders did little to hide the racism that underlay their continued subjugation of dark-skinned people.

Japan's representatives proposed that a clause on racial equality be included in the Covenant of the League of Nations. "The equality of states being a basic principle of the League of Nations," read the clause, "the High Contracting Parties agree to accord, as soon as possible, to all alien nationals of States members of the League, equal and just treatment in every respect, making no distinction, either in law or fact, on account of their race or nationality."

From left to right: British prime minister David Lloyd George, Italian premier Vittorio Orlando, French premier Georges Clemenceau, and Wilson at the Paris Peace Conference. Most of the lofty rhetoric of Wilson's Fourteen Points was rejected by the other Allies, who were out for revenge, new colonies, and naval dominance in the postwar world.

The British rejected the clause outright. It raised "extremely serious problems" for the British Empire, explained Lord Robert Cecil, a British cabinet member.

Vladimir Lenin wasn't invited to the Paris peace talks, but his presence was felt throughout. He predicted that the capitalist powers would never abandon their colonies or accept Wilson's vision of solving conflicts in a peaceful manner.

He was right.

Twenty-seven nations met in Versailles, just outside Paris, on January 12, 1919, to hammer out peace terms. The task ahead was enormous. Empires were collapsing. New countries were emerging. Starvation was rampant. Disease was spreading. Displaced persons were seeking refuge.

Visionary leadership was desperately needed to craft a meaningful and effective treaty, but the heads of state from Great Britain, France, and Italy found Wilson, who considered himself to be the "personal instrument of God," to be insufferable.

"Mr. Wilson bores me with his 14 points," Georges Clemenceau, the French prime minister, complained. "Why, God Almighty has only ten!"

British prime minister Lloyd George agreed, commenting, "I really think that at first the idealist President regarded himself as a missionary whose function was to rescue the poor European heathen."

Who was Wilson to preach? The Allies accused him of having betrayed his own Fourteen Points when he'd sent soldiers into the Russian Civil War. They pointed out that US troops were still stationed in Russia.

Ultimately, few of Wilson's Fourteen Points remained in the Treaty of Versailles. The victors—particularly Great Britain, France, and Japan—divided the former German colonies in Asia and Africa. They also carved up the Ottoman Empire. They called their new colonies "mandates," so the world wouldn't see their actions as extensions of prewar colonial exploitation. Wilson resisted the landgrab, but he ultimately went along. He rationalized his decision by arguing that the Germans had "ruthlessly exploited their colonies," denying their citizens basic rights, while the Allies had treated their colonies humanely—a view that was laughed at by the people who lived in those new mandates.

One of those people was a man from French Indochina named Ho Chi Minh. He questioned the right of the French to control Vietnam. As a nationalist, he believed that French Indochina had a right to govern itself free of colonial rule.

He knew firsthand that the lives of the poor differed greatly from the lives of the colonial elite in regions of the world under Western control. In

At the Paris Peace Conference, Ho Chi Minh visited Wilson and the US delegation. He carried a petition demanding Vietnamese independence.

a rented tuxedo and a bowler hat, Ho carried a petition to the Paris Peace Conference and met with Wilson and other US delegates. He demanded independence for the Vietnamese.

But like other non-Western world leaders who attended the peace talks, Ho would learn that it would take an armed struggle to win liberation, not the goodwill of colonial powers. Later, Ho became the revolutionary leader of North Vietnam. Ultimately, he and his army defeated the French in the Battle of Dien Bien Phu in 1954, which paved the way for America's disastrous involvement in the Vietnam War.

As for the Germans, they protested that the treaty terms were severe, with reparations totaling $33 billion—less than one fifth what France demanded but more than double what Germany had expected. Germany's ability to pay was greatly compromised by its loss of colonies and Polish-speaking territories. Adding to the financial burden was Germany's surrender of the port of Danzig and the Saar coal region. And the "war guilt clause," which pinned the blame on Germany for starting the war, left an especially bitter taste.

The House of Morgan (later known as J. P. Morgan & Co.), concerned about protecting its interests, also influenced the treaty. Thomas W. Lamont, one of the firm's leading partners, traveled to Versailles as one of two Treasury Department representatives for the American delegation. Lamont and other bankers wanted to ensure that the interests of the House of Morgan were well protected. Lamont had advocated for Germany to pay $40 billion. Later, Morgan would contend that Germany had gotten off easy.

The Rise of Fascism

As Germany would soon see, its reparations were worse on paper than in practice. Beginning in 1921, the actual payments were adjusted downward based on Germany's ability to pay.

Article 231 of the Versailles Treaty—that humiliating "war guilt clause"—did not actually use the word "guilt." Rather, it made Germany responsible for paying for "all the loss and damage" resulting from "a war imposed by the aggression of Germany and her allies."

In the 1920s, Adolf Hitler and other right-wing Germans would exploit the postwar sense of victimization. Little of the fighting had taken place on German soil, and this led them to believe that Germany had surrendered when victory was possible—and close at hand. Many believed, as Hitler did, that their leaders had stabbed them in the back.

Just as American workers were fighting for increased wages and improved working conditions, so were workers in Italy. There, leftist demonstrators and strikers clashed with armed fascisti who were followers of Benito Mussolini. Mussolini, the leader of the Fascist Party, was originally a member of the

Benito Mussolini wearing different uniforms, circa 1935. The Italian dictator claimed to have invented the word "fascist."

Italian Socialist Party before switching to fascism. He claimed to have invented the word, which the *Enciclopedia Italiana di Scienze, Lettere ed Arti*, an Italian encyclopedia, defined as "corporatism," or "the merger of state and corporate power." Mussolini was convinced that Italy needed a dictator to fix Italy's social, economic, and political problems. Once established as that dictator, he eliminated free speech and opposition.

Later, the US ambassador to Italy would praise Mussolini's anti-communism and his willingness to use strong-arm methods to put down labor strikes.

World War I marked the end of European dominance and the rise of the war's two real victors: the United States and Japan. For the next ten years, American businessmen and bankers would expand rapidly around the globe. New York would replace London as the center of world finance, and soon the US domination of the world economy would begin.

Oil companies would help lead the way.

13

Disillusionment

Soon after the armistice was signed, Britain's Lord Curzon pronounced that "the Allied cause had floated to victory upon a wave of oil." The United States was part of that wave, having met 80 percent of the Allies' petroleum needs.

But now that the war had ended, oil companies were poised to grab whatever new territory they could. In 1920, Royal Dutch Shell said, "We must not be outstripped in this struggle to obtain new territory. . . . Our geologists are everywhere where any chance of success exists."

Shell trained its sights on Venezuela in South America. There, General Juan Vicente Gómez's government offered friendly, stable conditions. Venezuela seemed much more welcoming than Mexico, where conditions were still unstable and oil production was declining. In his book *The Prize*, Daniel Yergin describes Gómez as a "cruel, cunning, and avaricious dictator who, for twenty-seven years, ruled Venezuela for his personal enrichment."

Worried about losing out to British oil companies, US companies

The brutal reign of Venezuelan dictator Juan Vicente Gómez's made his country a favorite of American and British oil companies, who helped him amass a great fortune.

soon joined the competition for Venezuelan oil. These companies overlooked the fact that Gómez had an army of local strongmen and a network of spies. They also overlooked the fact that Venezuelans who disagreed with Gómez were arrested and treated with "medieval severity."

Despite Gómez's known cruelty, the United States was ready to help him, if that's what was necessary to protect Royal Dutch Shell's oil supplies. In 1923, for example, when the United States learned that a revolution was brewing, it sent a Special Service Squadron to Venezuela as a show of support for Gómez. The rumors, it turned out, were unfounded.

In 1922, Gómez turned to US oil companies for help in writing parts of Venezuela's Petroleum Law. The oil companies obliged, writing a business-friendly law that allowed them to reap massive profits.

But the law didn't protect oil company workers or the environment. Unsafe working conditions and a lack of oversight and regulation meant that spills and accidents happened frequently, hurting workers and the environment. One oil blowout in 1922 spread twenty-two miles. It released nearly one million barrels of oil into Lake Maracaibo.

Gómez's family and friends bought up choice properties and sold them to foreign companies. Venezuelan oil production jumped from 1.4 million barrels in 1921 to 137 million in 1929, making it second only to the United States in total output and first worldwide in exports. Americans owned two of the top three oil companies that dominated the Venezuelan market: Gulf and Pan American. At the time of Gómez's death, the two companies were responsible for 60 percent of oil production in Venezuela.

While Gómez became extremely wealthy, ordinary Venezuelans were mired in poverty.

By the time Gómez died in 1935, his fortune was worth an estimated $200 million and his land holdings totaled 20 million acres. Venezuelans celebrated his death.

It would take until 1945 for the leftist Democratic Action Party of Venezuelan president Rómulo Betancourt to succeed in taking power and to forge a relationship with oil companies that better protected the country's interests. Though Betancourt would be ousted three years later, progressive reformers would establish a legacy of nationalist and anti-imperialist resistance to the exploitation of Venezuela's resources by foreign oil interests.

Disillusioned Americans

For many years, people believed that the United States was so disgusted by the war and the complicated European entanglements that ensued from it that it withdrew from the world stage and plunged into a period of isolationism. This isn't true. Historians have long since discredited the isolationist myth.

It's true that the war had left a bitter taste in the mouths of most Americans. The nature of the fighting—the trench and chemical warfare—and the shaky postwar settlement combined to undermine the glory of the war itself.

Americans were disillusioned. The war to make the world safe for democracy had failed in its purpose. Nor was there hope that this war would end all wars. Sure, some people clung to the belief that the United States had engaged in a great crusade for freedom and democracy, but for others, the phrase rang hollow.

Although Woodrow Wilson had gushed, "At last the world knows America as the savior of the world," political opponents did not treat him like a savior. At home, both the Left and the Right attacked him.

Wilson fought back. He toured the country, trying to rouse support for the Treaty of Versailles so that the United States could join the League of Nations. He tried to explain that it was the only way the United States could solve the problems caused by the treaty.

But Senators Borah, La Follette, Norris, and Johnson denounced the league as a group of "imperialists" who were bent on defeating revolutions and defending their own imperial designs. Borah charged that the treaty was "a cruel, destructive, brutal document" that had produced "a league to guarantee the integrity of the British Empire."

Norris condemned the treaty provision that handed Shandong, the birthplace of Chinese philosopher Confucius, to Japan as "the disgraceful rape of an innocent people." Apparently, some thought the land that had given us the wisdom of Confucius was not capable of self-determination.

Isolationists and others who opposed the treaty wanted guarantees that the United States wouldn't be drawn into military actions without authorization by Congress. Opponents feared that a body such as the League of Nations would be an expensive organization that would draw the United States into European politics.

Wilson was confused. How could this have happened?

George Creel, who had headed the Committee on Public Information—the US government's official wartime propaganda agency—explained to the president how it happened. Wilson's own wartime policy had deprived him of domestic political allies. "All the radical, or liberal friends of your

THIS LEAGUE OF NATIONS BRIDGE WAS DESIGNED BY THE PRESIDENT OF THE U·S·A·

KEYSTONE USA

BELGIUM FRANCE

ENGLAND ITALY

THE GAP IN THE BRIDGE.

As this December 1919 *Punch* cartoon shows, the Senate's rejection of US participation in the League of Nations rendered the league largely ineffectual. Wilson had helped guarantee the league's defeat by silencing potential anti-imperialist allies in the United States during the war.

anti-imperialist war policy were either silenced or intimidated," said Creel. "The Department of Justice and the Post Office were allowed to silence and intimidate them. There was no voice left to argue for your sort of peace. *The Nation* and *The Public* got nipped. All the radical and socialist press was dumb."

Amid all this discord, Wilson presented the Versailles Treaty and its Covenant of the League of Nations to the Senate for a vote. The league would be an international organization, headquartered in Geneva, Switzerland, designed to facilitate international cooperation and security and provide a council for resolving disputes. "Dare we reject it and break the heart of the world?" he asked the Senate.

They dared. By seven votes, the treaty and the League of Nations failed to pass the US Senate.

By 1920, Americans had had eight years of Woodrow Wilson's idealism. They looked forward to what the next president, Warren G. Harding, would call "a return to normalcy." The next three presidents—Harding, Coolidge, and Hoover—would seek ways to expand US economic interests in Latin America without resorting to the heavy-handed gunboat diplomacy that Roosevelt, Taft, and Wilson had used.

Harding pledged that, unlike Wilson, he "would not empower an Assistant Secretary of the navy to draft a constitution for helpless neighbors in the West Indies and jam it down their throats at the point of bayonets borne by United States Marines."

Nor would Harding do other things that Wilson had done. Harding promised that the United States would be a good neighbor: "I [will not] misuse the power of the Executive to cover with a veil of secrecy repeated acts of unwarranted interference in domestic affairs of the little republics of the Western Hemisphere, such as in the last few years have not only made enemies of those who should be our friends, but have rightfully discredited our country as their trusted neighbor."

Far from becoming isolationist, the United States would find more effective ways than warfare to expand its empire.

Harding and his Republican successors would make more friends among US bankers than among the people who lived in those little republics. In 1922, *The Nation* magazine reported that revolutionaries had sparked an uprising against the extremely unpopular president of Nicaragua. The revolutionaries captured a fort overlooking the capital. In response, the commander of the US Marines who were already stationed there alerted them that he would use artillery if they didn't give up control of the fort.

Latin America had twenty independent republics. But in several republics, according to *The Nation*, the governments were fictitious. US bankers actually ruled the puppet governments. And to make matters worse, US troops backed up the bankers.

This, the magazine continued, reduced at least five countries—Cuba, Panama, Haiti, and the Dominican Republic, along with Nicaragua—to the status of colonies. At least four others—Guatemala, Honduras, Costa Rica, and Peru—were in the process of becoming colonized by US bankers.

"How far is this to go?" asked *The Nation*. "Is the United States to create a great empire in this hemisphere—an empire over which Congress and the American people exercise no authority, an empire ruled by a group of Wall Street bankers at whose disposal the State and Navy departments graciously place their resources? These are the questions which the people, the plain people whose sons die of tropic fever or of a patriot's bullet, have a right to ask."

Wilson's Conflicted Legacy

In many ways, Wilson's failures provided a fitting capstone to a decade in which the United States' unique mixture of idealism, militarism, greed, and realpolitik propelled the nation toward becoming a world power.

Wilson had proclaimed, "America is the only idealistic nation in the world." He acted as if he believed it was true. He hoped to spread democracy. He hoped to end colonialism. He hoped to transform the world. He supported self-determination and opposed formal empire. He had promised that the United States would "never again seek one additional foot of territory by conquest." Yet he intervened repeatedly in other nations' internal affairs, including Russia, Mexico, and countries throughout Central America.

He encouraged reform, but he held a deep mistrust of the kind of fundamental, and at times revolutionary, change that would actually improve people's lives.

He championed social justice, but he believed that property rights were sacrosanct and must never be infringed upon.

He endorsed human brotherhood, and yet, believing that nonwhites were inferior, he resegregated the federal government.

He extolled democracy and the rule of law, yet he oversaw extreme abuses of civil liberties.

He condemned imperialism, yet he propped up the global imperial order.

He proclaimed a just, nonpunitive peace, but he went along with a harsh, retributive peace that inadvertently helped create the preconditions for the rise of Adolf Hitler and the Nazis.

His inept performance at Versailles contributed to the Senate defeat of the treaty and inclusion in the League of Nations.

Thus, the "war to end all wars," the war "to make the world safe for democracy," would have consequences that went far beyond the horrors on the battlefield. The United States would never join the League of Nations, rendering the league powerless in the face of fascist aggression in the 1930s.

Later, it would be revealed that US bankers and arms manufacturers—dubbed "merchants of death"—had raked in huge profits. This created widespread skepticism about foreign involvements at a time when the United States needed to contend with a coming "axis of evil": Germany, Italy, and Japan.

PART TWO

The New Deal:
"I Welcome Their
Hatred"

14

The Stock Market

The 1920s is often remembered as a decade of fun and indulgence. People referred to it as "the Roaring Twenties" and "the Jazz Age." While that image of gangsters, flappers, and frivolity is certainly exaggerated, Americans did do all they could to put the "Great War" behind them.

It was a decade during which most Americans prospered. Three Republican presidents would occupy the White House. The gap between the wealthiest 1 percent and the rest of the population widened sharply.

In 1923, Calvin Coolidge became the thirtieth US president, after Warren G. Harding became ill and died while on a speaking tour. Known as "Silent Cal," Coolidge was a small-government conservative who cut taxes on the wealthy, eased business regulations, and balanced the budget. During his presidency, business boomed, but workers and the poor weren't so lucky. As a result, many Americans were barely making ends meet.

Other changes were also occurring. The 1920 census showed

that for the first time, the majority of Americans lived in urban areas rather than rural ones. During the war and after, millions of people had migrated from farms to factories, particularly African Americans who relocated from the south to the north in pursuit of work and opportunity. This was called the "Great Migration." It would continue for decades. Blacks sought a better life in the north, where they earned significantly higher wages, but social conditions were often deplorable and discrimination persisted.

As the decade progressed, interest in buying and selling stocks skyrocketed, with get-rich-quick mania sweeping the nation. Investors borrowed at stunningly low interest rates and often made a killing on the market. Others borrowed to fuel consumption. Cars, radios, and other in-demand goods were bought on credit. Advertisements were everywhere, warning people if they didn't look, smell, or sound right, they would face humiliation. With the economy expanding on such a shaky foundation, some experts warned that a crash was coming.

When Coolidge decided not to run for a second term, Herbert Hoover, the popular secretary of commerce, threw his hat into the ring. In the ensuing contest, promising "a final triumph over poverty," he easily defeated New York Democrat Al Smith, the first Catholic to run atop a major party ticket.

At his inauguration on March 4, 1929, Hoover characterized the 1920s as a "great period of recovery" and thanked Coolidge for his "wise guidance." He proclaimed a future "bright with hope."

Following Hoover's victory, the stock market continued to climb, peaking on September 3, 1929. But over the following few weeks, the market began to drop. On October 29, 1929, a day known as "Black Tuesday," the stock market crashed. Panic set in. Stock prices plummeted to record lows. The United States plunged into the worst depression in its history. It is known as "the Great Depression." Hoover proved powerless to stop it.

The Bank Takes a Holiday (With Your Money)

The economic situation in the United States continued to worsen as the 1930s rolled in.

On October 31, 1932, Nevada's Lieutenant Governor Morley Griswold declared a twelve-day bank holiday. Around the state, banks closed. Depositors rushed to their banks to find them shut, their doors and windows locked. They didn't want everyone to withdraw all the money from the banks at the same time. Mayors and governors across the nation anxiously eyed the situation, wondering if they should follow suit.

A crowd gathers outside the New York Stock Exchange following the October 29, 1929, stock market crash.

Worried investors stand outside a bank hoping to withdraw their money before it's too late.

Things began to unravel when Michigan declared an eight-day bank holiday on February 14, 1933, closing 550 state and national banks. *The New York Times* tried to assure nervous readers that "there is no reason why [Michigan] should be taken as a precedent."

The *Times* was wrong. Soon after, Maryland and Tennessee closed banks. So did Kentucky, Oklahoma, and Alabama as panicky depositors lined up to get their money out while they still could.

Between 1930 and 1932, one fifth of US banks failed. Others tottered on the edge of closure. Many Americans lost their life savings. By 1933, economic problems seemed insurmountable. The jobless rate stood at 25 percent. Farm income plummeted by 60 percent. Industrial production was down by more than 50 percent. The banking system had collapsed. Bread-lines formed in every town and city. Homeless walked the streets.

The Rest of the World

Most of the world was in even worse shape than the United States. Unlike the United States, the belligerents of World War I hadn't experienced the period of relative prosperity of the 1920s. Those countries had not yet fully recovered from the devastation of the war.

Benito Mussolini was firmly in power in Italy after years of dictatorial rule. Adolf Hitler and his National Socialists had come to power in Germany by exploiting both postwar grievances and economic hardship.

Mussolini and Hitler appealed to nationalism—an extreme form of patriotism marked by a feeling that one's country is superior to other countries. Hitler was also viciously anti-Semitic, trying to blame Germany's problems on the Jews.

Trouble was also brewing in Asia. In September 1931, Japanese forces seized Manchuria, a resource-rich and contested region bordered by the Soviet Union, China, and Korea, and they continued their advances from there.

Banksters

By 1932, mistrust of Wall Street financiers was at an all-time high. This mistrust prompted the Senate to investigate the banks' role in causing the economic collapse.

The Senate Committee on Banking and Currency appointed former New York County Assistant District Attorney Ferdinand Pecora to lead the hearings. He exposed fraud and wrongdoing on the part of the nation's top bankers who were guilty of obscenely high salaries, unpaid taxes, hidden bonuses, unethical loans, and more.

The committee blistered the nation's leading bankers for what the committee's chair, Peter Norbeck, called a "wild stock market boom." Norbeck

People stand in a breadline, waiting to be fed at a mission house under the Brooklyn Bridge, New York.

argued that the banks' "promotion schemes" were "just a polite way of robbing the public."

As a result, Charles E. Mitchell, one of the most powerful men in the country, was forced to resign as chairman of National City Bank. Mitchell managed to win an acquittal on charges of defrauding the government of $850,000 in income taxes, which could have landed him a ten-year prison sentence.

Bankers were nothing more than "banksters," according to magazines such as *The Nation.* "If you steal $25, you're a thief," wrote the magazine. "If you steal $250,000, you're an embezzler. If you steal $2,500,000, you're a financier."

Enter Franklin Delano Roosevelt

The world Franklin Delano Roosevelt confronted when he was inaugurated president on March 4, 1933, was vastly different from the one in which he ran for vice president thirteen years earlier. The prosperity of the post-war 1920s had long since vanished.

During his campaign, Roosevelt had given little indication of the kind of economic policies he would adopt to combat the crisis. At times, he attacked President Herbert Hoover from the right for spending too aggressively and unbalancing the budget. At other times, he acknowledged the suffering of the people and called for a "New Deal." Now he had to solve some very real and very practical problems.

Despite the misery and despair wrought by the Great Depression, America's mood was upbeat. With Roosevelt's election, there was a

Soon-to-be president Franklin Delano Roosevelt (*right*) and President Herbert Hoover ride to Roosevelt's inauguration. The inauguration inspired much optimism.

sense of buoyant optimism in the air. Americans were eager to see a new president who acted on the belief that "nothing is impossible for the United States."

The *New York Times* captured the national excitement: "Americans are a people of invincible hope. They have exhibited an extraordinary patience in enduring hardships which millions of them have somehow come to believe will be mitigated or removed by the mere fact of MR. ROOSEVELT'S entering the White House. . . . No President of the United States ever came to greater opportunities amid so great an outpouring of popular trust and hope."

Roosevelt decided to act boldly. The country was behind him. The Democrats controlled both houses of Congress, and people wanted action. Will Rogers later commented on the president's early days: "If he burned down the capitol, we would cheer and say, 'Well, we at least got a fire started anyhow.'"

Roosevelt's much-anticipated inaugural address rallied the nation to the fight. His declaration that "the only thing we have to fear is fear itself" seems, in retrospect, to have been out of touch with reality, given the magnitude of the nation's problems. But Roosevelt connected with a deeper reality— Americans' desperate need for renewed hope and confidence.

This was the challenge that faced Franklin Delano Roosevelt as he rode toward the US Capitol on March 4, 1933. He was about to be sworn in as president, and he had inherited a mess.

15

"People Can't Eat the Constitution"

During his first days in office, Roosevelt focused on jump-starting the economy and getting Americans back to work with a series of reforms that he called the "New Deal." The New Deal would provide relief for the poor, help spur the recovery of the economy, and enact laws to reform the American economic system.

After the stock market crash, the bank failures across the country, and the public anger at the "banksters," Roosevelt knew that conditions were ripe for dramatic changes in the banking system. Several advisers urged the president to nationalize the banks. But Roosevelt didn't. Instead, on his first full day in office, Roosevelt took a much more conservative approach—he declared a four-day national bank holiday.

While the banks were closed, Roosevelt met with the nation's top bankers. He also called a special session of Congress to pass emergency legislation to establish a series of badly needed banking regulations.

On March 12, 1933, President Roosevelt spoke to Americans over the radio in his first "fireside chat." He addressed listeners as

President Roosevelt sits at his desk during one of his radio addresses, called a "fireside chat."

"my friends" and communicated directly with them in terms they could all understand. "I want to talk for a few minutes with the people of the United States about banking."

This first of about thirty fireside chats succeeded in calming the public's fear about the banking crisis. In his speech, Roosevelt thanked the American people for their "fortitude and good temper."

At Roosevelt's insistence, Congress passed the Emergency Banking Act, which was largely written by the bankers themselves and restored the banking system without radical change.

Congressman William Lemke criticized Roosevelt's actions: "The president drove the money changers out of the Capitol on March 4th—and they were all back on the 9th."

Roosevelt's actions show fundamentally conservative instincts. He would save capitalism from the capitalists. Yet the means he would use to save capitalism would be bold, visionary, and humane.

As president, he laid out an ambitious recovery program during his first 100 days in office. It included the Agricultural Adjustment Administration, to save farming; the Civilian Conservation Corps, to put young men to work in forests and parks; the Public Works Administration (PWA), to coordinate large-scale public works projects; and the Glass-Steagall Banking Act, which separated investment and commercial banking and instituted federal insurance of bank deposits.

Roosevelt's solution to the banking crisis would serve as a model for how he would handle most issues. He demonstrated that he valued both democracy and capitalism.

A Civilian Conservation Corps (CCC) crew works in Idaho's Boise National Forest.

Fixing the banking problem was the first step. But fixing the banks alone could not remedy the nation's ailing economy. "We have provided the machinery to restore our financial system," Roosevelt told the American people during that first fireside chat. "It is up to you to support it and make it work."

The NIRA and NRA

In another fireside chat, Roosevelt told the American people of his plan "to get many hundreds of thousands of the unemployed back on the payroll by snowfall" and to ensure "a better future for the longer pull."

To achieve these goals, Roosevelt successfully pushed Congress to pass the National Industrial Recovery Act (NIRA), which he considered "the most important and far reaching legislation ever enacted." At its center was the National Recovery Administration (NRA). The NRA wasn't completely new. It was modeled in part on the War Industries Board, which had been directed by Bernard Baruch during World War I.

The NRA suspended antitrust laws. This move effectively ended laissez-faire capitalism—that is, capitalism without government interference. Under the NRA, each industry drew up its own code covering wages, prices, production, and working conditions. The largest corporations dominated the code-setting process, with labor and consumer groups playing, at best, a minor role.

President Roosevelt chose General Hugh Johnson to head the NRA. Johnson's leadership fueled allegations that the New Deal was fascist. Johnson did not hide his fascist sympathies. In September 1933 at an NRA parade in New York, *Time* magazine reported, "General Johnson, his hand raised in a continuous fascist salute, had declared the parade to be 'the most marvelous demonstration I have ever seen.'"

Johnson even gave Frances Perkins, the US Secretary of Labor and the

A restaurant window displays its NRA Blue Eagle poster, showing its support for the agency that created codes of fair business practices.

country's first female cabinet member, a copy of Raffaello Viglione's fascist tract *The Corporate State*. Eventually, Roosevelt removed Johnson from his position because of his strange behavior, abrasive personality, heavy drinking, and habit of antagonizing labor. In his farewell speech, Johnson celebrated the "shining name" of Benito Mussolini, Italy's fascist dictator.

American Fascists?

There was great uncertainty about where Roosevelt was taking the country during his first term. Many liberals applauded the NIRA legislation. But some observers compared the United States with fascist Italy and feared a form of American fascism.

"The tremendous concentration of power in the hands of the president, the new codes under the National Industrial Recovery Act regulating competition, the fixing of minimum wage rates, of maximum working hours in industry, and the general policy of economic planning and co-ordination of production, all strongly suggest essential features of the Italian fascist programme," wrote *The Quarterly Review of Commerce.*

While some businessmen preferred laissez-faire economics, hating government interference in any form, others welcomed government assistance in stabilizing the economy and limiting disruptive competition.

Some feared that FDR's New Deal would propel America toward fascism. Despite the numerous right-wing groups that emerged during the 1930s, the fascist threat never took hold in the United States as it had in Italy and Germany. That is not to say that Italy's prime minister Benito Mussolini and Germany's Adolph Hitler lacked admirers.

Henry Luce, the publisher of *Time* and *Fortune* magazines, openly supported Mussolini. In 1934, *Fortune* praised Italian fascism, saying that it embodied "certain ancient virtues of the race [including] discipline, duty, courage, glory, sacrifice."

Many members of the American Legion felt the same way about fascism. The organization's commander, Alvin Owsley, considered Italian fascism a model for fighting every element that threatened democracy, including the forces of the left. "The fascisti are to Italy what the American Legion is to the United States," Owsley declared. In 1930, the American Legion invited Mussolini to address its national convention.

Elected officials also praised the ultraconservative Mussolini. "If this country ever needed a Mussolini, it needs one now," proclaimed Pennsylvania Senator David Reed.

Like Mussolini, Hitler had numerous defenders in the United States too. Many shared his anti-Semitic views. Some were elected officials, such as Republican Congressman Louis T. McFadden of Pennsylvania, who took to the floor of the House in May 1933 to decry the international Jewish conspiracy.

This so-called conspiracy was based on deeply anti-Semitic lies. It maintained that Jews, especially bankers, were plotting to take over the world. McFadden declared, "This country has fallen into the hands of the international money changers. Is it not true that in the United States today the Gentiles have the slips of paper while the Jews have the gold and the lawful money?"

Of course, there was no such conspiracy. There never has been. But to prove his point even further, McFadden read passages from *The Protocols of the Elders of Zion*. This widely distributed publication was part of an anti-Semitic conspiracy to spread the false idea that Jews control the world and that they are responsible for the world's problems. Though the contents of *The Protocols* were entirely made up, rendering it a complete work of fiction, many people believed its lies and still do today.

One of those people was Father Charles Coughlin, the infamous "radio priest" of Royal Oak, Michigan. Father Coughlin took to the airwaves to spew his anti-Semitic vision. His weekly publication *Social Justice* published the *Protocols* in installments. He urged followers to join the Christian Front, an armed militia.

A 1938 Gallup poll reported that 10 percent of American families owning radios listened to Coughlin's sermons on a regular

A childhood bully, Benito Mussolini formed Italy's Fascist Party and eventually made himself dictator.

REICHSKANZLER
ADOLF HITLER

Many people in the United States shared Hitler's fascistic, racist, and anti-Semitic views.

basis and 25 percent did so occasionally. Of these listeners, 83 percent approved of the priest's messages. In 1940, *Social Justice* had more than 200,000 readers weekly.

Even farther to the right were the so-called shirt movements in the United States. They were inspired by Mussolini's Blackshirts and Hitler's Brownshirts.

An American extremist named William Dudley Pelley believed Jews and communists were trying to take over the world. Pelley founded the Silver Legion in 1933, which may have enlisted as many as 25,000 members that year. They wore silver shirts and established chapters in nearly every state.

Other extremist groups included the Jayhawk Nazis (Kansas), Knights of the White Camelia (West Virginia), Khaki Shirts (Philadelphia), Crusader White Shirts (Tennessee), and Christian Mobilizers (New York City).

One of the most violent organizations was the Midwest-based Black Legion. It had split off from the Ku Klux Klan in 1925. Wearing black robes instead of the Klan's white sheets, the legion had an estimated membership of 60,000 to 100,000 in 1935. Its leader, Virgil Effinger, spoke openly about the need for mass extermination of American Jews. In 1937, the federal government cracked down on the group.

Even soon-to-be vice president Harry Truman once applied for membership in the Ku Klux Klan before thinking better of it.

Abandoning the Gold

In 1933, the money of most countries was backed by gold. It was—and had been for centuries—the unquestioned anchor of the global monetary system. In country after country, a dollar or its equivalent could be traded for its value in gold. In 1932, the value of one ounce of gold was $20.69, a price that had remained remarkably stable for close to 100 years. That meant that if a person held one dollar, he or she knew that it was worth approximately one twenty-first of an ounce of gold. This was known as the "gold standard."

When the Depression hit, people panicked. What if their paper money lost its value? Many traded in their paper money for gold and hoarded it. This created a dangerous situation for governments: the possibility of running out of gold.

Roosevelt realized that if the United States stayed on the gold standard, there simply would not be enough money in the economy to fuel a sustainable economic recovery. There needed to be more cash in the system than the gold standard would allow. If the government cut its ties with gold, it could print more money and pump it into the economy as needed. Roosevelt ultimately decided to suspend the gold standard to spur inflation and kick-start economic growth. Faith in the US economy would now be tied not to the value of an ounce of gold, but to the US government itself.

Baloney Dollars

Roosevelt received a mixed response to his suspension of the gold standard. Some businessmen and bankers supported his decision. Others denounced it.

Abandoning the gold standard was a commitment to "baloney dollars," said former presidential candidate Al Smith, who had become a New Deal critic. "The Democratic party is fated to be always the party of greenbackers, free silverites, rubber dollar manufacturers, and crackpots."

The Federal Reserve Board called the currency decision a "tragic illusion." The New York Chamber of Commerce rejected a resolution to support Roosevelt and the new monetary policy.

Congressman Louis McFadden even accused Roosevelt of partaking in the fictitious Jewish conspiracy to take over the world. McFadden claimed that the president's abandonment of the gold standard "had given gold and lawful money of the country to the international money Jews of whom Franklin D. Roosevelt is the familiar."

Roosevelt sent a letter to the US Chamber of Commerce's annual convention, asking members to "stop crying wolf" and "to cooperate in working for recovery."

But they didn't. The businessmen's attacks on Roosevelt and New Deal policies intensified. By October 1934, *Time* magazine noted that the attacks had become personal: "It was no longer a matter of Business v. Government but of Business v. Franklin Delano Roosevelt."

Roosevelt didn't stop there. He repudiated his earlier support for joining the League of Nations. He even took steps to reduce the country's 140,000-man army.

This upset Secretary of War George Dern and General Douglas MacArthur. MacArthur told the president that he was endangering the country's safety. This infuriated Roosevelt, and the tension boiled over.

"The President turned the full vials of his sarcasm upon me," MacArthur later wrote in his memoir. In response to Roosevelt's sarcasm, MacArthur spoke recklessly: "[I] said something to the general effect that when we lost the next war, and an American boy, lying in the mud with an enemy bayonet through his belly and an enemy foot on his dying throat, spat out his last curse, I wanted the name not to be MacArthur, but Roosevelt."

Roosevelt grew livid. "You must not talk that way to the President!" he roared.

MacArthur became overwrought. He apologized to the president and offered his resignation as chief of staff. He rushed out of the Oval Office and vomited on the White House steps.

Democratic Strength

Roosevelt was an astute politician. In creating the New Deal, he had stood up to corporate executives and Wall Street bankers. The 1934 midterm elections showed that the country had moved to the left. More and more Americans sided with Roosevelt.

The Democrats drubbed the opposition, winning twenty-six of the thirty-five Senate races. This gave them a 69–25 advantage over Republicans in the Senate. In the House of Representatives, the Democrats led 322–103.

The New York Times called the election the "most overwhelming victory in the history of American politics." It gave the president "a clear mandate" and "literally destroyed" the right wing of the Republican Party.

This was a wake-up call for Republicans. "Unless the Republican party is delivered from its reactionary leadership and reorganized in accordance with its one-time liberal principles," warned William Borah, an Idaho Republican senator, "it will die like the Whig party of sheer political cowardice." He criticized his party for opposing the New Deal "without offering a program of [its] own in place of it." Borah complained that when Republicans ask their leaders for an alternative to the New Deal, "they are offered the Constitution. But people can't eat the Constitution."

Universal Health Care

All in all, the combination of a left-leaning Congress; an energized, progressive population; a resurgent labor movement; and a responsive and caring

President Roosevelt made possible the greatest period of social experimentation in US history.

Still, Roosevelt had more work to do. Perhaps emboldened by the country's support, he saved his heaviest artillery for his annual message to Congress on January 3, 1936.

Over national radio, Roosevelt lashed out at his enemies on the right. "We have earned the hatred of entrenched greed," he proudly noted. "They seek the restoration of their selfish power. . . . Give them their way and they will take the course of every autocracy of the past—power for themselves, enslavement for the public."

It was an election year. As Roosevelt campaigned for a second term in 1936, he continued his harsh attack on business. He highlighted the list of progressive achievements during his first four years in office. The Works Progress Administration (WPA) and other government programs had put millions of unemployed back to work in government jobs. The economic and banking systems had been reformed. For the first time, the government had sided with workers against employers and unfair labor practices. The government had nurtured the growth of unions. Social Security guaranteed a degree of comfort in old age that few workers had previously enjoyed. The tax burden was shifting increasingly to the wealthy.

"We had to struggle with the old enemies of peace—business and financial monopoly, speculation, reckless banking, class antagonism, sectionalism, war profiteering," Roosevelt said before supporters at Madison Square Garden in New York City. "They had begun to consider the Government of the United States as a mere appendage to their own affairs. We now know that Government by organized money is just as dangerous as Government by organized mob. . . . They are unanimous in their hate for me—and I welcome their hatred."

Voters agreed. The revitalized Democrats thrashed the Republicans at every level. Roosevelt defeated his opponent, Kansas governor Alf Landon, 523–8 in the Electoral College. He won every state except Maine and Vermont. The Democrats also controlled the House, 331–89, and the Senate, 76–16.

The *Chicago Tribune* saw the lopsided vote as a ringing endorsement of the president's agenda. "The result of the election is a vote of confidence in Mr. Roosevelt and the New Deal," declared the conservative newspaper. "He will enter upon his second term with what amounts to a blank check signed yesterday by an overwhelming majority of the American people."

But then Roosevelt took a political misstep. He mistakenly believed that the end of the Depression was in sight. Eager to balance the budget, administration officials decided to cut spending.

Roosevelt targeted the WPA and the PWA for deep cuts. Almost overnight, the economy plummeted. Stocks lost one third of their value, and corporate profits fell by 80 percent. Unemployment skyrocketed and millions lost their jobs.

The 1937 economic collapse was so stunning that Roosevelt and other administration officials believed it was staged by businessmen seeking to bring the president down.

Still the administration moved forward with its progressive plan. There was one fundamental human need that had yet to be addressed: health care.

In 1938, Roosevelt's administration supported a national movement to create a sweeping national health care system. The movement was sparked by the Committee of Physicians for the Improvement of Medical Care, a group of prominent physicians based largely at the nation's most prestigious medical schools. They openly defied the conservative American Medical Association (AMA).

Health care was a right, Roosevelt's administration argued, not a privilege. This position was supported by labor unions and a broad range of reform-minded organizations.

In late February 1939, New York Senator Robert Wagner submitted his administration-backed bill for a national health program. He claimed that no legislation had received "more widespread approval" from the American people.

But the American Medical Association vehemently opposed the legislation and denounced its supporters.

The AMA was backed by a new conservative coalition that had formed between Southern Democrats and Republicans. Faced with the AMA's opposition to the issue and with the approaching 1940 elections to attend to, Roosevelt wanted to avoid a nasty fight. He abandoned the effort.

Few people realize how close the United States came to adopting a national health care plan in 1938 and 1939.

16

"Why Should Russians Have
All the Fun?"

During the 1930s, as Americans suffered through the stock market crash, failed banks, and an unemployment rate that reached a high of 25 percent, the Soviet Union's economy seemed to be booming. There, communism appeared to be producing a livelier, more equal society. It also seemed to offer an effective alternative to free-market capitalism, which was floundering at the time. How could this be? How could Soviet communism be outperforming American capitalism?

In 1928, Soviet leaders announced their first Five-Year Plan, designed by Joseph Stalin. The plan promised a rational, centralized economy that would create abundance by unleashing science and technology. It relied on rapid industrialization of the Soviet Union and collectivization of agriculture.

Soviet leaders intended to transform the country into a modern socialist state. They built thousands of new factories and turned individual farms into large state-owned farms, which they believed would raise enough grain to feed a growing army of urban workers.

RUSSIA DID IT

SHIPYARD WORKERS—You left the shipyards to enforce your demands for higher wages. Without you your employers are helpless. Without you they cannot make one cent of profit—their whole system of robbery has collapsed.

The shipyards are idle; the toilers have withdrawn tho the owners of the yards are still there. Are your masters building ships? No. Without your labor power it would take all the shipyard employers of Seattle and Tacoma working eight hours a day the next thousand years to turn out one ship. Of what use are they in the shipyards?

It is you and you alone who build the ships; you create all the wealth of society today; you make possible the $75,000 sable coats for millionaires' wives. It is you alone who can build the ships.

They can't build the ships. You can. Why don't you?

There are the shipyards; more ships are urgently needed; you alone can build them. If the masters continue their dog-in-the-manger attitude, not able to build the ships themselves and not allowing the workers to, there is only one thing left for you to do.

Take over the management of the shipyards yourselves; make the shipyards your own; make the jobs your own; decide the working conditions yourselves; decide your wages yourselves.

In Russia the masters refused to give their slaves a living wage too. The Russian workers put aside the bosses and their tool, the Russian government, and took over industry in their own interests.

There is only one way out; a nation-wide general strike with its object the overthrow of the present rotten system which produces thousands of millionaires and millions of paupers each year.

The Russians have shown you the way out. What are you going to do about it? You are doomed to wage slavery till you die unless you wake up, realize that you and the boss have not one thing in common, that the employing class must be overthrown, and that you, the workers, must take over the control of your jobs, and thru them, the control over your lives instead of offering yourselves up to the masters as a sacrifice six days a week, so that they may coin profits out of your sweat and toil.

71 ⌐═⌐

The Russian Revolution inspired American workers, as illustrated by this leaflet from the Seattle General Strike.

Surplus crops would be sold, and the money earned would pay for future industrialization.

The Soviets' Five-Year Plan appealed to many American intellectuals. It seemed to be an intelligent plan that ensured abundance. Why leave the economy to the whims of individual capitalists who cared only about maximizing their own profits?

Socialists and progressives were also inspired. In 1929, Oswald Garrison Villard, editor of *The Nation*, described the Soviet Union as "the greatest human experiment ever undertaken."

And perhaps most remarkably, the socialist economy seemed to be thriving, while the world's capitalist economies were collapsing. In 1931, *The Christian Science Monitor* reported that not only was the Soviet Union the only country that escaped the Great Depression, its industrial production had jumped an astronomical 25 percent the previous year. "While banks crash . . . abroad, the Soviet Union continues in an orgy of construction and national development," wrote a correspondent for *The Nation*. Similar reports also came from more conservative publications such as *Barron's*, *Business Week*, and *The New York Times*.

And then *The New York Times* reported that the Soviet Union intended to hire foreign workers. *Business Week* reported that desperate jobless Americans stampeded Soviet offices in the United States looking for work; 100,000 Americans applied for 6,000 Soviet jobs.

Before the world's eyes, Soviet society seemed to be undergoing an incredible transformation from agrarian backwardness to industrial modernization.

Many American intellectuals had begun to see the Soviet Union as a place of intellectual, artistic, and scientific vibrancy. "For Russians, the world is exciting, stimulating, challenging," wrote economist Stuart Chase in 1931. The next year, he added, "Why should Russians have all the fun of remaking a world?"

A literary editor for the *New Republic* visited the Soviet Union. He wrote that he felt as if he were "at the moral top of the universe where the light never really goes out."

In *Betrayal of Trust*, Laurie Garrett wrote about Russia during the 1920s:

> A vast network of sanitation and epidemiology was created, eventually reaching into nearly every village in the nation. Medical schools and sanitation training centers were constructed all over the Soviet Union . . . As a result, diseases that were responsible for killing large numbers of Soviets were almost eradicated entirely by 1991.

Workers Unite

The news from Russia encouraged some Americans to seek alternatives to capitalism. Though they would eventually learn the terrible truth about Stalin's cruelty, the Soviet Union's industrial success and the promise of greater equality compelled them to join the Communist Party of the United States of America. As a result, the party experienced profound growth during the 1930s.

In 1933, as the economy showed early signs of recovery, workers united in their struggle for better working conditions. In 1934, major labor strikes occurred in Toledo, Minneapolis, and San Francisco. A national textile strike rocked the country. Workers turned to Musteites, Trotskyists, and communists for leadership.

In the past, jobless workers had often been used as strikebreakers who would cross picket lines. This time, newly formed Unemployed Councils and Unemployed Leagues brought in jobless workers to support the strikes rather than take strikers' jobs.

With such broad support from the working class, strikes often spread to other industries. In some instances, these general strikes shut down entire cities. When a communist-led general strike shut down San Francisco, the *Los Angeles Times* called it "an insurrection, a communist-inspired and led revolt against organized government."

The Oregonian feared for Portland and called for presidential intervention. "San Francisco, paralyzed, is in the throes of violent insurrection," reported the newspaper. "Portland faces the practical certainty of a general

Workers turned to radical groups for leadership, and the unemployed often supported the strikers rather than taking jobs as strikebreakers. Pictured here is a march of the unemployed in Camden, New Jersey.

Evicted sharecroppers set up camp along Highway 60, New Madrid County, Missouri.

strike within a few days that will similarly paralyze this city."

The *San Francisco Chronicle* complained, "The radicals have wanted no settlement. What they want is revolution."

For workers, this was a welcome change. For thirteen years, the labor unions had taken a pounding and suffered sharp declines in membership. But the New Deal had helped to level the playing field between management and labor. Now the labor movement began to penetrate heavy industry with the formation of the Congress of Industrial Organizations (CIO) in 1935.

Communists played a major role in the organizing. Before, strikes often led to violent and bloody confrontations. Now, workers used new tactics such as sit-down strikes. In the right circumstances, these peaceful tactics proved effective.

Economic hardship was felt especially by black families, who suffered the double sting of racism and poverty. By 1932, urban black unemployment reached over 50 percent in the South. The North fared no better; in Philadelphia, black unemployment topped 56 percent.

The Depression had eliminated an entire category of jobs traditionally called "Negro jobs." Now, according to Richard Wormser in *The Rise and Fall of Jim Crow*, blacks competed with desperate whites for work as cooks, porters, elevator operators, maids, busboys, and garbagemen. In some cities, people shouted, "City jobs are for white men." In Mississippi, unemployed white men killed black workers.

African Americans, struggling for both jobs and civil rights, thought the NAACP was moving too slowly. Some turned to the Communist Party and its front organizations. The communists organized interracial unions and led demonstrations to help needy workers get jobs and relief payments and to block evictions.

Communism also appealed to intellectuals who rejected the shallow materialism and anti-intellectualism of the 1920s. The search for a more vibrant culture had motivated many of America's leading writers to relocate to London and Paris throughout the decade.

"One couldn't help being exhilarated at the sudden and unexpected collapse of the stupid gigantic fraud," wrote social commentator Edmund Wilson, referring to the fall of the stock market and the failure of the banks. "It gave us a new sense of freedom and it gave us a new sense of power to find ourselves still carrying on while the bankers, for a change, were taking a beating."

But then the news from Russia turned. Reports leaked out of catastrophic famine and starvation; political trials and repression; ham-fisted bureaucracy, secret police forces, and brutal prisons.

It would take more than twenty years for the world to learn about the forced labor camps called "gulags." They would learn about the violence, the hard labor and unsanitary conditions, the stifling of organized religion, the purging of military leaders, and the more than 13 million people who died under Stalin's despotic rule. Paranoid and cruel, Stalin had transformed what looked like a workers' paradise into a brutally repressive state.

How to "Save" the USA

The Great Depression was devastating for many Americans. However, the New Deal ensured that the United States and capitalism would survive. Its programs were not radical, but they were robust enough to help turn the Depression's tide. Roosevelt's reforms were more pragmatic than ideological, but he was willing to allow government to play a vastly bigger role than any of his predecessors or critics could have imagined.

This made him enormously popular with the American people. It made him incredibly unpopular with right-wing businessmen and bankers.

To many banksters and big business moguls, Roosevelt was the enemy.

17

"The Time Has Come"

In August 1934, a group of right-wing businessmen and bankers announced the formation of the American Liberty League. They claimed that Roosevelt's New Deal was violating the US Constitution because it changed the form of government.

"If the American people wish to change the form of their government from a federal republic with limited powers to an absolute dictatorship or to state socialism, they can do so by appropriate amendments to the Constitution," wrote league chairman Jouette Shouse, who had once supported Roosevelt. "One basic purpose of the American Liberty League is to see that this contract is complied with—faithfully, honestly, completely, and without evasion."

The American Liberty League was the brainchild of members of the wealthy du Pont family, owners of the largest chemical company in the world. The league included du Pont brothers Irénée, Pierre, and Lammot, as well as in-law and top executive Robert "Ruly" Carpenter. Carpenter recruited John Raskob, the former chairman of the Democratic National Committee, to the cause.

Raskob had been a strong proponent of shifting the tax burden from the wealthy to the working class. He had engineered du Pont's purchase of General Motors and had served as chief financial officer in both corporations.

Top executives from other corporations also joined the American Liberty League: GM president, Alfred Sloan; National Steel Corporation president, Ernest Weir; Sun Oil Company president, J. Howard Pew; and General Foods chairman, E. F. Hutton. The famous aviator Charles Lindbergh was invited to serve as president of the league, but he turned down the offer.

The American Liberty League went public on August 22, 1934. The group announced its intentions: to combat radicalism, defend property rights, and uphold the Constitution.

The league also announced plans to recruit two to three million members and hundreds of thousands of contributors. It unfurled a massive "education" campaign to stem the liberal tide. "There is one very clear lesson to be learned from history," stated one of its pamphlets, "namely that governmental disregard for property rights soon leads to disregard for other rights."

Despite the league's publicity campaign, it recruited only 125,000 members and 27,000 contributors at its peak. Few of its members were active, so most of the league's funding came from the du Ponts and a handful of other right-wing businessmen.

In November 1934, highly decorated retired Marine General Smedley Butler testified to Congress that two Liberty League members, William Doyle and Gerald MacGuire, tried to recruit him to organize a military coup against the Roosevelt administration. A reporter for the *New York Evening Post* and *The Philadelphia Record* corroborated Butler's testimony. He testified that he heard McGuire say, "We need a Fascist government in this country to save the Nation from the Communists who want to tear it down and wreck all that we have built in America. The only men who have patriotism to do it are the soldiers and Smedley Butler is the ideal leader. He could organize one overnight."

Major General Smedley Butler was recruited to lead a military coup to oust President Roosevelt and install a fascist government.

Butler rejected their offer. "If you get the 500,000 soldiers advocating anything smelling of Fascism," he warned, "I am going to get 500,000 more and lick the hell out of you, and we will have a real war right at home."

Butler recounted his entire story to the House Special Committee on Un-American Activities, headed by John McCormack of Massachusetts and Samuel Dickstein of New York. MacGuire denied Butler's charges, but after hearing the testimony, the committee reported that it had been "able to verify all the pertinent statements made by General Butler."

In what became known as the "Business Plot," the House committee concluded that "attempts to establish a fascist organization in the United States . . . were discussed, were planned, and might have been placed in execution when and if the financial backers deemed it expedient."

It was shocking to learn that the unscrupulous businessmen and bankers who called themselves the American Liberty League had concocted a plan for a fascist takeover of the American government. But a second set of hearings would prove just as unsettling.

The Nye Committee

At the end of the First World War, Dorothy Detzer's twin brother, Don, came home in a hospital ship. He had been gassed, and he soon died from mustard poisoning. Dorothy was devastated. She wanted to know the truth about the munitions industry and its profits during wartime.

Dorothy Detzer lost her twin brother, Don, who died from mustard gas poisoning in World War I. She lobbied for disarmament and economic justice. Here, she is shown speaking to the Senate Committee on Foreign Affairs.

Should the government have entered the war in 1917? Did the munitions industry influence the government's decision to enter the war? Is it ethical for an industry to reap enormous profits at the cost of the lives of American soldiers like her brother?

A tireless peace activist, Dorothy took her questions to Capitol Hill. There, she approached twenty senators, asking each to sponsor hearings on the munitions industry. But each senator turned her down. Finally, she approached Senator Gerald Nye from North Dakota. He didn't believe the United States should become involved in foreign wars. He agreed to sponsor Dorothy's proposal.

At last, perhaps, she would find justice for her brother.

Senator Nye headed the Special Committee on the Investigation of the Munitions Industry, which became known as the Nye Committee. Like Dorothy, Nye wanted to find out the truth about the munitions industry and its profits during the war.

In February 1934, Nye proposed one of the most remarkable congressional investigations in US history. He called upon the Senate Foreign Relations Committee to investigate the individuals and corporations involved in manufacturing and selling arms, munitions, and other implements of war.

The investigation would target steel, airplane, and automobile manufacturers; arms and munitions makers; and shipbuilders. The committee wanted some answers too. How had these industries profited from World War I? Should the United States have gotten involved in such a costly foreign war?

As word spread about the hearings, peace groups around the country organized support. Other progressives rallied to the cause. Tensions were heating up in Europe. Nobody wanted to be drawn into war.

Roosevelt voiced his approval of the hearings. He urged stronger international steps to curb the "mad race in armament which, if permitted to continue, may well result in war."

He blamed the munitions industry. "This grave menace to the peace of the world," said Roosevelt, "is due in no small measure to the uncontrolled activities of the manufacturers and merchants of engines of destruction."

Dorothy Detzer could not have agreed more.

On the hot Tuesday morning of September 4, 1934, hundreds of people jammed the room in the Senate office building, eager to observe the Senate hearings that journalists were calling "historic." The senators were reopening a seventeen-year-old debate over whether the United States should have entered the war, why it did, and who stood to gain.

Nye promised that "when the Senate investigation is over, we shall see that war and preparation for war is not a matter of national honor and national defense, but a matter of profit for a few."

While the nation waited for the hearings to begin, two extremely timely books appeared: *Merchants of Death* by H. C. Engelbrecht and F. C. Hanighen, which was chosen as a Book-of-the-Month Club selection, and *Iron, Blood, and Profits* by George Seldes. The two books detailed the sordid dealings of US munitions makers and their compatriots in other parts of the world. The books fueled public anger and focused more attention on the Senate hearings.

New York publisher Doubleday reprinted in pamphlet form a startling exposé of the European arms industry titled "Arms and the Men." It had first appeared as an article in *Fortune* magazine. "According to the best accountancy figures," stated the article, "it cost about $25,000 to kill a soldier during the World War. . . . [E]very time a burst shell fragment finds its way into the brain, the heart, or the intestines of a man in the front line, a great part of the $25,000, much of it profit, finds its way into the pocket of the armament maker."

The Nye Committee hired eighty researchers and accountants to comb the

Gerald Nye headed the Nye Committee, which investigated those who profited from World War I.

account books of the leading corporations in the United States. The committee members were astonished at their findings. The American people will be "amazed by the story of greed, intrigue, war scare propaganda and lobbying," promised Senator James Pope of Idaho. He added that the information would "shock the entire Nation when disclosed."

The facts were so disturbing that the seven members of the committee recommended turning over the manufacture of war materials to the government from that point on, so that no private industrialist could ever again reap the benefits from war.

On September 12, 1934, four members of the du Pont family took the stand: Felix, Irénée, Lammot, and Pierre. They were grilled about the firm's enormous profits during the war years. The company had received orders of $1.2 billion between 1915 and 1918—an increase of 1,130 percent over company orders in the four years prior to the war. Stockholders had also benefited. During the war, du Pont had paid 458 percent dividends on original par value stock. Du Pont "made extremely good profits," Pierre admitted to the Senate committee.

The committee also learned that Army Chief of Staff General Douglas MacArthur had gone to Turkey in 1932. While there, he had "apparently talked up American military equipment to the skies in discussions which he had with the Turkish general staff," according to an executive of the Curtiss-Wright Corporation, an aircraft manufacturer.

Senator Nye didn't think such a sales pitch was appropriate. "It looks to me like Gen. MacArthur was pretty much of a salesman. It makes one begin to wonder if the Army and Navy is just a sales organization for private industry."

The hearings produced one eye-opening revelation after another. They exposed the fact that US and foreign arms dealers had divided foreign markets through cartel arrangements, shared secrets and profits, and even designed German submarines that were busy sinking American ships during World War I.

And that wasn't all. The Senate learned the troubling news that American companies were engaged in helping Germany rearm. Officials of the United Aircraft Corporation and Pratt & Whitney had sold planes and aircraft equipment to Germany. But, the officials claimed, the sales were for commercial use, not military use.

The fact that such American companies were helping Germany defy the Treaty of Versailles outraged Senator Nye. "Do you mean to say that through all of these negotiations you hadn't the ghost of an idea that Germany was buying for military purposes?" Nye asked.

Secretary of State Cordell Hull was incredulous too. He reiterated that US policy had been to oppose the sale of any military equipment to Germany since 1921.

To the committee and countless other Americans, the heads of these US companies were guilty of aiding the enemy—and reaping huge profits on the backs of American soldiers.

Taking the Profits Out of War

Support for the hearings inspired both conservatives and liberals to suggest ways to penalize companies that profited from war. In late September, John Thomas Taylor, the legislative representative of the American Legion, supported a plan to have the government seize 95 percent of any abnormal profits during wartime.

Senator Nye announced that he would introduce legislation that would raise income taxes to 98 percent on all incomes above $10,000 on the day the United States entered a war. This was one way to entirely eliminate war profits. But, Nye said, it was preferable to have the government take over the entire arms industry in the event of another war.

Nye gave a national address over NBC Radio in which he defended his plan to nationalize the arms industry and sharply increase wartime taxes. "Do that and then observe the number of jingoists diminish," he said. He called the businessmen "international racketeers, bent upon gaining profit through a game of arming the world to fight itself."

Public pressure was building for decisive action. Roosevelt decided to defuse the issue. Four months after the hearings began, he announced that he had asked a high-powered group of government and industrial leaders to come up with a plan to end war profiteering.

"The time has come to take the profits out of war," Roosevelt told reporters.

18

The Profiteers

Behind closed doors at the White House, Roosevelt met with his own carefully selected committee. He left the Nye Committee out in the cold.

Nye Committee members were furious. They accused Roosevelt of trying to restrict their inquiry before the investigation was completed.

Others were skeptical about Roosevelt's motives. A *Washington Post* columnist suggested that the politically savvy Roosevelt was stealing the spotlight from Senator Nye, who was making headlines. Another *Post* columnist claimed that the American munitions companies under investigation "have got to the Administration and that it is trying to take them off of the spot." In other words, some charged, the Roosevelt administration was being influenced by the munitions companies themselves.

Perhaps no one was more mistrusting than Nye himself. He believed that the government was in bed with the arms dealer.

"The departments of our governments are really codefendants with the munitions industry and the profiteers," said Nye.

Refusing to let the administration steal its thunder, the Nye Committee came out with more headline-grabbing exposés. The du Ponts offered an easy target. *The Washington Post* headlined a December 1934 article: 800% WAR PROFIT TOLD AT INQUIRY; DU PONT DEAL UP.

The article also listed individuals whose earnings exceeded $1 million, thanks to war profits. The list included six members of the du Pont family, four Dodges, three Rockefellers, three Harknesses, two Morgans, two Vanderbilts, two Whitneys, and one Mellon.

Soon more revelations would come to light. The profits of the Bethlehem Shipbuilding Corporation jumped from $6 million before the war to $48 million once the war started. Eugene Grace, president of Bethlehem Steel, revealed that he had received personal bonuses of $1,575,000 and $1,386,000.

The more blood that Nye drew, the shriller the attacks on him and the committee became. But letters supporting the Nye Committee and its work poured in—more than 150,000 in the first four months of the investigation. Support remained strong. The American public wanted to know the truth about those who profited from the war.

In December 1934, Nye met with Roosevelt. Afterward, Nye assured reporters that he had been mistaken about the president's motives. The president supported the investigations. He had assured Nye that no new legislation would be forthcoming until the investigation had run its course.

Growing Tensions in Europe

Meanwhile, tensions were mounting in Europe. Adolf Hitler had been appointed chancellor of Germany the year before, on January 30, 1933. One month later, he used a fire set in the Reichstag to consolidate his dictatorial stranglehold

Adolf Hitler used an attack on the Reichstag to eliminate his political opposition.

on the country and to eliminate all opposition. He also announced his plans to rearm Germany, in defiance of the Treaty of Versailles. In October, he withdrew Germany from the League of Nations. In early January 1934, he signed a ten-year nonaggression pact with Poland to secure Germany's eastern border. Five years later, he would violate this agreement and invade Poland.

But Germany wasn't the only problem. Other aggressive and expansionist states—Japan in Manchuria and Italy in Abyssinia—were also threatening the peace.

Alarmed at the mounting unrest in Europe, the Nye Committee warned the public about another war looming on the horizon. Senator Pope thought it "paradoxical" that governments around the world were aiding munitions manufacturers. These countries, said Pope, "seem to be in the grip of some monster that is driving them to destruction. Preparations for the next war are feverishly under way. That it is inevitable is widely assumed."

The Nye Committee contemplated opening a new line of inquiry. Members of the National Education Association had passed a resolution declaring that they were "shocked and outraged by the iniquitous greed for profits on the part of the American munitions manufacturers." The educators asked committee members to investigate "the propaganda in newspapers, schools, motion pictures and radio carried forward to increase the fear of war and promote the sale of munitions." They especially wanted the newspapers published by William Randolph Hearst to be investigated.

Nye considered the request. Such an inquiry would fall within the committee's mandate. But in the end, he decided against it.

American Folly

In late March 1935, a Senate bill to ban war profits started to take shape. *The New York Times* described it as "a plan that is admittedly the most radical in the history of the government." *The Washington Post* agreed, describing it as "a plan so drastic in its confiscatory features that six months ago it would have been scoffed at. . . . It went beyond anything that Senator Gerald P. Nye, dapper chairman and most radical member of the committee, ever thought of recommending."

Roosevelt responded positively to the bill, so the committee members put their proposals into legislative form. The legislation proposed drafting corporate executives into the army, closing all stock exchanges in wartime, taking over all essential industries and services, and prohibiting all commodity speculation.

Significantly, the legislation included Nye's provision for government seizure of all corporate profits above 3 percent and of all individual earnings above $10,000 in wartime to prevent the US government from having to borrow to finance war efforts.

The ultimate objective of the legislation was to get Americans to think long and hard before getting involved in another war and to take the profit motive away from large corporations. If corporate executives and the wealthy had to fight, or if their hard-earned incomes were going to be confiscated, they might not be so quick to support wars. Nye commented, "The bill is drastic because war is a drastic thing. The tax collector who comes for one man's money is not nearly so solemn and forbidding as the draft officer who knocks at another man's door and calls for his young son."

Senate staff researcher John Flynn told the committee, "The profits in war, the spiraling of prices, the uncivilized scrambling for the shameful fruits of national disaster, can be prevented in only one way, and that is to prevent inflation at the beginning. In 1917 and 1918 we had our war and we sent the bill to our children and grandchildren. In the next war we must resolve, as intelligent as well as civilized beings, that while one part of the population—the army—fights in the field, the other part, that stays at home, will pay the bills."

The committee worked and reworked the proposal. In early May, Nye introduced his bill to the Senate. He promised that this would be only the first of several bills to come out of his committee. "We believe the opinion of the American people is behind this bill," said Nye. "We think that now, when the whole world is troubled by rumors of wars, is the time to serve notice on our own people and on the world that America does not intend to use another war as an instrument to make a foolish and futile effort to make a few people rich."

And Nye was right. The public was behind the bill. There was something ethically and morally wrong with American bankers and industrialists reaping huge profits from a war that killed Americans and foreign soldiers. Yet the conundrum was how easy it was to convince men to go to war and give up their lives.

In his 1933 Nobel Peace Prize lecture, Norman Angell raised a crucial question: "There are many who say in effect that public opinion has little to do with war, that it is explained by the influence of the vested interests who profit by it—armament makers or groups of capitalists. Why are the mass of men, millions, powerless in this matter as against a tiny minority, a few dozen or a few score or a few hundred who profit by the general disaster? There are undoubtedly some who say to the millions in effect: 'We should like you to go to war because it would expand our profits.' But why do the millions obey?"

Angell asked, "Suppose that the building industries, in which there is far more money invested than in the armament industry, aware that it would make enormous profits if people could be persuaded to burn down their cities, said: 'Kindly burn down your homes.' We know that the millions would not obey. Why is it relatively easy for a few armament makers to persuade men to go to war, to give their lives, and quite impossible for the much larger group who would benefit by another form of general destruction to persuade men to destroy their property?"

Angell answered his own question. "[B]ecause the folly of burning down houses is plain," concluded Angell, whereas "the folly of the policies which lead to war is not so plain."

Solutions to Combat War Profiteering

The Nye Committee presented the Senate with three options to stop US industrialists from turning war into a profitable business. One option prohibited making loans to warring nations or their citizens. A second denied passports to citizens entering war zones. And a third embargoed arms shipments to warring nations if such shipments might involve the United States in conflicts.

The Senate Foreign Relations Committee approved the first two measures and was debating the third when Secretary of State Hull convinced committee members to keep US options open in dealing with other nations. A crisis in Ethiopia was developing, and the Senate decided to reconsider all measures before finalizing actions.

The Senate adjourned in September. Pressure continued to mount for dramatic action. The conservative *Chicago Tribune* called the committee's resolutions a "communistic defense act." It warned that the outbreak of war would allow the president to "communize the American nation as completely as Lenin communized Russia."

The Real Reason for War

Woodrow Wilson was no longer alive to speak on behalf of his administration's position on wartime commercial interests, but his former secretary of war, Newton Baker, did so in a letter to *The New York Times*.

In the letter, Baker denied that there had been any discussion of protecting private US commercial or financial interests in the years leading up to America's entry into the Great War. "America's safety from future wars cannot be secured by muzzling bankers or disabling munitions makers," Baker insisted.

Four days later, Thomas Lamont of J. P. Morgan & Co.—the same banker who had represented the US Treasury at the Treaty of Versailles negotiations—agreed with Baker. He blamed Germany's aggression for America's entry into the war and said it had nothing to do with US business interests.

In early 1936, the committee resumed its investigation and sought to answer an important question: Was it true that the House of Morgan and other Wall Street firms had pushed the United States into the war in order to recoup the enormous sums they had lent the Allies?

Both sides prepared for a showdown. Nye Committee members had been poring over the books and files of J. P. Morgan for almost a year. They examined more than two million letters, telegrams, and other documents.

J. P. Morgan spokesmen denied allegations that the money the bank had lent the Allies was "worthless unless America entered the war" and "that the holders of these loans urged our Government into the war 'to make the loans good.'"

"The loans were always good," said the powerful banker. "No one feared for their safety."

Nye took to the radio again to make his case to a national audience. "After we had started stretching our American neutrality policy to accommodate commercial interests to the extent of permitting loans, the Allied powers were never in doubt as to what America would ultimately do," he explained. "They knew what we didn't seem to realize, namely that where our pocketbook was, there would we and our hearts ultimately be."

During the first hearing in September 1934, the committee released documents showing that President Wilson had allowed bankers to loan money to the warring countries in 1914. In later hearings, Nye and his fellow committee members tried to show that the United States had, in fact, never been neutral. They tried to prove that Wilson used German submarine warfare merely as an excuse to enter the war.

Then Nye dropped one last bombshell. He alleged that Wilson had learned about the Allies' secret treaties before the United States had entered the war and then falsified the record by telling members of the Senate Foreign Relations Committee that he had found this out much later.

The Nye Committee investigations showed that Wilson had, in effect, taken the country into the war on false premises. Furthermore, the president had undermined neutrality by allowing loans and other support to the Allies. He had deliberately exaggerated claims of German atrocities and covered up his knowledge of the secret treaties.

It wasn't a war to further democracy. It had been a war to redivide the spoils of empire.

Infamous Charges

The investigation screeched to a halt. Senate Democrats were furious that the committee had tarnished the reputation of the dead president.

"I do not care how the charges were made," said Senator Tom Connally, a Texas Democrat. "They are infamous."

Connally lambasted Nye, saying, "Some checker-playing, beer-drinking back room of some low house is the only place fit for the kind of language the Senator from North Dakota, the chairman of the committee—this man who is going to lead us out toward peace—puts into the record about a dead man—a great man, a good man, and a man who, when alive, had the courage to meet his enemies face to face and eye to eye."

The senator accused Nye and the committee of an "almost scandalous effort to besmear and besmut the records of America in the World War."

The controversy split the committee. Two members, Senators James Pope and Walter George, left the hearing in protest. Pope then returned and read a statement in which he and George expressed resentment at "any effort to impugn the motives of Woodrow Wilson and to discredit his great character."

The two men regretted that the purpose of the investigation had shifted. They feared that the chance of securing "remedial legislation" was slipping away. They questioned the integrity of the committee's investigation. However, they did not resign from the committee. They would return for the final vote.

Senator Arthur Vandenberg added that he admired President Wilson, but economic motives had provided "an inevitable and irresistible impulse" for getting the United States into the war. He wanted to ensure it never happened again. He took pride in the committee's accomplishments. "History has been rewritten in the last 48 hours," he said. "It is important that history should be revealed in all its nakedness, no matter what it shows."

Nye assured Pope and George that he had no bad feelings toward Wilson and had, in fact, voted for him in 1916. He promised to continue his efforts "as long as there is a possibility of lessening the chances of our being drawn into war."

The bloodletting continued. To Carter Glass, the seventy-eight-year-old senator from Virginia, Gerald Nye had committed "infamous libel" and made an "unspeakable accusation against a dead President, dirt-daubing the sepulchre [sic] of Woodrow Wilson."

"Oh, the miserable demagogy, the miserable and mendacious suggestion, that the House of Morgan altered the neutrality course of Woodrow Wilson!" cried Senator Glass, pounding his hand on the desk so hard that blood spurted over his papers. His colleagues cheered in support.

Nye offered no apologies. Instead, he read letters and documents that showed that "the United States entered the war knowing the spoils had been agreed upon. Yet we were told news of secret treaties came as a bombshell at the peace conference."

Nye accused his critics of using the Wilson issue as a "smoke screen." Their real intention, he insisted, was to "seize upon any weapon and resort to any subterfuge to kill legislation which threatens the bloody profits to be made from war."

It looked to Nye as though the committee had hit a roadblock and that the Senate would not approve the $9,000 needed to continue the investigation. But Nye was wrong.

The public weighed in loud and clear. Mail sacks bulging with letters arrived on Capitol Hill, urging that the inquiry continue. The American public wanted the full story to be told.

The Senate unanimously approved $7,369 to finish the probe, but the funding came with advice. The committee should stick to living people and not invade the "cemeteries and catacombs" of the dead, said Senator Connally. In other words, let President Wilson rest in peace.

"Should the manufacture and sale of war munitions for private profit be prohibited?" asked a Gallup poll in March 1936. An overwhelming number of Americans—82 percent—believed that it should. The strongest support came from Nevada, where 99 percent favored eliminating profits. The weakest support—perhaps it's no surprise—came from Delaware, headquarters of du Pont, where 63 percent answered yes.

Ordinary Americans could see through the smokescreen. "The profit system in munitions has been leading us to war for generations," said a grocer in western Pennsylvania.

The Final Report

The Nye Committee issued its long-awaited third report in April 1936. The report concluded, "While the evidence before this committee does not show that wars have been started solely because of the activities of munitions makers and their agents, it is also true that wars rarely have one single cause, and the committee finds it to be against the peace of the world for selfishly interested organizations to be left free to goad and frighten nations into military activity."

Four members of the committee—Gerald Nye, Bennett Champ Clark, James Pope, and Homer T. Bone—called for outright government ownership of the munitions industry. The three remaining members—Walter George, W. Warren Barbour, and Arthur Vandenberg—called for "rigid and conclusive munitions control."

However, the bill to remove profits from war had been assigned to a subcommittee chaired by Tom Connally, one of Nye's biggest critics. The bill got bogged down. Finally, the committee produced a watered-down version, which failed to get the necessary votes.

The Nye Committee had failed to nationalize the arms industry or curb the profits of war.

19

Death Calculators

Since his appointment as chancellor in January 1933, Adolf Hitler had been ruthlessly eliminating any opposition to his power. He didn't want a multiparty government system. He wanted a one-party rule by his National Socialist Party.

Under the pretext of patriotism and devotion to Germany, Hitler had been imprisoning and murdering communists, Social Democrats, and labor leaders. American newspapers reported these events, as well as the spread of anti-Semitic propaganda and the vicious attacks on Jews.

It became a central goal of the National Socialist Party to identify all Jews living in Germany. Out of a population of 67 million people, 523,000 were Jews, or less than 1 percent of the population. To find them, Nazi officials searched community, church, and government census records.

The Nazis had a device that helped them catalog people: an IBM punch card and card-sorting system. Germany had used the machines to help tabulate its 1930 census information.

"World Peace Through World Trade"

The International Business Machines Company—IBM, for short—was headed by an American named Thomas J. Watson. His motto was: "World peace through world trade."

The name of IBM's German branch was Dehomag. After meeting Hitler in 1937, Watson spoke to the International Chamber of Commerce in Berlin. He conveyed Hitler's message of peace. "[T]here will be no war," Watson promised. "No country wants war; no country can afford it."

A few days later, Watson turned seventy-five years old. As a birthday present, Hitler gave him a medal: the Grand Cross of the German Eagle. It was a thank-you for IBM's punch card and card-sorting machines that helped the Nazis locate and identify Jews. The Nazis stamped the Jews' identity cards and passports with a *J*.

IBM's machines became a vital part of Hitler's campaign to exterminate Jews and other targeted minorities. The machines could be found in every major concentration camp.

What did men like Thomas Watson and other corporate officials at the New York headquarters know? Did they know that the top management at IBM's German subsidiary were rabid Nazis? Did they know they were supplying the machinery for mass murder? Or were profits too important?

Another Hero for Hitler

In 1923, a *Chicago Tribune* reporter visited Adolf Hitler in his Munich office. The reporter noted that a large portrait of Henry Ford hung on the wall beside Hitler's desk.

"I wish I could send some of my shock troops to Chicago and other big American cities to help in the elections," Hitler told the reporter. "We look on Heinrich Ford as the leader of the growing Fascist Party in America."

The information from this Buchenwald concentration camp prisoner data card was entered onto a Hollerith punch card, also shown here.

A Hollerith Type III Tabulator with its control panel exposed.

SA men put up a sign on the front of a Jewish business that reads: "Not one penny to the Jews."

Nine years later, Hitler would tell readers of another newspaper, *The Detroit News*, "I regard Henry Ford as my inspiration." Henry Ford, the pioneering auto manufacturer, helped to spread hateful anti-Semitic ideas in the United States.

In Michigan, Henry Ford published a small-town newspaper called *The Dearborn Independent.* On May 22, 1920, the newspaper published its first anti-Semitic article and continued to attack Jews in ninety-one more editions. The articles blamed Jews for every possible ill in America and around the world. Labor strikes? It was the Jews' fault. Financial scandal? The Jews. The Depression? The Jews.

The Jewish plan, according to Ford's newspaper, was "to control the world, not by territorial acquisition, nor by military aggression, not by government subjugation . . . but by control of the machinery of commerce and exchange." Weekly articles also claimed that "the motion picture influence of the United States . . . is exclusively under the control, moral and financial, of the Jewish manipulators of the public mind."

The Dearborn Independent may have been a small-town paper, but since Ford published it, every Ford car dealership in the country carried it. The newspaper made its way into the hands of many potential customers. It boasted a peak circulation of 900,000. Other news outlets picked up the articles in *The Dearborn Independent* and republished them.

From 1920 to 1922, Ford published a collection of anti-Semitic articles that had first appeared in *The Dearborn Independent.* He titled the four-volume work *The International Jew: The World's Foremost Problem.*

The former head of the Hitler Youth organization testified at Nuremberg that this collection had helped shape his political views. "This book made . . . a great impression on my friends and myself," said Baldur von Schirach, "because we saw in Henry Ford the representative of success, also the representative of a progressive social policy. In the poverty-stricken and wretched Germany of the time, youth looked toward America, and . . . it was Henry Ford who, to us, represented America. . . . If he said Jews were to blame, naturally we believed him."

A Jewish shop owner clears broken glass from the front of his store.

Ford also sponsored the printing of 500,000 copies of *The Protocols of the Elders of Zion.* The fact that it had been exposed as a forgery didn't deter him.

Henry Ford did more than help the Nazis to spread anti-Semitic propaganda. By 1937, Ford's German subsidiary was making heavy trucks and troop carriers for the Wehrmacht—Germany's armed forces.

In 1938, four months after Germany had annexed Austria, Hitler presented Henry Ford with the Grand Cross of the German Eagle on Ford's seventy-fifth birthday, just as he had to Watson of IBM. He gave another medal to James D. Mooney, chief overseas executive of General Motors, the following month.

Like Thomas Watson, Henry Ford also believed that Hitler wanted peace. On August 28, 1939, Ford assured *The Boston Globe* that Hitler was just bluffing. The Germans "don't dare have a war, and they know it," he said.

Just days later, Hitler invaded Poland. As the German army steamrolled over the country, Ford still wasn't convinced. "There hasn't been a shot fired," Ford told a friend. "The whole thing has been made up by Jew bankers."

Doing Business with Nazis

The spirit of American capitalism was hard at work in Nazi Germany. American companies continued to develop, engage in trade, and accumulate wealth for investment.

After war broke out in 1939, the Ford and GM companies continued to control their German subsidiaries, which dominated the German auto industry. They even complied with German government orders to retool their machines for war production.

Ironically, when the United States demanded that Ford and GM retool their machines at home, both companies refused. The German operations were "highly profitable," explained Alfred P. Sloan, who headed GM. Germany's internal politics, insisted Sloan, "should not be considered the business of the management of General Motors." (Later, the company would comply.)

The GM-owned Opel company saw an opportunity to expand. It converted its 432-acre complex in Rüsselsheim to produce Luftwaffe warplanes. It provided 50 percent of the propulsion systems for Germany's JU-88 medium-range bombers. It also helped to develop the world's first jet fighter, the ME-262, which was capable of speeds of 100 miles per hour faster than the United States' P-510 Mustangs. And it built hundreds of thousands of trucks that played a crucial role in Hitler's blitzkrieg strategy.

During the war years, Ford's parent company lost effective control of the corporation when Ford-Werke supplied the Nazi regime with arms, employing prisoners from nearby Buchenwald concentration camp as slave labor.

In 1998, a former prisoner named Elsa Iwanoa brought a suit against the US automaker, contending she had been forced to work at a Ford plant in Germany. She claimed that the American company knowingly profited from slave labor.

The Ford Motor Company hired a small army of researchers and lawyers for its defense. It denied that it had helped the Nazis and that it had profited from slave labor. The automaker also claimed that it broke off contact with the Nazi government when the United States entered the war in December 1941—just as other American businesses had.

Just after the war, however, a report by US Army investigator Henry Schneider called Ford-Werke an "arsenal of Nazism." And, as Bradford Snell discovered during his congressional investigation into the auto

A German edition of Ford's collection, *The International Jew*, is shown here.

industry, through "their multinational dominance of motor vehicle production, GM and Ford became principal suppliers for the forces of fascism as well as for the forces of democracy."

Other American companies also continued to deal with the Nazis. At the start of the war, 250 American firms owned more than $450 million worth of German assets, with almost 60 percent owned by the top ten of those firms. These companies included Standard Oil, Woolworth, ITT, Singer, International Harvester, Eastman Kodak, Gillette, Coca-Cola, Kraft, Westinghouse, and United Fruit. Ford ranked sixteenth, holding just less than 2 percent of the total US investment. Standard Oil and GM topped the list, holding 14 and 12 percent, respectively.

Most of these companies were represented by the powerful law

IBM technology helped Nazis to locate Jews, herd them into boxcars, and transport them to concentration camps. Here, Jews await deportation from a Warsaw ghetto.

firm Sullivan & Cromwell, which counted the Bank for International Settlements—set up in Switzerland in 1930 to channel war reparations between the United States and Germany—among its clients. Sullivan & Cromwell was headed by future Secretary of State John Foster Dulles. His brother Allen Dulles, future head of the CIA, was a partner.

After the United States entered the war in 1941, the Bank for International Settlements continued to offer financial services to the Third Reich. But instead of channeling war reparations, it held much of the gold looted during the Nazi conquests of Europe. The transfer of capital allowed the Nazis access to money that normally would have been trapped in blocked accounts under the Trading with the Enemy Act.

During the Nuremberg trials, Secretary of the Treasury Henry Morgenthau was aghast by the bank's vile operations. He charged that twelve of the bank's fourteen directors were "Nazi or Nazi controlled." In 1998, Holocaust survivors sued the bank, claiming it held blocked accounts from that era.

Unintended Consequences

In the years that led up to World War II, while American capitalists and their companies piled up earnings from their overseas investments, Gerald Nye and his crack team of investigators succeeded in brilliantly revealing ugly truths about the influence of arms manufacturers and moneylenders. The Nye Committee exposed the ugly realities hidden beneath the lofty refrains to which American soldiers had marched off to war and to their death.

But the hearings led by Nye and the committee had two other effects that, with the wisdom of hindsight, are justly regrettable. First, they tended to oversimplify the causes of the First World War. Second, they reinforced the country's isolationist tendencies at precisely the worst time imaginable—when US influence might have helped to avert disaster.

The hearings justified the widespread belief that the United States should steer clear of entangling alliances and involvement in world affairs. For perhaps the only time in US history, powerful antiwar sentiment was actually misplaced in light of the true threat to humanity posed by fascistic and other dangerous forces.

PART THREE

World War II: Who Really Defeated Germany?

20

A Deal with the Devil

Most Americans view World War II nostalgically as the "good war." It was the war in which the United States and its allies triumphed over German Nazism, Italian fascism, and Japanese militarism.

The rest of the world remembers World War II as the bloodiest war in human history. By the time it was over, more than 60 million people lay dead, including 27 million Russians, between 10 and 20 million Chinese, 6 million Jews, 5.5 million Germans, 3 million non-Jewish Poles, 2.5 million Japanese, and 1.5 million Yugoslavs. Austria, Great Britain, France, Italy, Hungary, Romania, and the United States each counted between 250,000 and 410,000 dead.

Unlike World War I, which took one month for the Central and Allied forces to square off after the assassination of Austria's Archduke Ferdinand in 1914, World War II began slowly and incrementally. Japan fired the opening shots in 1931 in Manchuria.

Japan's Military Prowess

While the Western powers expanded their empires in the late nineteenth century, the rapidly modernizing and industrializing Japan sought its proper place among the world's leading nations. Japan demonstrated its new military might by defeating China in the Sino-Japanese War of 1894–1895 and then delivering a stunning defeat to Russia in the Russo-Japanese War exactly ten years later. It was the first time in almost 700 years—since the time of Genghis Khan—that an Eastern power had defeated a Western one. The Russo-Japanese War created a bitterness between Russia and Japan that would last for decades.

During the First World War, Japan allied itself with Great Britain and the United States. As an Allied country, Japan expected to win territories at the peace conference in Versailles in 1919, just as Britain, France, the United States, and other Allied countries had done.

Instead, Japan met great opposition, especially from the United States. From this, Japan learned the lesson that Western powers—the United States, Great Britain, and France—regarded imperialism very differently when it applied to an Asian country rather than a European power.

The Japanese were frustrated. Their leaders wanted security, equality, trade, access to foreign markets, and a proper place among the world's leading nations.

A crying baby sits at the bomb site of Shanghai's South Railway Station on Saturday, August 28, 1937, after the Japanese bombing during the Battle of Shanghai.

"[W]e feel suffocated as we observe internal and external situations," said Finance Minister Matsuoka Yosuke in January 1931. "What we are seeking is that which is minimal for living beings. In other words, we are seeking to live. We are seeking room that will let us breathe." That same year, Japan's Kwantung Army invaded China's northern province Manchuria, overwhelming the Chinese forces. Under Japanese control, Manchuria became one of the must brutally run regions in the world. This invasion arguably became the opening shot of what would evolve into World War II in the Pacific.

In 1937, full-scale war erupted in China as the powerful Japanese army captured city after city. In December of that same year, Japanese soldiers brutalized the citizens of Nanjing, killing 200,000 to 300,000 civilians and raping perhaps 80,000 women. Japan soon controlled the east coast of China, with its population of 200 million.

World leaders condemned Japanese aggression but did little to help China as Japan relentlessly bombed Chinese cities. Such actions were not only inhumane, they threatened US and other Western interests in the region. In July 1939, the United States tightened the noose around the Japanese economy by terminating its 1911 commercial treaty with Japan. This move cut off the flow of vital raw materials, such as oil, and banned US exports critical to the Japanese war machine.

Meanwhile, tensions mounted in the east as Russian and Japanese armies battled over the disputed border of Manchuria, leading the Soviets to claim their first victory in the war.

The Spread of Fascism

Germany and Italy also dreamed of conquest. In 1935, Hitler defiantly and openly began to rebuild Germany's military strength. Italy invaded Ethiopia to expand its colony in neighboring Eritrea. The United States and its allies

Hitler and Mussolini formed the Axis in 1936 and began a campaign of aggression in Ethiopia and Spain. Fearful of war, the Western democracies did little to stop them.

condemned this action, but they did nothing to stop it. Roosevelt knew World War I had left a very bitter taste in Americans' mouths. As the magazine *Christian Century* wrote in January 1935, "Ninety-nine Americans out of a hundred would . . . regard as an imbecile anyone who might suggest that . . . the United States should again participate in [another European war]."

As they watched Mussolini's aggression go unpunished, Germany and Japan concluded that the United States, France, and Britain had no stomach for war. In 1936, Mussolini and Hitler formed the Axis. The next year, Mussolini visited Hitler in Germany. As his train pulled into the station, swastika-waving crowds cheered the Italian prime minister. In Berlin, Hitler entertained Mussolini with a grand display of military power marked by thousands of goose-stepping Nazi soldiers. Mussolini declared that Italian fascism and German Nazism were "the only true democracies" and that they had two common enemies—liberalism and communism.

In July 1936, Spanish general Francisco Franco's fascist forces set out to topple Spain's democratically elected government. Hitler and Mussolini came to Franco's aid, providing planes, pilots, and thousands of troops. Germany would use the Spanish Civil War to test the weapons and tactics it later deployed against Poland and the rest of Europe.

"A Grave Mistake"

The Soviet Union rallied to Spain's defense. Stalin sent planes and tanks to the republican forces but couldn't come close to matching the massive assistance from Berlin and Rome. Tragically, Roosevelt and other Western capitalist leaders failed to join the Soviets in defending the Spanish republic against the fascists.

US officials and corporate leaders were troubled by the republic's progressive policies and tight regulation of business. They feared that if the republicans won, Spain would become communist. Following the British and French, the United States banned the shipment of weapons to both sides, which weakened the beleaguered and outgunned republican forces.

Ford, GM, Firestone, and other US businesses provided the fascists with trucks, tires, and machine tools. Texaco Oil Company, headed by pro-fascist Colonel Thorkild Rieber, promised Franco all the oil he needed—on credit. Roosevelt, furious, threatened an oil embargo and slapped Texaco with a fine. But Rieber persisted undeterred, supplying oil to Hitler. He was lionized in the pages of *Life* magazine.

Appalled by Western leaders' failure to act, thousands of progressive Americans joined with thousands more from around the world to fight for the republican cause. Many sacrificed their lives in this early attempt to stem the tide of fascism. But the Spanish fascists backed by Germany and Italy ultimately prevailed.

Ernest Hemingway (*center*) was one of the American volunteers who helped the Spanish Loyalists.

The Spanish republic fell in spring 1939, burying with it more than 100,000 republican soldiers and 5,000 foreign volunteers, along with the hopes and dreams of much of humanity. Franco would rule as Spain's dictator until his death in 1975.

By 1938, Roosevelt realized how foolish his neutral stance had been and tried to send covert aid to the republic. It was too little too late. His policy had been "a grave mistake," Roosevelt told his cabinet in January 1939. He warned that they would soon all pay the price.

And indeed they would. England, France, and the United States lost a golden opportunity to halt the spread of fascism. The Western democracies' spineless response to fascist belligerence in Ethiopia and Spain emboldened Hitler to believe that he could pursue his plans to conquer the rest of Europe. It also convinced Stalin that Great Britain, France, and the United States had no interest in taking collective action to slow the Nazis' advance.

Peace in Our Time

The international situation deteriorated further in 1938. The Germans annexed Austria. Then, under the Munich Agreement, the Allies appeased Hitler by giving him the Sudetenland, a primarily German-speaking area in Czechoslovakia. British prime minister Neville Chamberlain infamously proclaimed that the settlement had brought "peace in our time."

Chamberlain was sorely mistaken. In March 1939, Hitler struck again. This time, Germany invaded Czechoslovakia.

European leaders knew it was only a matter of time before Hitler moved against Poland. Chamberlain sternly warned Hitler that if he dared to invade Poland, Britain would declare war on Nazi Germany.

President Roosevelt knew Chamberlain's warning wouldn't stop Hitler. The British and French, he insisted, had abandoned the helpless Czechs and would "wash the blood from their Judas Iscariot hands."

But Roosevelt also knew that the United States itself was offering little support to those who wanted to stand up to the Nazi dictator.

Nor was the United States doing enough to help desperate Jews living in Germany and Austria. In 1939, the United States admitted its full quota of 27,300 German and Austrian immigrants—the only year in which it did so. But with hundreds of thousands of Jews trying to escape from the Nazis, US assistance proved woefully inadequate. Roosevelt made no effort to raise the low quotas established by discriminatory immigration legislation in 1924.

Blitzkrieg

Joseph Stalin understood that Germany would soon turn its eyes to the Soviet Union. For years, the Soviet dictator had implored the West to unite against Hitler and Mussolini. The Soviet Union even joined the League of Nations in 1934. But Soviet pleas were ignored.

After Hitler's assault on Czechoslovakia, Stalin again urged England and France to join in defense of Eastern Europe. His words fell on deaf ears.

Fearing a German-Polish alliance to attack the USSR, Stalin decided to buy time. In August, he struck a deal with his mortal enemy, Adolf Hitler. Hitler and Stalin shocked the world by signing a nonaggression pact with a secret provision dividing Eastern Europe between them. The two countries agreed to take no military action against each other for ten years.

In fact, the Soviet dictator had proposed a similar alliance with Britain and France. But neither would accept Stalin's demand to place Soviet troops on Polish soil as a deterrent to Germany. Hitler invaded Poland on September 1, 1939. Great Britain and France declared war on Germany. The Soviet Union invaded Poland on September 17 and soon took control of the Baltic states of Estonia, Latvia, and Lithuania.

Two German tanks cross the Zora River in Poland during the blitzkrieg of September 1939.

In late summer of 1940, the Luftwaffe began to mercilessly bomb London and other British cities. Here, smoke and flames rise from St. Paul's Cathedral in London.

After a brief respite in April 1940, Hitler unleashed his furious blitzkrieg, or "lightning war." In rapid succession, Denmark, Norway, Holland, and Belgium all fell to the Nazis. On June 22, France surrendered after only six weeks of fighting. Great Britain stood alone. To many, it looked as though Hitler was on his way to conquering all of Europe.

In the summer of 1940, Britain's prospects looked bleak. The German Air Force, the Luftwaffe, was pummeling Britain's cities, but it failed to destroy Britain's Royal Air Force. Germany canceled its plans for a cross-channel invasion in September.

Roosevelt wanted to help, but the neutrality legislation limited the aid he could offer to Britain. The United States could not loan money to warring nations nor sell arms or war materials. With US military preparedness at a low level and isolationist sentiment running high, there was little he could do.

The president also encountered resistance from cabinet members and military leaders who thought that Great Britain was lost and that resources should be concentrated on defending the homeland. Still, he maneuvered to get Great Britain as much military aid as he could. Knowing he was acting illegally, he bypassed the Senate and gave Great Britain fifty old naval destroyers in exchange for ninety-nine-year leases of air and naval bases on eight British territories in the Western Hemisphere. As the Battle of Britain raged on, Roosevelt was willing to let critics charge that he had illegally violated the Neutrality Acts to bolster British resolve.

In September 1940, Germany, Italy, and Japan formally concluded the Tripartite Pact, establishing the "Axis powers" alliance. Hungary, Romania, Slovakia, and Bulgaria joined soon thereafter.

That same month, Roosevelt signed into law the hotly contested Selective Training and Service Act. It established the first peacetime military draft in American history. The act required all men between the ages of twenty-one and thirty-five to register for the draft.

Roosevelt could see the war clouds drifting toward the United States. He knew the British were desperate for US involvement.

21

Radical Ideas

In 1940, as the Nazis steamrolled over Europe, President Roosevelt decided to run for a third term. Republicans, and even some fellow Democrats, were outraged. The Constitution didn't forbid three terms, but first president George Washington thought eight years was enough, and the tradition stuck. Even First Lady Eleanor Roosevelt didn't approve, but she stood by her husband and supported his candidacy.

Roosevelt ran against Republican Wendell Willkie, a millionaire from Indiana who made his fortune selling electricity. Willkie, who had been a Democrat, thought the New Deal went too far and had become a Republican. Many Republicans were angry that Willkie won their party's nomination so soon after switching parties. Former senator James Watson said, "If a [sinner] repented and wanted to join the church, I'd personally welcome her and lead her up the aisle to a pew, but . . . I'd not ask her to lead the choir the first night."

Roosevelt gave serious thought to choosing a new running mate.

As Roosevelt decides to run for a third term, the Germans bombed London and other major cities. Here, an aircraft spotter stands on the roof of a building in London. St. Paul's Cathedral is in the background.

The stakes were high. The nation might soon be at war. Roosevelt chose his secretary of agriculture, Henry A. Wallace.

Like Willkie, Henry Wallace had also switched parties. Some Democrats questioned Wallace's loyalty, but Roosevelt was certain that Wallace was the right person for the job. He knew what Wallace had done as secretary of agriculture. He was a man who could make intelligent—and tough—decisions.

Principles over Politics

When Henry Wallace became secretary of agriculture in 1933, farmers were in miserable shape. The price of cotton had dropped to five cents per pound. Warehouses were bursting with excess cotton. With so many workers unemployed, fewer people were buying goods. Farmers couldn't even sell cotton overseas because the Depression was worldwide. And yet another large cotton crop was sprouting. What was to be done with all the surplus?

Wallace believed if there was less cotton available to buy, demand would increase and the price would rise. He proposed paying farmers to cut their production. He believed that a lowered supply would increase demand and thereby raise prices. He decided to pay cotton farmers to destroy 25 percent of the crop that was in the ground and to let some fields lie fallow.

It was a difficult decision. Wallace had a degree in animal husbandry from Iowa State College. He believed that abundant food supplies were essential for a peaceful world. "To have to destroy a growing crop," he lamented, "is a shocking commentary on our civilization." But Wallace also knew how to collect and analyze data in order to help solve real-world problems.

The next decision was even more difficult. There were also too many hogs. On the advice of hog farmers, Wallace supported a program of slaughtering six million baby pigs that weighed under 100 pounds, or half the normal 200-pound market weight of adults.

People called it "pig infanticide" and "pig birth control."

Wallace agreed that it was just as inhumane to kill a big hog as a little one, but he fired back, "To hear them talk, you would have thought that pigs are raised for pets."

The thought of destroying crops and killing livestock in the midst of hunger and poverty turned people's empty stomachs. It saddled the New Deal with an image of callousness. Wallace regretted having to enforce such emergency measures—and the message such measures sent—that he was promoting recovery through scarcity. "The plowing under of ten million acres of cotton in August 1933, and the slaughter of six million little pigs in September 1933 were not acts of idealism in any sane society," he wrote later.

But Wallace also knew where the blame for such actions lay. "They were emergency acts made necessary by the almost insane lack of world statesmanship during the period from 1920 to 1932," he explained.

He made sure that some good came from the pig slaughter: 100 million pounds of pork, lard, and soap were distributed to needy Americans. "Not many people realized how radical it was," he reflected, "this idea of having the Government buy from those who had too much, in order to give to those who had too little."

It worked. The price of cotton doubled. Farm income jumped by 30 percent in one year.

"Wallace was a great secretary of agriculture," wrote historian Arthur Schlesinger Jr. "For the urban poor, he provided food stamps and school lunches. He instituted programs for land-use planning, soil conservation and erosion control. And always he promoted research to combat plant and animal diseases, to locate drought-resistance crops and to develop hybrid seeds in order to increase productivity."

The Responsibility of Science

Scientists held Henry Wallace in high regard. They considered him the most scientifically knowledgeable member of the Roosevelt administration and the scientific community's best ally.

In October 1939, scientists invited Wallace to participate in a panel at the New York World's Fair. His address was titled "What the Scientist Can Do to Combat Racism."

Wallace defined racism as "the attempts of individuals in certain groups to dominate others through the building up of false racial theories in support of their claims."

Wallace stated that scientists had a special responsibility to combat false theories like the lies the Nazis were spreading about race. Wallace said that scientists must "[prevent] the use of these theories for the destruction of human liberty."

He continued, "[The scientist's] motive comes from the fact that when personal liberty disappears scientific liberty also disappears. His responsibility comes from the fact that only [scientists] can give the people the truth. Only [scientists] can clean out the falsities in our colleges, our high schools and our public prints. Only [scientists] can show how groundless are the claims that one race, one nation, or one class has any God-given right to rule."

An outspoken antifascist, Wallace was devoted to principles over politics. This angered party "bosses," who controlled their party's votes and doled out political favors. It also angered party conservatives. But there was no doubt about it, Wallace was a champion of freedom and democracy. He was not a man who could be stifled.

With European democracy on life support, Roosevelt wanted Wallace as his running mate. But at the July 1940 Democratic Convention, the party bosses pushed back. It looked as though the Wallace nomination would go up in flames. Angry and frustrated, Roosevelt wrote a remarkable letter to the assembled delegates, telling them:

In 1940, Roosevelt selected the high-minded Henry A. Wallace as his running mate. Recognized as a "visionary," Wallace was an advocate of labor unions, national health insurance, public works jobs, and women's equality.

> The Party has failed . . . when . . . it has fallen into the control of those [who] think in terms of dollars instead of . . . human values . . . Until the Democratic Party . . . shakes off all the shackles of control fastened upon it by the forces of conservatism, reaction and appeasement, . . . it will not march to victory. . . . [T]he Democratic party . . . cannot face in both directions at the same time.

And then, in a shockingly bold move, Franklin D. Roosevelt declined the presidential nomination.

"A Grave and Serious Situation"

Eleanor Roosevelt saved the day. The first wife of a nominee ever to address a convention, she told disgruntled delegates that "we now face a grave and serious situation" and reminded them that this was "no ordinary time."

Indeed, the delegates didn't need to be reminded of the Nazi army that was threatening to conquer all of Europe.

Under intense pressure, the party bosses caved. Other convention delegates quickly followed suit. They put Henry Wallace's name on the ticket as Roosevelt's running mate. The party bosses lost this battle. They would, however, four years later, exact revenge.

Before the November 1940 election, Roosevelt promised that he would keep the United States out of the war. To an overflow crowd in Boston Garden, he declared, "I have said this before but I shall say it again. Your boys are not going to be sent into any foreign wars."

Republican candidate Wendell Willkie had not made an issue of foreign policy during the campaign. It was an unspoken agreement, and now Willkie felt that Roosevelt had betrayed it. Willkie spoke harshly. "That hypocritical son of a bitch!" he fumed. "This is going to beat me!"

And it did. Roosevelt and Wallace won 55 percent of the vote as Roosevelt became the first and last president to win a third term. In 1947, Congress passed an amendment limiting the president's time in office to eight years.

Working America into War

Roosevelt promised to keep Americans out of war, but the United States was actually inching closer and closer to the conflict. The United States was

First Lady Eleanor Roosevelt addressed delegates at the
1940 Democratic National Convention, telling them, "This
is no ordinary time." Here, Eleanor rides with Franklin D.
Roosevelt near their home in Hyde Park, New York.

already supplying Great Britain with much of its military needs, including
artillery, tanks, machine guns, rifles, and thousands of planes.

Over the radio, Roosevelt talked to the American people. "This is not
a fireside chat on war," he said. "It is a talk on national security. . . . If Great
Britain goes down, the Axis powers will control the continents of Europe, Asia,
Africa, Australia, and the high seas—and they will be in a position to bring
wgeration to say that all of us, in all the Americas, would be living at the point
of a gun—a gun loaded with explosive bullets, economic as well as military."

To keep Americans safe, the United States must become the "great arsenal
of democracy," Roosevelt proclaimed.

In early January 1941, to be able to send more aid to Britain, Roosevelt introduced a bill in Congress patriotically numbered HR 1776. The bill, called the Lend-Lease Act, would allow him to provide noncombat assistance to the increasingly desperate British without worrying about the "silly, foolish dollar sign."

Republican critics were angrier than ever. Thomas Dewey, who would later run unsuccessfully for president, warned that the bill "would bring an end to free government in the United States and would abolish the Congress for all practical purposes." The governor of Kansas, Alfred Landon, a former presidential candidate, called it "the first step toward dictatorship by Mr. Roosevelt." Landon saw the handwriting on the wall: "Step by step, he is working us into the war."

At a press conference the next day, Eleanor Roosevelt said she was "astonished and saddened" by the cold Republican response to the president's message.

Critics feared that loans to Great Britain would again draw the United States into war, as they had in 1917. Senator Gerald Nye, who had conducted hearings about US involvement in WWI, thought, "War is almost inevitable." A heated debate erupted in Congress. The Democratic senator from Montana dismissed the thought that Hitler would ever declare war on the United States and charged that the lend-lease program was "the New Deal's Triple A foreign policy—plow under every fourth American boy."

Infuriated, Roosevelt shot back, saying that the senator's comment was "the most untruthful . . . the most dastardly, unpatriotic . . . the rottenest thing that has been said in public in my generation."

Roosevelt had a great many defenders. They agreed that aiding Great Britain was the United States' best chance to avoid being drawn into the war.

"Hitler is a madman standing at the switch of the most powerful and destructive machine that the human brain ever devised," said the senator

These American-made howitzers are ready for transport to
Great Britain in 1941, as part of the lend-lease program.
Similar to a cannon, a howitzer is used to fire projectiles
with a high trajectory.

from Oklahoma. "America has only one chance to escape total war and that
chance is England. England is the only barrier between America and a bap-
tism of blood."

Congress overwhelmingly passed the Lend-Lease Act in March 1941,
allocating the first $7 billion of what would eventually total $50 billion to
fund the shipments of military supplies.

Prime Minister Churchill thanked the Americans profusely. He telegraphed the president, "Our blessings from the whole of the British Empire
go out to you."

Both Churchill and Roosevelt knew that, like it or not, the United States was on the path to war. "I would like to get them hooked a little firmer," Churchill confessed, "but they are pretty on now."

The American people, it turned out, were willing to hook themselves. Their sympathies lay entirely with the Allies. In 1939, a Gallup poll found that 84 percent of Americans wanted Great Britain and France to win the war. Only 2 percent were rooting for Germany. But 95 percent wanted the United States to stay out of the war.

Ironically, it would be Hitler who would bring a surprising ally to Great Britain.

22

Betrayal

In May 1941, Adolf Hitler decided that an invasion of Britain was still impossible. He called off the bombing raids and turned his attention to the Soviet Union.

On June 22, 1941, Germany double-crossed the Russians, breaking the 1939 nonaggression pact. Germany launched Operation Barbarossa, the code name for a full-scale invasion of the Soviet Union.

Stalin had ignored the warnings that such an attack was imminent. His forces were caught off guard as 3.2 million German troops attacked along a 2,000-mile front. Germany quickly pushed deep into the Soviet Union.

The Luftwaffe destroyed Soviet air units, and Hitler's army, the Wehrmacht, encircled Soviet forces. By fall, the Germans had captured much Soviet territory. The Soviets suffered terrible losses as the Nazis advanced toward the cities of Leningrad, Smolensk, and Kiev.

Nazi Onslaught

The Nazi assault sparked fears in London and Washington. Few people believed that the Soviets could withstand the Nazi onslaught. The US Army calculated that the Soviets would hold on for no more than three months and might even fold in four weeks.

American leaders worried that Stalin would conclude a separate peace with Hitler, as Lenin had done with Germany in 1918 with the Treaty of Brest-Litovsk.

Great Britain and the United States knew they must keep the Soviets in the war. If the USSR surrendered Russia, Great Britain was doomed. All of Europe would be lost.

German cavalry leave a Russian village in flames during the invasion.

If the Soviets could hold off 200 German units in the east, Britain would gain some breathing time. But in order to hold off the Germans, the Soviets would need supplies.

Churchill knew he would have to swallow to his long-standing hatred of communism. He pledged support for the Soviet Union and urged his allies to do the same. He promised "to destroy Hitler and every vestige of the Nazi regime."

A Missouri senator named Harry Truman also despised communism. He balked at the idea of offering such aid. "If we see that Germany is winning we ought to help Russia," he said. "And if Russia is winning, we ought to help Germany, and that way let them kill as many as possible."

But Roosevelt didn't share that view. He understood that helping Russia was necessary. He asked the Soviet ambassador to compile a list of items that the United States might provide. In July 1941, Roosevelt sent one of his closest advisers, Harry Hopkins, to Moscow to meet with Stalin.

To Hopkins, Stalin acknowledged that Germany was militarily superior. But the Russian winter, known for its subzero temperatures, was coming. The Soviets would use the lull in the fighting to be ready by spring. "Give us anti-aircraft guns and the aluminum [for planes and] we can fight on for three or four years," said Stalin.

Hopkins relayed the message. Roosevelt ordered the delivery of 100 fighter planes. More supplies would be on the way, he promised.

Americans Fail to Deliver

Some US military leaders didn't agree that the United States should send aid to the Soviets. Instead of helping the Soviets, the military leaders wanted to focus on US defenses and preparedness. Some British military leaders also objected to diverting badly needed supplies to the Russians.

Many didn't believe that a communist country deserved help. "We are not required by our national interests or our national dangers to join hands with a system of government which professes undying contempt for everything we regard as necessary in our way of living," editorialized the *Chicago Tribune*. He called Stalin "the greatest barbarian of modern times."

Many Americans agreed. A Gallup poll found that only 35 percent of respondents favored giving aid to the Soviets.

Roosevelt knew that Stalin had committed crimes against his own people, but he knew the Allies needed Russia. He ordered Secretary of War Henry Stimson and other cabinet members to speed delivery of military supplies to the Soviet Union the way it had to Britain. He also announced that a US delegation would head to Moscow to confer on providing more military aid.

On November 7, 1941, Roosevelt announced that the United States would extend lend-lease aid to the Soviet Union. The president offered a billion-dollar interest-free line of credit. It was to be repaid starting five years after the end of the war.

The Soviets were elated.

But the promised US aid to the Soviets never arrived. US shipments during the fall of 1941 fell "far, far short" of "the specified tonnage of materials of war," reported *The New York Times*.

The United States delivered less than half of what it had offered. US production was lagging, and military leaders who disapproved of the aid felt no need to hurry the supplies.

This dealt a crushing blow to the Soviets. Leningrad and Moscow were under siege. Ukraine was occupied, and the Red Army was suffering debilitating losses. The Soviets felt betrayed.

Behind the Scenes

Roosevelt wanted the United States in the war. He believed that Hitler was intent on world domination and had to be stopped. Somehow, he had to convince Americans that war was in the best interests of the United States. Somehow, he had to goad the Germans into an incident. Just as Woodrow Wilson had done, Roosevelt maneuvered quietly, provoking the Germans at sea, where Germany's U-boats were sinking a great number of British ships. This undermined US efforts to supply Great Britain.

In April 1941, Roosevelt began allowing US ships to provide vital intelligence to the British about the presence of enemy ships and planes. He soon authorized US ships to transport supplies to British soldiers in North Africa. Roosevelt knew this would precipitate direct confrontations with German U-boats. After one incident, a German communiqué charged Roosevelt with "endeavoring with all the means at his disposal to provoke incidents for the purpose of baiting the American people into the war." In September, after one of these allegedly unprovoked attacks, Roosevelt announced a "shoot on sight" policy toward German and Italian ships in US waters.

In August 1941, Roosevelt met secretly with Churchill in Newfoundland. The two leaders drew up the Atlantic Charter. Much like Wilson's Fourteen Points, the Atlantic Charter, which stated the ideal goals for a postwar world. Like Woodrow Wilson's Fourteen Points, the charter spelled out a democratic and progressive set of war aims.

It proclaimed self-government, equal access to trade and resources for victors and vanquished alike, a peace allowing "freedom from fear and want," freedom of the seas, disarmament, and a permanent system of general security.

Churchill feared that Roosevelt's proposed wording threatened Great Britain's colonial possessions. He added a clause stipulating that equal access to international wealth would be guaranteed only "with due respect for . . . existing obligations."

But could Great Britain count on the United States to join the war immediately? That's what Churchill wanted. But Roosevelt said no.

To his cabinet, Churchill later recalled the conversation. Roosevelt, Churchill told them, "said he would wage war, but not declare it, and that

In August 1941, President Roosevelt (*second from right*) stands with British prime minister Winston Churchill during the Atlantic Charter conference onboard HMS *Prince of Wales*. The charter renounced a number of imperialistic practices. It also proclaimed such themes as self-government and disarmament.

he would become more and more provocative. If the Germans did not like it, they could attack American forces. Everything was to be done to force an 'incident' that could lead to war."

War Provocations

Within days of Roosevelt's meeting with Churchill, the American destroyer USS *Greer*, together with a British Royal Air Force plane, detected a German submarine in the North Atlantic. The bomber released depth charges—deep-water explosives—but failed to damage the sub. The plane then turned around and headed back to base to refuel. The *Greer* continued on to track the submarine. Suddenly, the sub launched a torpedo at the *Greer*. The *Greer's* crew released depth charges. Neither vessel was damaged. Some time later, the two vessels engaged once more, but again, no damage was done.

The following week, President Roosevelt took to the radio. First, he made it sound like the sub's attack on the *Greer* was unprovoked. Second, he left out a key piece of information—that a British plane was also present and that it too was chasing the German sub. Third, he failed to mention that that plane had actually fired first when it released depth charges, provoking the sub's crew to respond. Roosevelt merely said that the German sub "fired first upon th[e] American destroyer without warning, and with deliberate design to sink her" in "defensive waters." He characterized the attack as "piracy—piracy legally and morally."

Additionally, Roosevelt asserted that the crew of the German sub knew positively that the *Greer* was an American vessel and fired with that knowledge. However, two days prior to Roosevelt's speech, navy representatives had told him that there was "no positive evidence that [the] submarine knew [the] nationality of [the] ship at which it was firing."

Roosevelt then told the American people, "We have sought no shooting war with Hitler. We do not seek it now." His actions contradicted his words.

Ultimately, President Roosevelt got his wish, but it was not triggered by an incident in Europe or the North Atlantic, as most were anticipating. On December 7, 1941, a day he said would "live in infamy," the Japanese navy attacked the US naval base at Pearl Harbor, Hawaii, leaving almost 2,500 dead and sinking or disabling much of the US Pacific fleet.

Intelligence Failure

In Hawaii, the Americans were literally caught sleeping. At about eight o'clock on that Sunday morning, approximately 360 Japanese bombers and fighter planes swept down on the American naval base and nearby airfields at Pearl Harbor. Each plane bore the rising sun emblem of Japan's military flag on the underside of its wings.

"Everybody, out!" William Melnyk remembered his sergeant yelling. "The damn Japs are bombing us!"

Wave after wave of Japanese bombers dive-bombed the airfields and nearby areas. They dropped torpedoes and strafed ships, planes, and buildings. "I saw the planes strafing and bombing the base," said William F. Rudder Sr., an electrician. "I saw them strafing people who were on the roads. The planes would swoop down so low we could see the pilot's goggles."

The attack took about one hour and fifteen minutes—long enough to sink or damage 21 ships and 323 aircraft. A total of 2,388 Americans died; 1,178 were wounded. Of those killed, forty-eight were civilians, including a man who owned a small airport near Honolulu—the first to die—and the youngest, a ten-year-old girl. Sixty-four Japanese fighters died.

There were many warning signs about the attack. Roosevelt and others

A US Navy gunner managed to shoot down this Japanese bomber over Pearl Harbor, as evidenced by the thin line of smoke trailing in its wake.

On December 7, 1941, flames rise from the US naval base at Pearl Harbor during the Japanese bombardment.

knew an assault from Japan was coming. Codebreakers had intercepted messages that warned that an attack was imminent. But the messages never revealed exact naval or military plans and few anticipated that the attack would be in Hawaii. Most believed that Hawaii was too far from Japan to be a target. It was an intelligence failure on a colossal scale.

Conspiracy theories about the Pearl Harbor attack have grown. Just as theories have circulated about the attacks on September 11, 2001, many people believed in 1941—and continue to believe today—that Roosevelt allowed the attack in order to draw the United States into the war. While the circumstances surrounding US lack of readiness remain suspicious, the evidence that top leaders knew the attack was coming at Pearl Harbor and allowed it to happen is not conclusive.

The next day, Great Britain and the United States declared war on Japan, but the Soviet Union did not. Three days later, Germany and Italy declared war on the United States. The bloodletting and chaos would soon engulf the globe.

Churchill later wrote, "Hitler's fate was sealed. Mussolini's fate was sealed. As for the Japanese, they would be ground to powder. . . . I went to bed and slept the sleep of the saved and thankful."

A Sleeping Giant Awakened

The United States had stood in the way of Japan's conquest for years. When the Nazis took over France and Holland, Japanese leaders moved to grab their rich colonies. Though some Japanese army officers had argued that Japan should join Germany and first knock out its old Russian adversary to the north, other strategists prevailed. As a result, Japan invaded French Indochina to the south in July 1941, seeking the resources and bases needed to fortify its position in the region.

The United States responded by completely embargoing petroleum exports to Japan. Its supplies dwindling, Japan's leaders decided to secure oil from the Dutch East Indies.

With the United States and its allies focused on the European theater, the Japanese conquest proceeded largely unimpeded: Thailand, Malaya, Java, Borneo, the Philippines, Hong Kong, Indonesia, Burma, Singapore. Citizens of those countries often greeted the Japanese as liberators from their prior European colonial oppressors. President Roosevelt said privately, "Don't think for a minute that Americans would be dying in the Pacific . . . if it hadn't been for the short-sighted greed of the French and the British and the Dutch." However, citizens of those countries realized quickly how cruel the Japanese could be.

The Japanese bombed Pearl Harbor because they feared the US fleet might stand in their way. But Japan had failed to deliver the knockout blow that it desperately sought. The Allies began a counteroffensive led by General Douglas MacArthur and Admiral Chester Nimitz. In June 1942, US forces defeated the Japanese navy at Midway Island and began fighting the Japanese for control of islands in the Pacific. This would become known as the "island-hopping strategy." Ultimately, the United States would gain the upper hand in the Pacific and gain possession of islands closer and closer to mainland Japan. This proximity would prove essential when it came time to bomb Japan from the air. The sleeping giant—the United States—had awakened.

23

Russia, Disappointed

By the late fall of 1941, the Germans had overrun Ukraine and captured much Soviet territory. Stalin had intended to use the winter to prepare the Soviet war machine. To do so, he counted on his first request: the promised aid from the United States and Britain.

But now that the United States had entered the war, it had to meet its own defense obligations. This made it difficult to fulfill its commitment to the Soviet Union.

In December 1941, the United States had delivered only about 25 percent of the tonnage of promised supplies. Furthermore, much of what had been shipped was defective. How could the Soviets stave off and overcome the German forces without the necessary supplies?

Roosevelt worried about a "Russian collapse" because of US negligence. The lack of outside support may have left the Soviets weak, but they refused to collapse. Despite suffering catastrophic losses in the early months of the war, the Red Army defeated Germany in the Battle of Moscow in the fall and winter of 1941–1942. For the first time, the mighty German war machine had been stopped.

Roosevelt understood that the Soviets were bearing the brunt of the fighting. In May 1942, he told General MacArthur: "I find it difficult . . . to get away from the simple fact that the Russian armies are killing more Axis personnel and destroying more Axis material than all the other twenty-five United Nations put together."

Furthermore, Roosevelt said, it was only logical that the United States seek to deliver all promised munitions to the Soviets. He also knew that the delays and failures to deliver the promised military equipment had cost him an opportunity to win Stalin's trust, and he understood how crucial that trust would be.

The United States was still hoping for Soviet assistance in the war against Japan and Soviet cooperation in shaping the postwar world following the defeat of Germany and Japan.

Stalin had made two additional requests of the United States and Great Britain. Perhaps if the United States delivered on these requests, Roosevelt would regain the upper hand.

Stalin demanded territorial concessions. Once Germany was defeated, Stalin wanted to retain the lands that the Red Army had seized after the 1939 nonaggression pact with Hitler. These lands were the Baltic states of Lithuania, Latvia, and Estonia, eastern Poland, and parts of Romania and Finland.

The British were inclined to go along but felt caught in a difficult bind. They needed Soviet help to survive the war and US assistance to preserve their empire after the war. Churchill pressed Roosevelt to give Stalin the territorial concessions Russia desired. He warned Roosevelt that a break with the Soviets would bring down Churchill's government, which would be replaced by a "Communist, pro-Moscow" government.

Roosevelt refused to budge and instructed British Foreign Secretary Anthony Eden to make no postwar commitments during his trip to Moscow in late December 1941. Stalin responded angrily to Eden's rebuff of his demands, leading Churchill to appeal to Roosevelt again. "The Atlantic

Charter," he insisted, "ought not to be construed so as to deny to Russia the frontiers which she occupied when Germany attacked."

Having failed to receive all of the promised aid or territorial gains, Stalin pressed harder for his most significant demand: a second front against Germany in Europe. This would force Germany's military to fight on two fronts and ease pressure on desperate Soviet forces.

Stalin urged the British to invade Nazi-occupied France. He pressed the British to send twenty-five or thirty divisions to the Soviet Union.

Roosevelt agreed that a second front was the best hope for staving off Soviet defeat. As General Dwight D. Eisenhower explained, "We should not forget that the prize we seek is to keep 8,000,000 Russians in the war." It was the only way to beat Germany.

Roosevelt wanted to launch an invasion of Western Europe at the earliest possible date. He sent his advisers Harry Hopkins and General

Soviet soldiers used the winter to prepare for war against the Germans. Stalin counted on promised US aid.

George Marshall to convince Churchill to go along with the plan for a second front.

The two men carried a letter from Roosevelt. "Your people and mine demand the establishment of a front to draw off pressure on the Russians," Roosevelt reminded Churchill, "and those peoples are wise enough to see that the Russians are killing more Germans and destroying more equipment than you and I put together."

Churchill responded, "I am in entire agreement in principle with all you propose, as so are the Chiefs of Staff."

Convinced he had British support, Roosevelt asked Stalin to send his minister of foreign affairs and a trusted general to Washington, DC, to discuss the urgent task of creating a second front in Europe later that year.

To the visiting Soviet officials, Roosevelt laid out a breathtaking vision for postwar collaboration. The victors, he explained, would "keep their armaments" and form "an international police force." The police force would consist of four policemen: the United States, the United Kingdom, the Soviet Union, and China. They would disarm the Germans and their allies and "preserve peace by force."

The second front, Roosevelt said, would begin later that year.

Stalin was delighted with this plan and the promise to establish a second front. But he was unsettled when he learned that the formation of this front meant that the United States would have to cut back its aid to the Soviet Union by as much as 60 percent.

Still, the second front was Stalin's main priority, and Roosevelt planned to deliver.

"Not One Step Backward"

Stalin was soon disappointed again. The British, he learned, had no intention of going along with the plan. The British argued that they lacked sufficient

Wearing a flight suit, a Soviet pilot stands next to his I-16 airplane painted with the words "For Stalin."

troops and that they could not muster enough ships to transport invading forces across the English Channel.

Even worse, Churchill convinced Roosevelt to postpone the promised invasion. Instead, the British and US forces would mount an invasion of Nazi-occupied North Africa. Such an invasion was the key to the oil-rich Middle East, where the British had important colonial interests that were being threatened by Hitler's forces. For the British, it was imperative to secure North Africa, the Mediterranean, and the Middle East in order to hold on to the Persian and Iraqi oil reserves. The British also wanted to maintain their access to India and the rest of their empire through the Suez Canal and Gibraltar.

And there was more. Before the war, enormous oil reserves had been discovered in Saudi Arabia, Kuwait, and Qatar—and Hitler's forces were threatening these interests. The new oil reserves reinforced the British desire to protect this region.

Intent upon keeping the Axis powers out of the Middle East, Great Britain diverted troops and tanks there. When Britain argued that it didn't have adequate troops to launch a much-needed second front in Europe, it was because it had troops and tanks stationed in the Middle East, protecting the oil reserves.

Soviet leaders were fit to be tied. They believed the British and US governments had decided to allow the Soviet Union to be bled dry while fighting the Nazis as the capitalist Allies secured their global interests. After the Soviets defeated the Germans, they figured, the Allies would march in to set the peace terms.

To make matters worse, Stalin's minister of foreign affairs, Vyacheslav Mikhailovich Molotov, was so grateful for the pledged second front that he had not pressed for territorial demands. The Soviets felt as though all three of their demands had been denied: aid, territorial gains, and the second front. Stalin felt betrayed and used.

Relations among the Soviets, Americans, and British hit rock bottom in the fall of 1942, just as the Nazi onslaught against Stalingrad began. Hitler's forces had laid siege to Leningrad for more than a year, and now they attacked Stalingrad. The city was of particular importance because it blocked the German road to the Soviet oil fields in Baku. Loss of the oil fields would have spelled doom for the Red Army. The city was also Russia's center of communications and industry.

The Soviets could not let Stalingrad fall. Stalin's order was "Not one step backward."

Abandoned Plans

The Soviets weren't the only ones angered by the about-face. US Army Chief of Staff George C. Marshall was furious about the diversion of troops to North Africa. The United States had delayed major operations against Japan in the Pacific in order to expedite victory in Europe. Now those plans for victory in Europe were being abandoned in an attempt to secure British "imperial" interests in the Middle East, South Asia, and southern Europe.

It didn't make sense to Marshall. He dismissed the invasion of North Africa as "periphery pecking." Marshall was so angry that he proposed reversing course and taking on the Japanese before confronting the Germans.

General Eisenhower, who would actually lead the invasion, shared

Marshall's disgust with the change in plans and predicted that the day they decided to invade North Africa would go down as the "blackest day in history."

Some US leaders believed that the British were afraid to take on the Germans and the fearless Soviets were not. Chief of Naval Operations Admiral Ernest King sneered that the British would never invade Europe "except behind a Scotch bagpipe band."

Whether deterred by fear or spurred on by imperial interests, the British never had any intention of directly engaging the powerful Wehrmacht army. Instead, they designed a strategy based on sea power and attacking Hitler's southern flank, protected by weaker Italian forces.

The Soviet Union's Heroic Struggle

For many Americans, the Nazi-Soviet Pact of 1939 had confirmed their worst suspicions about Soviet communism. This caused an outpouring of anti-Soviet feeling in the first two years of the war.

But as the Soviets now battled the backstabbing Nazis, stories about the Soviets' courage captured America's imagination and sympathy. The American people's attitude toward the Soviet Union began to undergo a profound shift. Goodwill toward the Soviet Union abounded. Many hoped this would lay the basis for friendship and collaboration after the war.

Within days of the attack on Pearl Harbor, Soviet diplomat Maxim Litvinov visited the US State Department. There, state officials applauded the Soviet Union's "heroic struggle" against the Nazis. The 1941–1942 winter campaign would end in a Russian victory.

Before long, many Americans were talking about the brave Soviet people and their willingness to sacrifice and adapt themselves to war conditions. "It would need a Tolstoy to describe the heroic endurance of the men and women who have made these things possible," wrote Ralph Parker, a *New York Times* correspondent, in April 1942.

A group of women and elderly men dig a trap to halt the German advance on Moscow.

In June 1942, a *New York Times* book reviewer credited the Red Army with winning the war and saving humanity. Of course, the war wasn't over yet—one of the bloodiest battles was yet to be fought—but that didn't stop the reviewer, Orville Prescott, from proclaiming, "The vast armaments, the fighting skill and magnificent courage of the Red Army may prove to have been the decisive factors in the salvation of the human race from Nazi slavery."

General MacArthur, the commander of the US Army Forces in the Far East, described the Red Army's 1941–1942 victory over the Nazis as "one of the greatest military feats in history."

Hollywood pitched in too. It had avoided making films about the Soviet

Union, but that changed in July 1942, when at least nine movies about the Soviet Union were in production or under consideration by major studios. Five significant motion pictures eventually appeared: *Mission to Moscow, The North Star, Song of Russia, Three Russian Girls,* and *Days of Glory.*

Second Front Now

On the American home front, a consensus was building that the war could not be won without a second front. "The Russians have done most of the fighting and most of the dying," acknowledged *The Atlanta Constitution.* Even though a second front would bring tragedy to many American homes, it "must . . . be done if the war is to be won."

Pulitzer Prize–winning journalist Leland Stowe reminded readers, "In thirteen months the Russians have suffered more than 4,500,000 in killed, wounded, and prisoners . . . twenty times the total American casualties in the first World War." Stowe stressed, "Soviet Russia is the one great power which is indispensable as an ally of the United States—if we are going to win the war."

With the steady barrage of pro-Soviet and pro–second front coverage, the American public increasingly supported the cause. In July 1942, a Gallup poll reported that 48 percent of Americans wanted the United States and Great Britain to attack immediately; 34 percent wanted to wait until the Allies were stronger.

Americans pasted bumper stickers on their cars that read: SECOND FRONT NOW. Readers flooded newspapers with letters calling for an attack on Hitler's forces in Europe. Twenty-five thousand people rallied in New York's Union Square.

Support for the second front was building in all directions. Thirty-eight leaders of the Congress of Industrial Organizations, a federation of labor unions, told Roosevelt that "only immediate land invasion of Western Europe

On September 24, 1942, 25,000 Americans rallied in New York's
Union Square to demand that the United States open a second
front to relieve some of the tremendous pressure on Russia in
its fight against Germany.

will guarantee winning the war." Wendell Willkie, the 1940 Republican Party
nominee for president, added his endorsement.

The Soviet Union could not hold out alone forever. It needed another
point of attack against the Germans. It needed the United States and Great
Britain to deliver on their promise. It needed the second front now.

24

The God of War

Despite the public demand for a second front in Europe, US and British troops headed off to North Africa. Without the promised support and aid, the Red Army was left to its own devices as the Nazis swarmed down on Stalingrad.

At Stalingrad, from July 1942 until February 1943, more than a million soldiers were engaged on each side. The Germans were pushing to take control of the Soviet Union's rich oil fields in the Caucasus. The Soviets were determined to stop them at all costs. The six-month battle was fierce, the human toll horrific. Casualties exceeded three quarters of a million on each side, and civilian deaths totaled more than 40,000.

The Soviets vanquished the Nazis. After its colossal defeat, the German army began a full-scale retreat from the eastern front. Hitler, stunned by the surrender of twenty-three generals and the Sixth Army's 91,000 troops, lamented, "The God of War has gone over to the other side."

The momentum had shifted. The Red Army was on the offensive and moving west.

The Soviets had turned the tide of the war without most of the promised help from the British and the Americans. Stalin wouldn't owe them any favors. This would put the British and the Americans on the defensive at the bargaining table.

To make matters worse, Roosevelt and Churchill decided to land in Sicily to take on the weaker Italian forces. Once again, they postponed the formation of a second front and the opportunity to make their nations relevant in determining the outcome of the war.

Still, the Red Army continued its advance toward Germany at an enormous cost. In November 1943,

A Soviet soldier bandages the leg of another soldier during the Battle of Stalingrad.

Stalin commemorated the anniversary of the Russian Revolution. In his speech, he celebrated the survival and future resurgence of the Soviet state.

He decried the Nazis' murder and pillage and promised revenge against the German invaders: "In the districts they seized, the Germans have exterminated hundreds of thousands of our citizens. Like the Medieval barbarians of Attila's hordes, the German fiends trample the fields, burn down the villages and towns, and demolish industrial enterprises and cultural institutions. . . . Our people will not forgive the German fiends for these crimes."

Uncle Joe

On November 28, 1943, Roosevelt, Churchill, and Stalin met for the first time in the Soviet embassy in Tehran, Iran. The strategy meeting would be the first of the World War II conferences to be held among the "Big Three" Allied leaders.

Roosevelt had tried unsuccessfully to exclude Churchill from the four-day meeting. The year before, Roosevelt had told Churchill, "I can personally handle Stalin better than either your Foreign Office or my State Department. Stalin hates the guts of all of your top people. He thinks he likes me better and I hope he will continue to do so."

Stalin invited Roosevelt to stay in the Soviet embassy, and he did. The next morning, Roosevelt arrived early and was wheeled into the conference room. Stalin was already there. Churchill arrived half an hour later.

Roosevelt initially found Stalin cold and aloof. He feared he would not be able to develop rapport with the Soviet leader. Finally, before one of the meeting sessions, Roosevelt apologized to Churchill for what he was about to do.

During the meeting, Roosevelt teased Churchill about his Britishness, his cigars, and his habits. This annoyed Churchill, but the more Churchill scowled and turned red, the more Stalin smiled. "I kept it up until Stalin was laughing with me," said Roosevelt later, "and it was then that I called him 'Uncle Joe.' . . . He laughed and came over and shook my hand."

Once he had broken the ice with Stalin, Roosevelt made important headway. The United States and Great Britain pledged to launch the long-delayed second front in France the following spring. Stalin agreed to enter the war against Japan after Germany was crushed.

Roosevelt then acceded to the Soviet-desired territorial changes in Eastern Europe. This would grant Stalin the Polish territory that the Soviets had gained under the 1939 nonaggression pact with Germany.

In agreeing to this, Roosevelt asked that Stalin implement the territorial changes in a way that would not offend world opinion. He also proposed that the Soviets hold votes on important questions in the Baltic states.

Stalin rejected that request. Roosevelt urged him to reconsider. He reminded Stalin that he would allow the Soviets considerable latitude in shaping those countries' futures.

Roosevelt came away from the conference encouraged that the trust he had established with Stalin would moderate the Soviet leader's demands. He felt assured that he had convinced Stalin that free elections in Eastern

Stalin (*left*), Roosevelt (*center*), and Churchill (*right*) were in a smiling mood when this picture was taken at the Russian Embassy in Tehran, Iran.

Europe would produce governments friendly to the Soviet Union.

In January 1944, as the Red Army advanced into Poland, US Secretary of War Henry Stimson discussed Poland's future with US Secretary of State Cordell Hull. Hull considered it essential to establish the principle of "no acquisition by force."

Stimson believed there were other, more realistic considerations, such as "feelings that would actuate Russia."

"She had saved us from losing the war," Stimson explained later. "She prior to 1914 had owned the whole of Poland including Warsaw and running as far as Germany and she was not asking for restitution of that."

In Lublin, Poland, the Soviet Union quickly set up a government that would be friendly to Soviet interests. The new Polish government excluded representatives living in London, who were hostile to the Soviet Union. The exiled Poles would feel betrayed by Churchill and Roosevelt.

Later that year, the Red Army moved into Romania, Bulgaria, and Hungary, all of whom had supported the Axis powers. When the United States and Great Britain complained that they were allowed only a token role in the occupation of these countries, Stalin replied that the Soviet Union had been given only a token role in the occupation of Italy.

Finally, the Second Front

On the night of June 5, 1944, Winston Churchill said to his wife, "Do you realize that by the time you wake up in the morning, twenty thousand men may have been killed?"

Minutes after midnight, Allied paratroopers dropped into German-occupied Normandy, France. By dawn, 5,000 Allied ships blanketed the Normandy coast. Thirteen thousand Allied planes thundered over the German fortifications. It was D-day.

The long-awaited second front had opened. In all, more than 100,000

Allied troops and 30,000 vehicles landed on the Normandy beach. More than 4,000 soldiers died during the landing alone, and 5,000 more would later be killed or wounded.

That fall, the Germans launched another offensive, but it was too late. After much fighting, by January 1945, the Germans were in full retreat.

By that point, the Soviets, despite having suffered catastrophic casualties, were occupying much of Central Europe. Now the Allied forces were approaching Germany from the east and the west.

Until the invasion of Normandy, the Soviet Union had almost

Under heavy Nazi machine-gun fire, American soldiers land on June 6, 1944 on the Normandy coast.

On June 6, 1944, in Times Square, New York City, crowds gather to learn the latest news about the long-awaited second front.

single-handedly battled the German military. While the Red Army was regularly engaging more than 200 enemy divisions, the Americans and the British together rarely confronted more than ten. Churchill admitted that it was "the Russian Army that tore the guts out of the German military machine."

25

The Road to a New World Order

By the summer of 1944, Allied victory finally appeared within grasp in both Europe and Asia. Italy had already left the war. The German army was in headlong retreat. And following US victory at Saipan in July 1944, Japanese leaders were coming to realize that defeat was inevitable. Japan's new prime minister Kuniaki Koiso still clung to the hope that securing one more major victory would enable him to get better surrender terms from the Americans.

But the end of the war was still months off in Europe and a year away in Japan. And then the job of rebuilding much of the world would begin. The challenge was enormous. Much of Europe and large parts of Asia lay in ruins. Agriculture and industry had been devastated. Transportation and communications ties were severed. Cities had been leveled, often burned to the ground. Homeless and displaced people sought shelter. Orphans roamed the streets. What would the victors do to put the world back together again?

An abandoned boy holds a stuffed animal and sits amid the ruins following a German aerial bombing of London. Throughout Europe, cities and farms lay in ruins. Displaced people searched for food and family members.

A Shift in Power

Though Germany would not surrender for another ten months, the writing was on the wall. In anticipation of an Allied victory, in July 1944, the United States invited friendly governments to send delegates to a conference in Bretton Woods, New Hampshire. In total, 730 delegates attended the conference, held one month after the Allied invasion of Normandy. It was the attendees' job to figure out what the postwar world would look like.

Conferees approved US plans to establish two major economic institutions: the development-minded World Bank and the finance-minded International Monetary Fund. The United States, which controlled two thirds of the world's gold, insisted that the postwar economic system, known as the Bretton Woods system, would be anchored by both gold and the US dollar. This ensured that America's economic superiority would continue for the foreseeable future. The United States would, in essence, become banker to the world—and would secure its place at the forefront of a postwar capitalist order.

Soviet representatives attended the conference but later declined to ratify the final agreements. They charged that the new institutions were "branches of Wall Street." A Soviet official commented that "at first sight," the Bretton Woods institutions "looked like a tasty mushroom, but on examination they turned out to be a poisonous toadstool."

The British understood that the new order would further erode their empire. Although Churchill had railed in late 1942, "I have not become the King's First Minister to preside over the liquidation of the British Empire," the balance of power had shifted toward the United States.

"Hands Off the British Empire"

Some critics have questioned the sincerity of Roosevelt's anticolonial efforts during the war. Roosevelt was never the passionate crusader against colonialism that his vice president Henry Wallace was, but he repeatedly expressed outrage at the colonizers' unjust and inhumane treatment of their subject populations.

Roosevelt's son Elliott reported his father's stern words to an "apoplectic" Churchill in 1941. "I can't believe that we can fight a war against fascist slavery," Roosevelt had said to Churchill, "and at the same time not work to free people all over the world from a backward colonial policy." Roosevelt pressed Churchill to end Britain's rule in India and beyond.

During a press conference in February 1944, Roosevelt publicly condemned British colonial rule in Gambia in western Africa, which he had seen firsthand the year before. "It's the most horrible thing I have ever seen in my life," he declared. "The natives are five thousand years back of us . . . the British have been there for two hundred years—for every dollar that the British have put into Gambia, they have taken out ten. It's just plain exploitation of those people."

Roosevelt criticized the French for their treatment of the 30 million inhabitants of Indochina—known today as Vietnam, Laos, and Cambodia—saying they were no better off after 100 years of French rule.

Roosevelt spoke repeatedly about a postwar trusteeship system that would prepare the colonies for independence. He insisted that Indochina should not be given back to the French, as Churchill and French resistance leader Brigadier General Charles de Gaulle demanded.

"France has had the country—thirty million inhabitants—for nearly one hundred years," said Roosevelt, "and the people are worse off than they were at the beginning. . . . The people of Indo-China are entitled to something better than that."

Churchill made it clear that he would not permit Roosevelt to use Indochina as a wedge to force full-scale decolonization. Great Britain did not want to lose its control over its established colonies or territories.

"'Hands off the British Empire' is our maxim," said Churchill. "And it must not be weakened or smirched to please sob-stuff merchants at home or foreigners of any hue."

Both Washington and Moscow paid close attention to the anti-colonial ferment. If the plan to decolonize was realized, the new or emerging Third World countries would become potential allies. These countries might provide military bases, resources, and markets for trade.

Despite Stalin's support, Roosevelt backed off from aggressively pressing the point with Great Britain. At that time, he feared rupturing the wartime alliance with Great Britain. With even less justification and more tragic consequences in the long run, he also backed off from pressing the point on Indochina.

Still, Roosevelt remained resolute on the subject of decolonization. The next year, on April 5, 1945, Roosevelt, in the presence of Philippines president Sergio Osmena, promised that once Japanese troops were ousted from the Philippines, the United States would grant the Filipinos "immediate" independence. Roosevelt would not live to make good on that promise.

Churchill withstood US pressure to grant India independence after the war, but that victory wouldn't last. The Indian people would take matters into their own hands.

A Naughty Document

In October 1944, as Roosevelt championed an end to colonialism, Stalin and Churchill held a secret meeting halfway around the world. The meeting was code-named "Tolstoy."

Churchill hoped to resolve a growing impasse over Poland. Stalin insisted that the government in Poland be friendly to the Soviet Union. He couldn't take chances. Germany had invaded Russia via Poland twice in twenty-five years. He wanted recognition of the communist-led government that was already in power. Churchill wanted to include Poles living in London who were fiercely anti-communist and fiercely anti-Soviet. Stalin labeled them terrorists.

Sitting in front of a fireplace in the Kremlin, Churchill cracked some of his favorite Polish jokes. The two leaders then set about defining broader British and Soviet spheres of influence and laying the groundwork for Western recognition of Soviet interests in Poland.

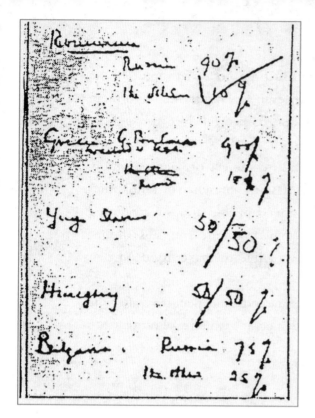

In October 1944, Stalin and Churchill met in Moscow. They outlined an agreement for the British and Soviet spheres of influence on this scrap of paper.

On the back of a scrap of paper, Churchill proposed the share of influence that Britain and the Soviet Union would exert: the Soviet Union would get 90 percent in Romania and 75 percent in Hungary and Bulgaria; Great Britain would get 90 percent in Greece; Yugoslavia would be split 50–50.

Stalin took the piece of paper, paused, and made a large check mark with a blue pencil. Then he handed it back to Churchill, who commented, "Might it not be thought rather cynical if it seemed we had disposed of these issues, so fateful to millions of people, in such an offhand manner. Let us burn the paper."

But Stalin urged Churchill to hold on to the historic scrap of paper, which Churchill called a "naughty document."

It was exactly the kind of deal that Roosevelt had set out to prevent.

Stalin quickly delivered on his part of the bargain, giving Great Britain 90 percent of Greece. Two months after meeting with Churchill, Stalin stood aside as British troops brutally suppressed a left-wing uprising in Greece. Honoring his agreement with Churchill, Stalin refused to support the leftists, despite the fact that they had the backing of much of the Greek population. Great Britain's behavior shocked the American public.

"A Great Hope to the World"

In early February 1945, Roosevelt, Stalin, and Churchill met for a second time at Yalta, a city in Crimea on the Black Sea. The time had come to finalize a postwar plan, including what to do with Germany. By now, Roosevelt was very ill. Those who saw him noticed how much weight he'd lost, how thin his face had grown, his shortness of breath.

Each of the leaders arrived at the summit with definite goals that reflected their desires for the shape of the postwar world. These desires represented their fundamentally different geopolitical and strategic views, and they had caused deep rifts. The Soviet Union was preoccupied with security. Great Britain sought to preserve its empire. The United States wanted Soviet assistance in ending the war in the Pacific, fashioning a world economy, and establishing a United Nations to preserve the peace.

Germany, Stalin insisted, must be permanently weakened so that the Soviet Union never again suffered a German attack. The Soviet Union had paid an enormous price in repulsing the German invasion. It has been estimated that 27 million Soviet soldiers and citizens lay dead, and much of the nation was in ruins. The United States and Great Britain had helped the Soviet Union defeat Germany, but their efforts and losses paled beside those of their Soviet ally. By comparison, Great Britain suffered between 400,000 to 450,000 total deaths; the United States, more than 410,000.

America had emerged from the war economically and militarily stronger than ever. But its diplomatic leverage was compromised by its failure to deliver the relief and assistance it had promised Stalin during the darkest hours of the war.

American leaders, however, had one major card to play: the promise of postwar economic assistance to help the Soviets rebuild their shattered nation. The once-powerful British were in the weakest position, no longer able to press their claims independently. Great Britain now depended on

Churchill (*left*), Roosevelt (*center*), and Stalin (*right*)—the Big Three—met at Yalta in February 1945. They overcame serious differences over the future of Poland and the rest of Europe to reach a series of agreements, which ignited optimism in both the United States and abroad.

US goodwill and largesse to retain its status as a major power in the postwar world.

These differences would play out in the debate over Poland. "The question of Poland is not only a question of honor but also a question of security," declared Stalin. "Throughout history, Poland has been the corridor through which the enemy has passed into Russia." It was a matter "of life and death for the Soviet Union."

Moscow had installed a pro-Soviet regime in Poland. Now Stalin demanded recognition of the communist-led government that was operating out of the eastern city of Lublin, Poland. But Roosevelt and Churchill supported the Polish government-in-exile in London, most of whose members were virulent anti-communists. Stalin accused them of being terrorists.

The three leaders compromised. They set up a Polish Provisional Government of National Unity. British, US, and Soviet ambassadors were to consult with the Polish leaders, and free elections, open to all "democratic and anti-Nazi parties," were to be held. The three leaders agreed on the Curzon Line as the eastern border, but they disagreed on the western boundary. This was left for future resolution.

The agreements were vague. Roosevelt's chief of staff, Admiral William D. Leahy, warned him, "This is so elastic that the Russians can stretch it all the way from Yalta to Washington without technically breaking it."

Roosevelt agreed, saying, "I know, Bill—I know it. But it's the best I can do for Poland at this time."

He understood that he had little leverage at Yalta. He was more excited about getting Stalin to agree to the "Declaration on Liberated Europe," which promised to establish broadly representative governments through free elections. The Big Three agreed to divide the soon-to-be-conquered Germany into four military zones with each ally controlling one. The fourth zone would be controlled by France.

The Soviet Union wanted reparations from Germany to assist in the massive task of rebuilding, but Stalin, Churchill, and Roosevelt were unable to reach an accord on postwar German reparations. They established a reparations commission, which based discussions on a figure of $20 billion. Half of this money would go to the Soviet Union.

Stalin agreed to come into the war against Japan three months after the end of the war in Europe. In return, the United States promised territorial and economic concessions in East Asia that would largely restore to Russia what it had lost to Japan in the 1904–1905 Russo-Japanese War.

The news of the Yalta summit ignited a kind of optimism that hadn't been felt for decades. Former President Herbert Hoover called the conference a "great hope to the world."

The Death of a President

The Soviets shared in post–Yalta optimism, but they could not be sure about the man next in line behind Roosevelt. Roosevelt's health was failing rapidly. On March 1, 1945, exhausted from his trip, for the first time in his presidency, he addressed the Congress sitting, not standing.

"I hope that you will pardon me for this unusual posture of sitting down during the presentation of what I want to say," Roosevelt began. "But I know that you will realize that it makes it a lot easier for me not to have to carry about ten pounds of steel around on the bottom of my legs; and also because of the fact that I have just completed a fourteen-thousand-mile trip."

Despite the rumors that he was ailing, Roosevelt assured Congress, "I was well the entire time. I was not ill for a second. . . . I come from the Crimea conference with a firm belief that we have made a good start on the road to a world peace."

He praised the "heroic advance" of American troops in Germany and the "gallant Red Army." The two armies would soon meet in Germany and bring the war with the Nazis to an end. He went on to say, "Hitler has failed."

"There can be no middle ground here," Roosevelt declared. "We shall have to take the responsibility for world collaboration, or we shall have to bear the responsibility for another world conflict."

In closing, Roosevelt praised the American people and stated his wish for a better world. "I am confident that the American people will accept the results of this conference as the beginning of a permanent structure of peace upon which we can begin to build, under God, that better world in which our children and grandchildren, yours and mine, the children

This is the last known photograph of Roosevelt, taken on April 11, 1945, while on a brief vacation in Warm Springs, Georgia.

and grandchildren of the whole world, must live and can live. And that, my friends, is the only message I can give you, for I feel very deeply, and I know that all of you are feeling it today and are going to feel it in the future."

Those who saw Roosevelt address Congress that night noticed how rapidly the president's health was failing. His personal doctor had diagnosed Roosevelt's problem as the "flu" and bronchitis. In truth, he was suffering from hypertension, heart disease, and left ventricular cardiac failure, as well as bronchitis.

Over the next few weeks, disagreements with the Soviets surfaced over Poland and other issues. This raised vexing questions for Roosevelt about the future of the relationship. But he never lost hope that the "Big Three" nations would continue to work together in peace and friendship.

In his last telegram to Churchill, Roosevelt advised: "I would minimize the general Soviet problem as much as possible because these problems, in one form or another, seem to arise every day and most of them straighten out."

On March 29, 1945, Roosevelt took a brief working vacation to his cottage refuge—dubbed the "Little White House"—in Warm Springs, Georgia. There, on April 11, he worked quietly inside the cottage. The next afternoon, he complained of "terrific pain" in the back of his head. Roosevelt suffered a massive stroke and died.

26

A New President

On April 12, 1945, Harry Truman went to House Speaker Sam Rayburn's office in the Capitol. The vice president had two things on his mind: playing poker and making a dent in Rayburn's latest shipment of whiskey.

Upon arrival at Rayburn's office, Truman was told to call the White House press secretary right away. Truman did, and Steve Early told him to rush right over.

At the White House, Eleanor Roosevelt informed Truman that the president had died. The news stunned Truman. Roosevelt had assured everyone that he was fine, that he had bronchitis, that was all. Even Roosevelt's personal doctor had said so.

After regaining his bearings, Truman expressed his regrets and asked if there was anything he could do. Mrs. Roosevelt replied, "Is there anything we can do for you? For you are the one in trouble now."

Truman was shockingly unprepared for that moment. He had

been vice president for only eighty-two days. During that time, he had met with Roosevelt only twice. They had never spoken about any of the substantive issues facing the nation.

In fact, most astoundingly, Truman did not know that the nation was building an atomic bomb. Neither Roosevelt nor any of the other top officials had ever informed the lightly regarded vice president.

And now Harry S. Truman was president.

"Pray for Me Now"

Outside the Capitol the next day, President Truman ran into a group of reporters. One asked how his first day on the job was going.

"Boys, if you ever pray, pray for me now," answered Truman. "I don't know whether you fellows ever had a load of hay fall on you, but when they told me yesterday what had happened, I felt like the moon, the stars, and all the planets had fallen on me. I've got the most terribly responsible job a man ever had."

Another reporter yelled out, "Good luck, Mr. President."

Truman responded, "I wish you didn't have to call me that."

It was not false humility. Truman sincerely felt he was in way over his head and told everyone he met with that it was all a mistake and he was not qualified to be president.

Some agreed with Truman, including Secretary of War Henry Stimson and Roosevelt's former vice president Henry Wallace, who now held a cabinet position as secretary of commerce. They feared that Truman would be putty in the hands of some of the hard-liners. Stimson anticipated that the greatest pressure would come from Churchill. It was imperative, he felt, to advise the new president of the "past differences between Britain and America."

Roosevelt had spelled out the most crucial difference between the two

This photograph of Harry S. Truman was taken eight days after Roosevelt's death. Truman turned to advisers for a quick education.

nations at his March 16 cabinet meeting. "The President indicated considerable difficulty with British relations," wrote Assistant Secretary of the Navy H. Struve Hensel in his diary. "In a semi-jocular manner of speaking, he stated that the British were perfectly willing for the United States to have a war with Russia at any time and that, in his opinion, to follow the British program would be to proceed toward that end."

Truman knew he needed to be brought up to speed about what was going on in the world.

The Education of President Truman

The next day, Truman turned to Secretary of State Edward Stettinius Jr. for advice. Many considered Stettinius a lightweight politician. He'd had little influence with Roosevelt.

Stettinius held a different view of Stalin and the Soviets than Roosevelt had. He didn't trust the Soviets. He told Truman the Soviets were deceitful. In a memo, Stettinius complained that since the Yalta Conference in February, the Soviets "have taken a firm and uncompromising position on nearly every major question."

He charged the Soviets with acting unilaterally in the liberated areas. He added that Churchill felt even stronger than he did on these matters.

Churchill wasted little time confirming Stettinius's view. He dashed off cables and sent British Foreign Secretary Anthony Eden to visit Truman.

The British ambassador to the United States also sized Truman up. The new president "was an honest and diligent mediocrity," decided Lord Halifax. "A bungling if well meaning amateur" surrounded by "Missouri County court-house caliber" friends.

After meeting with Stettinius, Truman turned to another man for advice. He met with his old Senate mentor James F. Byrnes, who had been part of the US delegation at Yalta. Truman assumed that Byrnes had accurate knowledge about what transpired at the conference. It would be many months before Truman discovered that that was not the case.

Truman admitted his abject ignorance and implored Byrnes to tell him everything "from Tehran to Yalta" and "everything under the sun."

The president relied on Byrnes to give him accurate information. But Byrnes reinforced Stettinius's message that the Soviets were breaking the Yalta agreement. He told Truman that he needed to be resolute and uncompromising with the Soviets.

Henry Wallace (*right*) stands apart from James Byrnes (*left*) and Truman (*center*). Byrnes would later push Truman to fire Wallace from his cabinet.

Byrnes also gave Truman his first real briefing about the atomic bomb. Byrnes described the bomb as "an explosive great enough to destroy the whole world" and it "might well put us in a position to dictate our own terms at the end of the war." He did not specify to whom the United States would be dictating terms.

The president trusted Byrnes so much that he made clear his intention to appoint him secretary of state as soon as Stettinius got the United Nations off the ground.

Truman's close friend and appointments secretary painted an unflattering picture of the relationship between Truman and Byrnes: "Mr. Byrnes came from South Carolina and talked to Mr. Truman and immediately decided that he would take over," wrote Matthew J. Connelly. "Mr. Truman to Mr. Byrnes, I'm afraid, was a nonentity, as Mr. Byrnes thought he had superior intelligence."

Superior intelligence, perhaps, but between this unlikely pair, who would do so much to shape the postwar world, Truman had more formal education. He'd graduated from high school, whereas Byrnes had dropped out at age fourteen.

His Cause Must Live On

The US ambassador to the Soviet Union hurried to the Kremlin to inform Stalin of Roosevelt's death. There, Ambassador W. Averell Harriman found the Soviet leader profoundly saddened at the news. Stalin held Harriman's hand and bemoaned humanity's loss. He asked Harriman to convey his deepest condolences to Mrs. Roosevelt and the Roosevelt children.

Harriman tried to assure Stalin that he would develop an equally strong relationship with President Truman. Harriman called Truman "a man of action and not of words."

Stalin responded, "Roosevelt has died but his cause must live on. We will support President Truman with all our forces and all our will."

Harriman was usually a skeptical man, but he found himself moved by the depth of Stalin's emotion.

But Harriman still intended to bend Truman's ear about Soviet intentions. Like many of Truman's advisers, he came from a very privileged background, and he hated everything that smacked of socialism and taking from the rich and giving to the poor. Harriman was the son of a railroad millionaire who had helped found Brown Brothers Harriman, a powerful private bank. Another founding partner of the bank was Prescott Bush, father of future president George H. W. Bush and grandfather of president George W. Bush.

When the ambassador learned that Minister of Foreign Affairs Molotov was stopping off in Washington before heading to San Francisco for the United Nations' planning sessions, Harriman rushed to Washington too. He wanted to reach Truman before the Soviet minister did.

Arriving before Molotov, Harriman warned Truman that the United States was facing a "barbarian invasion of Europe" by the Soviets, and he urged the president to stand firm. He told Truman to tell Molotov that "we would not stand for any pushing around on the Polish question."

Harriman further reinforced the information that Churchill and Eden had already given Truman about Stalin's oppressive measures. As soon as the Soviet Union extended control over a country and imposed its system, he told Truman, the secret police moved in and wiped out free speech.

Harriman felt certain that the Soviets wouldn't risk a break with the United States. They desperately sought the postwar reconstruction aid that Roosevelt had dangled before them. Secretary of State Stettinius and Secretary of the Navy James Forrestal generally agreed with that assessment.

All three men encouraged Truman to take a tough stand with the Soviets on the Poland matter. But Truman would do more than that.

Tough-Guy Act

On April 23, less than two weeks after Roosevelt's death, Truman gathered his foreign policy advisers for a final meeting before sitting down with Molotov. Secretary of War Henry Stimson, Army Chief of Staff George Marshall, and Chief of Staff William Leahy offered Truman a more balanced point of view on the Soviet situation.

The Yalta agreement was elastic, after all.

Leahy cautioned Truman on the difficulty of alleging bad faith on the part of the Soviets. In fact, said Leahy, he would have been surprised if the Soviets behaved any differently.

Marshall, *Time* magazine's 1943 Man of the Year, spoke up. He contended that a break with the Soviet Union would be disastrous. The United States needed the Soviets to help defeat Japan.

Stimson showed the clearest understanding of the predicament. He urged Truman to act with greater sensitivity to Soviet concerns. The Soviet Union had been a trustworthy ally, said Stimson, often delivering even more than promised, especially in military matters.

Stimson reminded the president of Poland's great importance to Soviet security and acknowledged that "the Russians perhaps were being more realistic than we were in regard to their own security." He also added that very few countries outside the United States and Great Britain shared the United States' belief in free elections.

True to form, Truman masked his limited grasp of the issues with bluster and bravado. He promised to stand up to Molotov and demand that the Soviets stop breaking the Yalta agreement. As far as the United Nations was concerned, the United States would "go on with plans for the San Francisco conference, and if the Russians did not wish to join us they could go to hell."

Truman acknowledged to Ambassador Harriman that he didn't expect to get 100 percent of what he wanted from the Soviets, but he did expect to get 85 percent.

In his meeting with Molotov later that day, Truman put on his tough-guy act. Right away, he accused the Soviets of having broken the terms established in Yalta, particularly those regarding Poland.

Molotov tried to explain that Poland was a vital security issue for the Soviets. He pointed out that the agreement called for including friendly Poles, not the London group that was hostile to the Lublin government.

But Truman wouldn't hear it and rudely dismissed Molotov. When Molotov tried to raise other issues, Truman snapped, "That will be all, Mr. Molotov. I would appreciate it if you would transmit my views to Marshal Stalin."

Molotov objected to Truman's insulting behavior. "I've never been talked to like that in my life," he said.

"Carry out your agreements and you won't get talked to like that," Truman shot back.

Indignant, Molotov stormed out of the room. Years later, Molotov remembered Truman's "imperious tone" and "rather stupid" effort to show "who was boss."

One More Betrayal

Stalin was furious at Truman's undiplomatic dressing-down of Molotov. Germany had invaded the Soviet Union twice in twenty-five years, through Poland and Eastern Europe. He insisted on having friendly governments to his west and especially on his borders.

Stalin cabled Truman the following day, outlining what had actually occurred at Yalta. He contended that Roosevelt had agreed that the Lublin government would form the kernel of the new Polish government. Because "Poland borders on the Soviet Union," the Soviets had the right to a friendly government there. He said he didn't know if the governments of Belgium or Greece were really democratic, but he wouldn't object because they were vital to British security. He wrote, "I am ready to fulfill your request and do everything possible to reach a harmonious solution. But you demand too much of me . . . [Y]ou demand that I renounce the interests of security of the Soviet Union, but I cannot turn against my country."

Once again, Stalin felt betrayed.

27

The End Is Near

It was April 26, 1945, and things were going well on the battle-field in Europe. US and Soviet soldiers had joined up near Torgau, Germany, 4,500 miles from the shores of the United States and 1,400 bloody miles from the ruins of Stalingrad.

The soldiers were standing on the Elbe River, and their mood was joyous. Germany had not yet surrendered, but the war was nearing its end. They all knew it and were celebrating. Food abounded and liquor flowed—champagne, vodka, cognac, wine, beer, scotch.

Private First Class Leo Kasinsky called it "the best time I ever had in my life. . . . [The Soviets] gave us a wonderful meal and we had about sixty toasts." The twenty-eight-year-old Kings County, New York, enlistee was clearly impressed with the Soviet soldiers. "Boy," he said, "they don't even drink like that in Brooklyn."

The New York Times reported "toasts and songs and expressions of hope for the future in which America, Russia and Britain would stand together for enduring peace."

The celebration was taking place about ninety miles from Berlin as the crow flies, and while good cheer and optimism were flowing in Torgau, it was quite a different story in Berlin.

Five days earlier, the Russians had reached the northern suburbs of Berlin. Germany's capital was under siege. The Russians blasted and burned their way through the Berlin streets.

Hitler vowed that the Russians would suffer their worst defeat in Berlin. He called on the German people to defend Berlin. Many did fight to defend their city. Others hid first. They feared the Russians' revenge for Hitler's double-crossing and for the atrocities inflicted on the Russians by German soldiers.

A Soviet soldier raises the Soviet flag over the Reichstag in Berlin.

The United Nations

As Berlin was under siege, delegates from forty-six countries met 7,500 miles away in San Francisco for the United Nations Conference on International Organization. The delegates planned to discuss the creation of the United Nations Charter, whose goal was to maintain peace among nations worldwide.

The conference began on April 25. Drinks and toasts and songs of hope for the future should have flowed there, too. It should have been an occasion to celebrate a new era of international peace and reconciliation.

Instead, the early sessions were marred by tensions between Russia and the United States. Harriman met with members of the US delegation. He wanted to make sure, he said, that "everyone understands that the Soviets . . . were not going to live up to their post-war agreements."

He insisted that the Soviets would use any devious means at their disposal to dominate Eastern Europe. When he repeated these charges to reporters at an off-the-record press conference, several reporters grew irate. They called him a "warmonger" and walked out.

The US delegates did not show the same sort of skepticism as those disgruntled reporters. When Molotov requested to have the Lublin government seated to represent Poland, the delegates rejected his request. Yet the US officials successfully pressured Latin American representatives to seat Argentina's government despite its Nazi sympathies.

From the White House, Truman addressed the convention by direct wire. He recalled the "courageous champions" who "died to insure justice." He told them: "Let us labor to achieve a peace which is really worthy of their great sacrifice. We must make certain, by your work here, that another war will be impossible."

But Truman's get-tough tactics with the Soviet Union were not producing the desired results. He met twice with Joseph Davies, a former ambassador to the Soviet Union, and sought his counsel. Truman confessed to Davies that after his tirade, Molotov was "visibly shaken, blanched and went pale." Initially, this convinced Truman that "the tough method" clearly worked. The Soviets were backing down in San Francisco and not demanding recognition of the Lublin government.

But, Truman also noted, relations with the Soviets were deteriorating rapidly. "What do you think?" he asked Davies. "Did I do right?"

Davies spoke directly and honestly, giving the president an answer he didn't expect.

A Stickler for Reciprocity

Davies, a conservative corporate attorney, explained to Truman that Molotov had come to see him before his April 23 meeting with Truman. Roosevelt's death was a "great tragedy" to the Soviets, Molotov told Davies, because "Stalin and Roosevelt understood each other." Molotov wanted to know if Truman knew all the facts about Yalta.

Davies explained to Truman that the Soviets had always been "sticklers for reciprocity . . . between allies." For this reason, the Soviets accepted British-imposed governments in Africa, Italy, and Greece, even though they didn't represent the antifascist forces in those countries, because the Soviets understood that they were "vital interests" to the United States and Great Britain.

The Soviets expected the same consideration for their vital security interests in Poland. Davies reminded Truman that while the United States and Great Britain had been planning global strategy during the war, the Soviet Union had been doing all the fighting.

Truman was surprised to learn that the Soviets had even agreed not to press their territorial claims with Churchill "out of consideration for Roosevelt." He realized that he had been influenced and misled by Byrnes,

Stettinius, and others. He promised Davies that he would "clean out" the anti-Soviet people in the State Department who had misled him.

Davies pointed out how fundamentally the relationship with the Soviets had changed in the last six weeks. The British had acted as instigators.

He further warned Truman that if the Soviets decided that the United States and Great Britain were "ganging up on them," they would respond by out-toughing the West. They had done so before: When it became clear that the West would not help them stop the Nazis, they had concluded the 1939 nonaggression pact with Hitler.

Nobody wanted a repeat of that situation. Davies assured Truman that "when approached with generosity and friendliness, the Soviets respond with even greater generosity. The 'tough' approach induces a quick and sharp rejoinder that 'out toughs' anyone they consider hostile."

Davies agreed to set up a meeting between Truman and Stalin. Later, Davies recorded Truman's self-deprecating remarks in his diary: "It's no wonder that I'm concerned over this matter. It is a terrible responsibility and I am the last man fitted to handle it and it happened to me. But I'll do my best."

Davies wasn't alone in standing up for Stalin. So did Admiral William H. Standley, another former ambassador to the Soviet Union. Standley countered those who believed Stalin was up to no good.

Writing in *Collier's* magazine, Standley insisted that Stalin genuinely desired to cooperate with the United States to establish a durable world peace. The Soviet Union not only "desperately" needed a stable peace, Standley wrote, "but I am certain that [Stalin] desires it sincerely and fervently."

"The world," he added, "simply cannot stand another war."

German Defeat

On April 30, as the Russian army approached within a few hundred yards of Hitler's bunker, Hitler, his wife Eva Braun, and several of his closest advisers

An American army officer salutes as he enters the bunker in Berlin, Germany, where Hitler committed suicide. Two Russian soldiers guard the bunker.

and their families committed suicide. Over the radio, the German people were told that their führer had been killed at the head of his troops in the heroic Battle of Berlin.

A week later, on May 7, 1945, Germany surrendered. A US diplomat wrote that the Soviet people's joy was "indescribable." Crowds gathered in front of the US embassy in Moscow and shouted "Hurrah for Roosevelt!"

Stalin addressed two to three million people in Red Square. In his victory speech, he said, "The great sacrifices we made in the name of the freedom and independence of our Motherland, the incalculable privations and sufferings experienced by our people in the course of the war, the intense work in the rear and at the front, placed on the altar of the Motherland, have not been in vain, and have been crowned by complete victory over the enemy."

Americans also acknowledged the immensity of the Soviets' sacrifice and suffering. In June, prize-winning journalist Cyrus L. Sulzberger wrote in *The New York Times* that the Soviets' losses strained the imagination: "In terms of misery and suffering, of malady and disaster, of wasted man hours in a land where work is glorified, the loss is incalculable. It perhaps cannot be fully realized even by the masses of Russian people themselves."

Sulzberger understood that such devastation would have enduring consequences. He predicted that "this terrible suffering and unprecedented destruction" will "leave its marks not only upon the people and lands of the USSR, but upon future decisions and policies as well as psychological attitudes."

This meant that the Soviets would demand "allies of the surest sort" in Eastern Europe, the elimination of German military power, and the forging of friendly relations with the nations of central Asia and the Far East that bordered the Soviet Union.

Americans wanted to help ease Soviet hardship. Throughout the year, charitable events took place. On New Year's Day, the editors of *The Washington Post* urged Americans to remember Russian children as they celebrated their holiday and to "send them a tithe of our good fortune."

Even First Lady Bess Truman lent a hand. In July 1945, she became honorary chair of a nationwide drive to collect a million books to replace those destroyed by the Nazis. Each volume would bear the flags of the two nations along with a frontispiece inscription reading, *To the heroic people of the Soviet Union from the people of America.* Universities, schools, libraries, churches, and private individuals donated books. Truman himself donated a forty-volume collection of the works of George Washington, perhaps thinking that the Soviets would like to read about American history.

Numerous stories circulated about the bravery and generosity of Soviet soldiers and ordinary citizens. When Captain Ernest M. Gruenberg and two other US officers escaped from a POW camp, they made the journey to Moscow in just fourteen days. "We hardly ever walked," recounted the paratroop surgeon to *The Washington Post*. "Always there was a truck or train to haul us and no one ever asked for money or tickets. We were Americans and nothing, apparently, was too good for us. Everywhere people took us in. . . . [W]e made a grand entrance into Moscow in the car reserved for Russian officers—free, of course."

The Soviets were so willing to share their meager food supplies, said Gruenberg, that he believed he gained back the twenty-five pounds he had lost in prison.

The comradely feelings toward the Soviet people translated into optimism about the postwar relationship between the two countries.

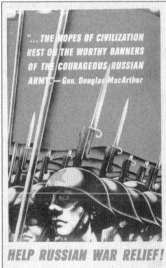

Led by the Russian War Relief, Americans gave generously to their struggling Soviet allies.

Another Kind of Reciprocity

Soviet soldiers related the atrocities they had seen while liberating concentration camps, including Majdanek, Sobibor, Treblinka, and Auschwitz, en route to Berlin. They reported on the terror, humiliation, deportation, and death that Jews and other victims had suffered.

"[The Red Army] saw the destroyed cities; it saw the mass-graves of Russian war prisoners, murdered or starved to death," wrote Alexander Werth, a war correspondent. "[I]n the Russian soldiers' mind, the real truth on Nazi Germany, with its Hitler and Himmler and its *Untermensch* [subhuman] philosophy and its unspeakable sadism became hideously tangible."

In a letter, a Russian soldier described the horror of a death camp to his wife:

> Yesterday we examined a death camp for 120,000 prisoners. Posts two meters high with electric fencing enclose the camp. In addition, the Germans mined everything. Watchtowers for armed guards and machine guns stand fifty meters apart. Not far away from the death barracks is the crematorium. Can you imagine how many people the Germans have burned there? Next to this exploded crematorium, there are bones, bones, and piles of shoes several meters high. There are children's shoes in the pile. Total horror, impossible to describe.

Soviet newspapers went out of their way to publish grisly accounts of the atrocities. By the time the soldiers reached German soil, their anger could not be contained. Seeking revenge for the havoc, devastation, and humiliation that German soldiers had wreaked on the Soviet people, the soldiers acted in unconscionable and inexcusable ways. They behaved brutally toward the Germans. German women paid an especially high price for Germany's crimes. In just a few weeks, more than 100,000 sought medical care for rape.

At first, Stalin did nothing to stop them. He later reversed course and ordered a halt to such horrific behavior.

The Soviet soldiers—and the world—would later learn about the Soviet Union's horrifying system of labor camps, the gulag. Historian Steven A. Barnes characterized it as "one of the most brutal institutions of [the] lethal twentieth century." Millions of people had been detained and made to perform hard labor. Many more were simply executed.

The Truth Comes Out

Although many of Truman's advisers assumed that Stalin would set up communist regimes throughout the territories occupied by the Red Army, Stalin was in no rush to institute revolutionary change. He recognized that the communists represented a minority element in most of these nations, though they had often played a leading role in anti-Nazi resistance movements. He had once remarked that communism fit Poland like a saddle fit a cow.

Far from initially imposing communist regimes, Stalin tried to restrain those seeking revolutionary change in both Western and Eastern Europe. He urged them to establish broader democratic coalitions.

More of a nationalist than an international revolutionary, Stalin thought first about what was in the interests of the Soviet Union. He expected the United States' support for postwar reconstruction, and he needed the Allies' cooperation in resisting the restoration of German power. He still saw the Germans as the primary threat to the Soviet Union.

Stalin told his communist allies not to follow the Bolshevik model but to move toward socialism under other "political systems"—for example, by a democracy, by a parliamentary republic, or even by a constitutional monarchy. He wanted nothing to disrupt his alliance with the United States and Britain. Hence, the governments he set up in Soviet-liberated Eastern and Central Europe were friendly to the Soviet Union but not communist-dominated.

A crowd cheers the arrival of Soviet troops in Prague, Czechoslovakia.

Feeling more conciliatory, Truman made an effort to improve relations with the Soviets. Churchill pressured Truman to maintain troops in their advanced positions until Britain and the United States had wrested concessions from the Soviets. But Truman resisted this pressure.

Gradually, the truth came out. Truman realized that Stalin's interpretation of the Yalta agreement conformed more closely to the truth than his own. His former mentor Byrnes admitted that he had left Yalta before the final agreement was concluded and that he hadn't participated in many of the critical meetings.

Truman also learned that Roosevelt had indeed agreed to a Soviet sphere of influence in Eastern Europe and that the United States and Britain had weak grounds for demanding a new government in Poland.

In late May, Truman sent Hopkins to meet with Stalin. They worked out an agreement on Poland that was similar to the formula established for Yugoslavia, where a provisional government had been formed. The agreement called for a postwar election to determine the future system of government and the economy.

Truman told journalists that this represented a "very pleasant yielding" on the part of Stalin. It gave him hope, he said, that future cooperation between the United States and the Soviet Union was possible.

The Number One Problem

In July 1945, Truman, Churchill, and Stalin met in Potsdam in occupied Germany. As Truman left for the meeting, he was more optimistic than he had been two months earlier.

Still, that month, *Life* magazine cautioned that "Russia is the No. 1 problem for America because it is the only country in the world with the dynamic power to challenge our own conceptions of truth, justice, and the good life." Just two years earlier, *Life* had put Stalin on its cover, hailing him as a hero.

The Potsdam Conference was amicable on the surface, but it would prove a setback to long-term cooperation. On July 16, the day before the Potsdam meeting started, the United States successfully tested its first atom bomb in New Mexico. Such a powerful weapon convinced Truman that the United States could get along just fine without catering to Soviet concerns. His behavior toward Stalin conveyed that message.

On his way back from Potsdam on the USS *Augusta*, Truman told a group of officers that it didn't matter if the Soviets were obstinate "because the United States now had developed an entirely new weapon of such force and nature that we did not need the Russians—or any other nation."

The only question now was about how to use the bomb. The Germans had already surrendered. The war in Europe was over.

That left Japan.

PART FOUR

The Bomb:
The Tragedy of
a Small Man

28

"Thank God for the Atom Bomb"

In May 1945, a young second lieutenant named Paul Fussell was about to be transferred from France to the Pacific. Like many other US infantrymen, he believed that a US invasion of Japan was imminent.

At twenty-one, the rifle platoon leader had seen plenty of action. He had been shot in the back and leg. He had recovered enough from his injuries to return to his unit, but his legs buckled and he fell to the ground every time he jumped from the back of a truck. Later, he would be classified as 40 percent disabled, but for now, the army deemed him fit enough for more fighting in the Pacific. The thought of more combat, he said, "made me breathe in and gasp and shake all over."

And then came the news of the atomic bombing of Hiroshima, Japan, on August 6, 1945. With great relief, Fussell realized that there would be no invasion. He would not have to rush Japan's beaches under assault, "firing while being machine-gunned, mortared, and shelled."

Thirty-six years later, he reflected on that moment of realization in his 1981 essay, "Thank God for the Atom Bomb." "For all the fake manliness of our facades, we cried with relief and joy. We were going to live. We were going to grow up to adulthood after all."

Fussell believed that the incineration of Hiroshima—and, three days later, Nagasaki—saved his life. The American people believed that the United States reluctantly dropped atomic bombs on Japan to save the lives of thousands of young men like Paul Fussell who were poised to die if the United States invaded Japan. Generations of Americans continue to believe it was so.

The story is really more complicated—and much more disturbing.

Entering Another World War

The United States entered the Second World War on December 8, 1941, after the bombing of Pearl Harbor. The Axis powers were on the march. The United States and its allies were losing.

Despite the surprise attack by Japan at Pearl Harbor, the United States trained its sights on first defeating the Nazis. Roosevelt insisted on the Europe-first strategy. The United States would fight Japan, but Roosevelt opposed "an all-out effort in the Pacific."

Defeating Japan, the president argued, would not defeat Germany, but defeating Germany would defeat Japan. The defeat of Japan, said Roosevelt, could be done "without firing a shot or losing a life." And so for Roosevelt, it was first things first. Defeat Germany, then Japan.

But when the United States entered the Pacific War, the Japanese fought fiercely, ensuring that US victory would come at an enormous cost. But US industrial production gave the American forces tremendous advantages. By 1943, US factories were churning out almost 100,000 planes a year. This dwarfed Japanese production, which totaled 70,000 during the entire war.

By the summer of 1944, the United States had deployed almost a hundred aircraft carriers in the Pacific, far more than Japan's twenty-five for the whole of the war. The United States was also capturing more and more Japanese-occupied territories. This eventually brought Japan itself within range of US bombers.

"I Told You So"

Science-fiction writers and scientists had long pondered the possibility of atomic energy. Some imagined its use for peaceful purposes; others imagined military purposes.

President Franklin D. Roosevelt signing the declaration of war against Japan on December 8, 1941.

Beginning in 1896, a series of scientific discoveries by Henri Becquerel and Marie and Pierre Curie of France, and Frederick Soddy and Ernest Rutherford of Great Britain, ignited public curiosity about radioactivity. These world-famous scientists and others talked about the enormous energy locked in matter and the possibility of blowing up the universe. But they also fantasized about the positive ways such energy might be put to use. Surely, they believed, such power could create a utopian society.

Some people became enamored with the healing powers of radium and other radioactive ingredients, which were infused into popular medicines. Advertisements promised that these products would heal all sorts of maladies, from baldness, and rheumatism to high blood pressure, flatulence, and even sexual disfunction.

Between 1927 and 1931, a wealthy American socialite, athlete, and industrialist named Eben Byers drank so much of a patent medicine called Radithor—somewhere between 1,000 and 1,500 bottles of it—that he lost weight, experienced bad headaches, and watched his teeth fall out and holes appear in his head. He required surgery to remove his upper jaw and most of his lower jaw. After Byers's death in 1932, *The Wall Street Journal* ran the headline THE RADIUM WATER WORKED FINE UNTIL HIS JAW CAME OFF.

H. G. Wells wrote the first atomic war novel, *The World Set Free*, in 1914. He described an atomic war between Germany and Austria on one side and England, France, and the United States on the other. In his story, the warring nations succeeded in destroying more than 200 cities by the "unquenchable crimson conflagration of the atomic bombs." Later, after atomic bombs were actually used in war, Wells proposed that his epitaph should read, "God damn you all, I told you so."

Wells's storytelling influenced a brilliant, quirky Hungarian physicist named Leo Szilard, who had left Germany soon after the Nazis came to power. Szilard had given extensive thought to the possibility of atomic energy. He tried to discuss the feasibility of such energy with the renowned British physicist Ernest Rutherford, but Rutherford dismissed the idea as the "merest moonshine" and threw Szilard out of his office. Undaunted, Szilard took out a patent in 1934 on how a nuclear chain reaction would work, mistakenly citing beryllium as the most likely element rather than uranium.

In December 1938, two German physicists stunned the scientific world by splitting the uranium atom. This accomplishment meant that Rutherford's "merest moonshine" was now a distinct possibility.

★ ★ ★

As the Nazis rose to power, leading Jewish scientists fled Nazi Germany. Many came to the United States. In the coming years, they would be joined by others escaping German and Italian fascism. They included Albert Einstein, Leo Szilard, Hans Bethe, Edward Teller, Enrico Fermi, Eugene Wigner, and John von Neumann.

News that the German scientists had split the uranium atom sent shivers down the spines of *émigrés*—those who had left their home countries for political reasons. They feared the consequences if a madman such as Adolf Hitler should ever get his hands on such a devastating weapon.

Germany did, in fact, begin an atomic research program. But unknown to Americans until late in the war, Germany had abandoned its atomic research early, opting instead to focus on weapons like the V-1 and V-2 rockets, which could be used immediately. Hitler had little interest in putting manpower and resources into a weapon he might not be able to use in the current war.

During the summer of 1939, *émigré* scientists proposed that the United States build its own atomic bomb as a deterrent. But US authorities weren't interested in building an atomic bomb—yet.

Feeling desperate, Szilard and fellow Hungarian physicist Wigner turned to Albert Einstein, the world's most famous and most respected scientist. They urged him to write to President Roosevelt to convince him that such a project was necessary.

Einstein did write a letter to Roosevelt, but he later regretted it. "I made one great mistake in my life," he told chemist Linus Pauling, "when I signed the letter to President Roosevelt recommending that the atom bombs be made."

In October 1939, Roosevelt authorized the US bomb project.

At first, the United States' atomic program moved at a glacial pace. Then came an important discovery: only 5 to 10 kilograms (about 11 to 22 pounds) of pure uranium were needed to build an atomic bomb, not 500 tons, as first calculated.

This is one of three letters that Albert Einstein wrote to President Roosevelt, urging him to authorize a US atomic research program.

On October 9, 1941, two months before the United States entered the war, Vannevar Bush, one of the country's top science administrators, met with President Roosevelt and Vice President Wallace. Bush explained the new information. This meant, he said, that an atomic bomb would be possible within two years.

Roosevelt gave Bush the go-ahead and the resources he requested.

More than $2 billion would fund the Manhattan Project, the secret effort to build the atomic bomb. The development of the atomic bomb would change the course of history. It would also change America—and America's relationship with Russia.

The Luminaries

One of the Manhattan Project's outposts was the Metallurgical Laboratory, which was set up at the University of Chicago. The "Met Lab," as it was known, was headed by Dr. Arthur Holly Compton. The goal was to produce a self-sustaining chain reaction in an atomic pile.

Compton asked Dr. J. Robert Oppenheimer, a brilliant and charismatic theoretical physicist, to bring together a team of extraordinary theoreticians to grapple with a number of important questions. Oppenheimer called his team the "luminaries."

In the summer of 1942, the "luminaries" had a scare so unsettling that it forced them to temporarily halt the project. During their deliberations, the physicists suddenly realized that an atomic detonation might ignite the hydrogen in the oceans or the nitrogen in the atmosphere and set the planet on fire.

As they made this stunning realization, abject fear engulfed the room. Oppenheimer stared at the blackboard and a look of "wild surprise" came over his face. The others looked equally shocked.

Oppenheimer hopped on a train and rushed east to confer with Compton, who agreed that the risk was too great—that unless the scientists could draw "a firm and reliable conclusion that . . . atomic bombs could not explode the air or the sea, these bombs must never be made." "Better to accept the slavery of the Nazis," Compton concluded, "than to run a chance of drawing the final curtain on mankind!"

But back in Berkeley, California, Hans Bethe performed additional calculations. He discovered that his fellow physicist Edward Teller hadn't accounted for the heat that would be absorbed by the radiation. This lowered the odds of blowing up the world to 3 in 1,000,000.

It was a risk the scientists were willing to chance.

A Black Day for Mankind

On December 2, 1942, the scientists at the Met Lab succeeded in creating the first sustained nuclear chain reaction. Given the lack of safety precautions, it's a wonder they didn't blow up the city of Chicago.

Szilard told Enrico Fermi that the date "would go down as a black day in the history of mankind." He was right.

The Manhattan Project now became a crash program. In 1943, Brigadier General Leslie Groves headed the Manhattan Engineering District. Groves had spent two years at MIT before entering West Point. Now he oversaw virtually all phases of the Manhattan Project: the scientific research, production, security, and planning for use of the bomb.

This is an artist's rendition of the first sustained nuclear chain reaction on December 2, 1942, in the top secret Met Lab at the University of Chicago. Afterward, Leo Szilard and Enrico Fermi shook hands in front of the reactors.

Under Groves's direction, plants were established in Oak Ridge, Tennessee; Hanford, Washington; and Los Alamos, New Mexico. The Los Alamos site, inconspicuously nestled in the beautiful Sangre de Cristo Mountains, was the base of secret operations.

Groves appointed Oppenheimer to head the secret Los Alamos laboratory. Most assumed the relationship between the two men would be a marriage made in hell, for they made an odd couple—opposites in every conceivable way. General Groves weighed more than twice as much as the pencil-thin scientist, who, at over six feet tall, weighed 128 pounds at the beginning of the project, 115 by the end. Groves came from poverty; Oppenheimer from wealth. They had different religious beliefs. They had different eating, smoking, and drinking habits.

They also held diametrically opposed political views. Groves was a staunch conservative, whereas Oppenheimer was an unapologetic leftist. Most of Oppenheimer's students, friends, and family members were communists. The scientist admitted that he was a member of just about every communist front organization on the West Coast. At one point, Oppenheimer had given 10 percent of his monthly salary to the Communist Party to support the republican forces in Spain.

The two men were opposites in

General Leslie Groves (*right*) and Dr. Robert Oppenheimer stand at ground zero of the Trinity Test. They examine the remains of the tower from which a test atomic bomb was detonated.

temperament as well. Whereas Oppenheimer was beloved by most who knew him, Groves was universally despised. His assistant described him as "demanding," "critical," "abrasive and sarcastic," "intelligent," "the most egotistical man I know," and "the biggest S.O.B. I have ever worked for."

Groves's gruff, bullying, take-no-prisoners style actually complemented Oppenheimer's ability to inspire and get the most out of his colleagues in driving the project to completion.

Oppenheimer's weapon was his sense of humor—and his ability to stand up to Groves. When the scientists and the military clashed over security provisions and other matters, Oppenheimer ran interference for the scientists. When Groves told him not to wear his signature porkpie hats because they made him too recognizable, Oppenheimer wore a full Native American headdress—and proclaimed he would continue to wear it until the end of the war. Groves ultimately relented.

29

The Man Who Would Be President

As work on the bomb steadily progressed at Los Alamos, so did the Allied effort in the Pacific.

In July, the Combined Chiefs of Staff, under General George Marshall—a future secretary of state, secretary of defense, and Nobel Peace Prize winner—adopted a two-pronged strategy to win the Pacific War: first, strangle Japan with an air and sea blockade and pummel the country with "intensive air bombardment"; then, with Japan's military weakened and morale lowered, invade.

In June 1944, as Allied forces advanced in both the European and Pacific theaters, Churchill and Roosevelt finally delivered on the long-delayed second front, landing 100,000 troops on the beach at Normandy, France. German forces, retreating from the Soviet advance, would now have to fight a real two-front war.

On July 9, 1944, a little more than a month after D-day, US forces took Saipan, a tropical island in the Pacific. The loss of life was enormous. Thirty thousand Japanese troops and 22,000 civilians were killed or committed suicide. The Japanese government had told

A torpedoed Japanese destroyer photographed in June 1942 through periscope as it sinks.

US soldiers use improvised litters to carry comrades who, from the lack of food and water on the May 1942 march from Bataan, Philippines, fell along the road.

A Japanese plane is shot down as it attempts to attack USS *Kitkun Bay* in June 1944, near the Mariana Islands.

the civilians of the horrors they would suffer at the hands of Americans if taken prisoner, leading many of them to throw themselves off "Suicide Cliff."

The United States counted 3,000 dead and more than 10,000 wounded in the nearly month-long combat—its highest battle toll to date in the Pacific. For most Japanese leaders, the calamitous defeat offered definitive proof that military victory could not be won. On July 18, 1944, Prime Minister Hideki Tojo and his cabinet resigned.

A Dangerous Man

As news of Tojo's resignation began to circulate, the Democratic National Convention opened in Chicago. Franklin D. Roosevelt easily secured the nomination for an unprecedented fourth term.

The real contest was over the vice presidency. Incumbent vice president Henry Wallace was enormously popular with the American people. His stature rose when he repudiated Henry Luce's vision of an "American Century"—a postwar world dominated by the United States. Luce had once been infatuated with Benito Mussolini and fascism. But now, he reasoned, it was America's obligation to lead.

"We must accept whole-heartedly our duty and our opportunity as the most powerful and vital nation in the world," wrote Luce, "and in consequence to exert upon the world the full impact of our influence, for such purposes as we see fit and by such means as we see fit."

Henry Luce's vision for America appeared in *Life* magazine on February 17, 1941, ten months before the United States entered the war.

Some were immediately suspicious. They noted that the appeal came from a media magnate who had recently defended fascism. Former New Deal administrator Raymond Moley urged Americans to reject this "temptation to drift into empire."

Henry Wallace deplored all empires— whether they were British, French, German, or American. In May 1942, Wallace spoke out against Luce's nationalistic vision. He called instead for the "Century of the Common Man."

"No nation will have the God-given right

Henry Robinson Luce was known as a man of missionary zeal and limitless curiosity. His company, Time Inc., included many popular publications, including *Time* and *Life* magazines. After his death in 1967, he became known for his prejudices.

to exploit other nations," said Wallace. "There must be neither military nor economic imperialism. . . . International cartels that serve American greed and the German will to power must go."

Wallace reminded Americans that the great revolutions of history had been rebellions of ordinary people—the American Revolution of 1775, the French Revolution of 1792, the Latin American Revolution of the Bolivian era, the German Revolution of 1848, and the Russian Revolution of 1917.

Each of these revolutions, observed Wallace, spoke for the common man. "Some went to excess," he acknowledged, but "people groped their way to the light."

Known as a visionary, Henry Wallace said that the really dangerous fascists are American fascists.

Wallace pointed to modern science as "a by-product and an essential part of the people's revolution." He harkened back to his days studying plant genetics and experiments to develop hybrid corn that produced a greater yield and resisted disease better than normal corn.

Science, he noted, "has made it . . . possible to see that all of the people of the world get enough to eat." And only when hunger was ended would peace be possible.

Wallace called for a worldwide "people's revolution." He spoke for the "common man," workers who wanted to join unions, African Americans who battled for civil rights, women who sought true equality, people around the world who struggled to end colonialist oppression. This earned Wallace the hatred of some. His enemies included Wall Street bankers, anti-union businessmen, Southern segregationists, opponents of women's equality, defenders of British and French colonialism, and conservative members of his own party.

Several months earlier, on April 9, 1944, Wallace had written an article on American fascism in *The New York Times.* "The really dangerous American fascists are not those who are hooked up directly or indirectly with the Axis," warned Wallace. "The FBI has a finger on those. The dangerous American fascist . . . would prefer not to use violence. His method is to poison the channels of public information . . . [using] the news to deceive the public into giving the fascist and his group more money or more power.

"If we define an American fascist as one who in case of conflict puts money and power ahead of human beings, then there are undoubtedly several million fascists in the United States," Wallace continued. "There are probably several hundred thousand if we narrow the definition to include only those who in their search for money and power are ruthless and deceitful. . . . They are patriotic in time of war because it is to their interest to be so, but in time of peace they follow power and the dollar wherever they may lead."

British prime minister Churchill so feared Wallace that he deployed Royal Air Force lieutenant and future writer Roald Dahl to befriend Wallace in order to spy on him. Dahl stole a pamphlet that Wallace had drafted called "Our Job in the Pacific."

British officials copied and transmitted the pamphlet to Churchill, who was aghast at Wallace's support for the "emancipation of . . . colonial subjects" in British India, Malaya, and Burma, French Indochina, the Dutch East Indies, and many small Pacific islands.

British leaders had no intention of giving up Great Britain's colonies. They pressured Roosevelt to censure Wallace and to part ways with him. William Stephenson, head of British intelligence, said, "I came to regard

Wallace as a menace and I took action to ensure that the White House was aware that the British government would view with concern Wallace's appearance on the ticket at the 1944 presidential election."

But most of the world respected and admired the vice president. This made Wallace all the more dangerous to those who feared him.

In March 1943, Wallace embarked on a forty-day, seven-nation goodwill tour of Latin America. He spoke in Spanish to his audiences and electrified them. In Costa Rica, 65,000 people turned out to greet him. That was just the beginning.

A crowd of 300,000 greeted his plane in Chile. More than a million cheered him as he walked through the streets of its capital, Santiago, arm in arm with President Juan Antonio Ríos. One hundred thousand people—20,000 over capacity—packed the stadium to hear him speak.

RAF Lieutenant Roald Dahl spied on Henry Wallace. Dahl, shown here in 1954, was a writer. Among his many works is *Charlie and the Chocolate Factory.*

What was it about Henry Wallace? Ambassador Claude Bowers summed up Wallace's visit in his report to Washington, DC: "Never in Chilean history has any foreigner been received with such extravagance and evidently sincere enthusiasm. . . . His simplicity of manner, his mingling with all sorts of people, his visit to the workers' quarters without notice . . . and his inspection of the housing projects absolutely amazed the masses who responded almost hysterically."

In Ecuador, Wallace spoke movingly at the University of

Guayaquil of the postwar future. "If the liberation of the people for which the fight is going on today with the blood of youth and the sweat of workers results in imperialism and oppression tomorrow, this terrible war will have been in vain," he declared. "If this sacrifice of blood and strength again brings a concentration of riches in the hands of a few—great fortunes for the privileged and poverty for the people in general—then democracy will have failed and all this sacrifice will have been in vain."

In Lima, Peru, 200,000 more welcomed Wallace. The trip was not only a personal triumph for Wallace; it was a tour de force. By the time it was over, a dozen Latin American countries had declared war on Germany, and twenty had broken off diplomatic relations with Germany.

Wallace was equally popular at home. A Gallup poll asked Democratic voters whether they viewed favorably or unfavorably each of the four leading contenders for president, if Roosevelt chose not to run for a fourth term. Wallace's favorability rating of 57 percent was more than double that of his nearest competitor.

Despite his popularity, his powerful enemies wanted him stopped. The Democratic Party bosses decided to oust the popular vice president and replace him with someone more to the liking of the party's conservatives. But the party bosses needed a candidate.

The Party Bosses

Oil millionaire Edwin Pauley served as treasurer of the Democratic Party. He had once quipped that he went into politics when he realized that it was cheaper to elect a new Congress than to buy up the old one.

Pauley and several other party bosses worked behind the scenes to replace Henry Wallace. They compiled a list of potential candidates and then chose an undistinguished senator from Missouri—Harry S. Truman.

The party bosses didn't pick Truman because he was qualified to be president. They gave little thought to the attributes that would be necessary to lead the United States and the world in the challenging times that lay ahead. Instead, they picked Truman because he had made few enemies and could be counted on not to rock the boat.

Born in 1884, Harry grew up on his family's Missouri farm. He struggled to win the affection of his father, John "Peanuts" Truman. Harry's father stood at only five foot four, but he relished beating up much bigger men to show how tough he was. He wanted the same toughness in his sons.

As a young boy, Harry was diagnosed with hypermetropia, or "flat eyeballs."

Harry Truman, pictured here at age thirteen, loved to read and played the piano.

Forced to wear Coke-bottle-thick glasses, he couldn't play sports or roughhouse with the other boys. "I was afraid my eyes would get knocked out if there was too much of a rough and tumble play," he explained.

Truman was picked on and bullied by the other boys. They would call him names and chase him home after school.

Economic hardship also plagued Truman. Although he was a good student with a serious interest in history, his family's economic circumstances made it impossible for him to attend college. His poor eyesight kept him out of West Point.

After graduating from high school, he bounced around for a while before returning to work on his father's farm. He suffered three failed business ventures. In 1917, he joined the National Guard.

He served bravely and honorably in France, with a unit that saw plenty of action in the First World War. He rose to the rank of captain.

At the age of thirty-five, Truman married Bess, whom he had known since the fifth grade. "She had golden curls and has . . . beautiful blue eyes," he wrote in his memoir. According to a relative, "there never was but one girl in the world for [Harry]."

Three years later, in 1922, his final business venture, a haberdashery, went belly-up. This left the thirty-eight-year-old Truman with a wife to support and limited prospects.

It was at that low point that a Democratic Party boss named Tom Pendergast offered to get Truman elected judge in Jackson County. Pendergast gave workers jobs and helped elect politicians. He became wealthy in the process.

During the campaign, Truman, who never rose above the bigotry of his rural Missouri upbringing, sent a ten-dollar check to the Ku Klux Klan. However, his plans were short-circuited when he refused to promise not to hire Catholics—a group the Klan despised almost as much as blacks and Jews.

Truman remained a loyal member of the corrupt Pendergast machine throughout the 1920s and 1930s, but he felt he was getting nowhere in life. On the eve of his forty-ninth birthday in 1933, he mused, "Tomorrow I'll be forty-nine, but for all the good I have done the forty might as well be left off."

The following year, when Truman had wearied of machine politics and was contemplating a return to the farm, Boss Pendergast picked him to run for the Senate. Truman didn't know that Pendergast's first four choices had turned him down.

Pendergast engineered Truman's entire election. When asked why he had picked someone as unqualified as Truman, Pendergast replied, "I wanted to demonstrate that a well oiled machine could send an office boy to the senate."

In 1940, President Roosevelt didn't endorse Harry Truman when he ran for reelection to the Senate. Truman barely won.

Truman was known derisively among his new Senate colleagues as "the senator from Pendergast." Shunned by most of them, he worked hard to gain respectability in Washington.

But he almost didn't get a second term. In 1939, Pendergast's dirty dealing landed him in prison for tax evasion. He was no longer in a position to help Truman.

Nor did Roosevelt come to his aid, refusing to endorse Truman's 1940 reelection bid. Without his patrons' or the president's backing, he was running third. Truman turned to another political machine in Missouri, the St. Louis Hannegan-Dickmann machine, for help while Pendergast languished in prison. He eked out reelection to the Senate by a razor-thin margin.

Just Five Feet More

The American people showed much better judgment than the party bosses who wanted to oust Wallace. When Gallup asked likely Democratic voters who they wanted on the ticket as vice president, 65 percent chose Henry Wallace. Like Wallace, they believed that the twentieth century should be the Century of the Common Man.

The American public overwhelmingly rejected James "Jimmy" Byrnes, the South Carolinian who believed in segregation and to whom Truman would later turn to for advice on foreign policy. In the poll, Byrnes received 3 percent of the vote.

Truman did worse. He came in last out of eight candidates, winning the support of only 2 percent of those polled.

But Roosevelt, whose health was failing and whose energy was depleted, was dependent on party bosses for reelection. He was not willing or able to fight for Wallace as he had done four years earlier. Roosevelt simply announced that if he were a delegate, he would vote for Wallace.

Party leaders made sure they had an iron grip on the convention, but the rank-and-file Democrats staged a rebellion. On the convention floor, an uproarious demonstration for Wallace broke out. In the midst of the demonstration, Florida Senator Claude Pepper realized that if he got Wallace's name into nomination that night, Wallace would sweep the convention and be back on the ticket as vice president.

As the demonstration went on, Pepper jumped to his feet and fought his way through the crowd. Just five more feet and he would reach the microphone and shout Wallace's name for nomination.

Boss Ed Kelly, the mayor of Chicago, spotted Pepper. He couldn't allow Pepper to reach the microphone and thwart the bosses' underhanded scheme. He had to stop Pepper.

And he did. Kelly yelled to the chairman, Senator Samuel Jackson, that the demonstration was a fire hazard. He demanded that Jackson immediately adjourn the meeting.

Jackson polled the delegates. A handful said yes to adjourning. The overwhelming majority shouted no. But Jackson declared that the motion had carried. He gaveled the session to a close.

There was no fire hazard. It was a ruse to keep Pepper from nominating Wallace. The next day, Jackson apologized to Pepper. "I knew if you made the motion," he explained, "the convention would nominate Henry Wallace. I had strict instructions not to let the convention nominate the vice president last night. I hope you understand."

"What I understood," Pepper later wrote in his autobiography, "was that, for better or worse, history was turned topsy-turvey that night in Chicago."

The next day, when the balloting began, Wallace was far ahead. But the bosses closed the doors and wouldn't let in more delegates. They offered ambassadorships, postmaster jobs, and other plum positions if delegates voted for Truman. Cash payoffs were made.

Bosses called every state chairman, telling each one that the fix was in and that Roosevelt himself wanted the Missouri senator as his running mate.

Truman finally prevailed on the third ballot.

If Pepper had reached the microphone and nominated Henry Wallace before the bosses forced the adjournment of the meeting against the will of the delegates, Wallace would have been nominated vice president. It would have been Wallace who became president in 1945, when Roosevelt died in office. Just five feet more, and the course of history might have been dramatically altered. Just five feet more, and there might have been no atomic bombings, no nuclear arms race, and no Cold War.

30

An Unconditional Surrender

As the Democrats were making deals to secure Truman's vice presidential nomination, the top secret Manhattan Project was progressing rapidly.

The scientists had worried that the Germans might develop an atomic bomb first, but in late 1944, the Allies discovered that the race was off. The Germans had abandoned their bomb project two years earlier.

The original rationale for the bomb project no longer applied: The United States did not need to create the atomic bomb as a deterrent to Germany. Realizing that, one scientist, Polish-born Joseph Rotblat, left the Manhattan Project. He would later go on to win a Nobel Peace Prize.

But the rest of the scientists were still fascinated by the research. They believed an atomic bomb could speed the end of the war. They pushed even harder to finish what they had started. They had developed two different bomb designs, one using uranium and the other plutonium.

A New President

If Wallace's ouster from the ticket represented the first major setback to hopes for a peaceful postwar world, and the development of the atomic bomb was the second, fate soon delivered a third devastating blow.

On April 12, 1945, with German surrender imminent, President Franklin Delano Roosevelt died after more than twelve years in office. The nation mourned its wartime leader and wondered about his successor.

Over the next four months, events unfolded at a dizzying pace. Truman faced some of the most momentous decisions in the nation's history.

Before his presidency, Truman did not even know about the Manhattan Project. After an emergency cabinet meeting on April 12—the day Roosevelt died—Secretary of War Henry Stimson finally let Truman in on the bomb secret. The next day, Truman received a fuller, more ominous briefing from Jimmy Byrnes, his old Senate mentor.

On April 25, Henry Stimson and General Leslie Groves met with Truman. They explained that they expected completion, within four months, of "the most terrible weapon ever known in human history, one bomb of which could destroy a whole city."

Soon, the two men warned, other nations would develop their own bombs. They warned that the fate of humanity would depend upon if and how such bombs were used and what was subsequently done to control them. "The world in its present state of moral advancement compared with its technical development would be eventually at the mercy of such a weapon," they said. "In other words, modern civilization might be completely destroyed."

Later, Truman wrote an account of the meeting. "Stimson said gravely that he didn't know whether we could or should use the bomb, because he was afraid that it was so powerful that it could end up destroying the whole world. I felt the same fear."

Germany was done. But Japan was still in the fight.

A Fierce Fight

Japanese soldiers fought fiercely and valiantly. Few ever surrendered. They believed that surrendering would dishonor their families and especially their emperor. Death on the battlefield brought the highest honor: eternal repose at Yasakuni Shrine.

At Tarawa, November 1943, out of 2,500 Japanese defenders, only 8 were taken alive. In just five weeks of combat at Iwo Jima, 6,281 US sailors and marines were killed and almost 19,000 wounded. At Okinawa, the biggest battle of the Pacific War, 13,000 Americans were killed or missing and 36,000 wounded. As many as 70,000 Japanese soldiers and more than 100,000 Okinawan civilians died, some of them taking their own lives.

Americans were also shocked to watch wave after wave of kamikaze pilots crash their planes in a last-ditch effort to sink or damage US ships.

As prospects worsened for Japan in 1945, some Japanese leaders began calling for "100 million deaths with honor." They preferred that their nation fight to the death rather than surrender.

But top US leaders, including General George Marshall and Secretary of War Stimson, dismissed such rantings and remained convinced that when defeated, Japan would surrender.

In early July 1945, Stimson presented the "Proposed Program for Japan." It stated that despite Japan's capacity for "fanatical resistance to repel an invasion," he believed that "Japan is susceptible to reason in such a crisis to a much greater extent than is indicated by our current press and other current comment. Japan is not a nation composed wholly of mad fanatics of an entirely different mentality than ours."

The debate over just how costly an invasion of Japan would have been has raged for decades. On June 18, 1945, the Joint Staff Planners met with Truman. They estimated it would cost 193,500 dead and wounded to take Japan. Some estimates were higher; some were lower.

Initially, Truman said that thousands would have died, but then he continually raised the number. He later claimed that Marshall had told him that half a million men could be lost in an invasion. But the basis for this number has never been found. Marshall's own estimates were much lower, as were those of General MacArthur, who was in charge of planning for the invasion.

Stimson's assessment of the Japanese people was astute. As the war dragged on, month after bloody month, the invasion no longer seemed necessary. By the end of 1944, the Japanese navy was decimated, having lost 7 out of 12 battleships, 19 out of 25 aircraft carriers, 103 out of 160 submarines, and 118 out of 158 destroyers. The air force was also badly weakened.

Japan's rail system was in tatters. Food supplies were shrinking, and public morale had plummeted. On the home front, things were so dire that some Japanese leaders feared a revolution.

Prince Fumimaro Konoe, who had served three times as prime minister between 1937 and 1941, sent a memo to Emperor Hirohito in February 1945. "I regret to say that Japan's defeat is inevitable," wrote the prince. "What we must worry about is a communist revolution that might accompany defeat."

Wartime propaganda portrayed the Japanese as a nation of suicidal fanatics who would never give up. But in the aftermath of US victory at Saipan in July 1944, Japan had quietly begun studies on how to end the war. Japanese desperation was growing by the day.

Publisher Henry Luce saw the situation firsthand when he visited the Pacific in the spring of 1945. "A few months before Hiroshima, I was with Admiral Halsey's Navy as it assaulted the coast of Japan," wrote Luce. "Two things seemed clear to me—as they did to many of the top fighting men I talked to: first, that Japan was beaten; second, that the Japanese knew it and were every day showing signs of increasing willingness to quit."

Even historian Richard Frank, whose book *Downfall* presents the most authoritative defense of the atomic bombings, observed, "It is reasonable to assume that even without atomic bombs, the destruction of the rail-transportation system, coupled to the cumulative effects of the blockade-and-bombardment strategy, would have posed a severe threat to internal order and subsequently thus impelled the Emperor to seek to end the war."

Why, then, if Japan was not a nation of suicidal fanatics and its prospects for military victory had vanished, did its leaders not surrender and ease the sufferings of its people?

Emperor Hirohito and his advisers must bear their share of the blame. But the answer to that question lies, in large measure, in the US surrender terms—two words, in fact.

At Casablanca in January 1943, President Roosevelt had called for the "unconditional surrender" of Germany, Italy, and Japan. He later claimed to have done so spontaneously, catching even Churchill by surprise.

In a letter to his biographer, Churchill supported that interpretation: "I heard the words 'unconditional surrender' for the first time from the President's lips at the [news] conference."

This, however, was not true. Roosevelt did not spontaneously call for "unconditional surrender," as Churchill claimed. Though "unconditional" had not been included in the official communiqué of the press conference, Roosevelt and Churchill had discussed it beforehand and agreed.

The ramifications of demanding an unconditional surrender from the Japanese would be enormous.

Terms of Surrender

The Japanese understood that "unconditional surrender" meant the destruction of the *kokutai* (imperial system). They feared the emperor would be tried as a war criminal and executed.

For most Japanese, such an outcome was too terrible to contemplate. They had been worshipping the emperor as a god since Jimmu in 660 BC.

General MacArthur understood what executing the emperor meant to the Japanese. A study by his Southwest Pacific Command explained, "To dethrone, or hang, the Emperor would cause a tremendous and violent reaction from all the Japanese. Hanging of the Emperor to them would be comparable to the crucifixion of Christ to us. All would fight to die like ants."

Realizing that, many statesmen urged Truman to soften the surrender terms.

Acting Secretary of State Joseph Grew, who had previously served as ambassador to Japan, knew the Japanese better than any other top administration official. In 1945, he pressed

Emperor Hirohito salutes as he rides on horseback ahead of his officers in this 1945 photograph.

Truman to assure the Japanese people that they could keep their emperor, if they chose. Otherwise, he warned, "Surrender by Japan would be highly unlikely regardless of military defeat."

Secretary of the Navy James Forrestal and Assistant Secretary of War John McCloy also urged Truman to change the surrender terms.

So did other US military leaders. Admiral William Leahy told a June meeting of the Joint Chiefs of Staff that he feared that "our insistence on unconditional surrender would result only in making the Japanese desperate and thereby increase our casualty lists."

Because they had intercepted Japanese communications that repeatedly emphasized the importance of the surrender terms, US officials understood how crucial they were.

Uncompromising Terms

Publicly, Japan's leaders stated their intention to fight to the bitter end. Privately, they were looking for a way out of the war. In May 1945, Japan's Supreme War Council met in Tokyo.

"The Big Six," as they were known, decided to solicit the help of the so-far-neutral Soviet Union. They hoped the Soviets would help them attain better surrender terms from the United States. In return, they offered the Soviet Union territorial concessions. They had no way to know that the United States had already offered Stalin a better deal.

A senior Japanese statesman met several times with the Soviet ambassador in Tokyo. The ambassador concluded that the Japanese were desperate to end the war.

On June 18, Emperor Hirohito informed the Supreme War Council that he wanted peace restored as quickly as possible. The council agreed to sound out the Soviet Union's willingness to broker a surrender that would safeguard the emperor and preserve the imperial system.

On July 12, Japan's foreign minister, Shigenori Togo, cabled ambassador to Russia Naotake Sato: "It is his Majesty's heart's desire to see the swift termination of the war. . . . [However], as long as America and England insist on unconditional surrender, our country has no alternative but to see it through in an all-out effort for the sake of survival and the honor of the homeland."

The next day, Togo cabled Sato: "'Unconditional surrender' is the only obstacle to peace."

Here was mounting evidence that changing the surrender terms could bring the war to a swift end. Yet, once again, Truman listened to James Byrnes, who was now secretary of state.

Byrnes insisted that the American public would not tolerate compromising on surrender terms. He warned the president that he would be crucified politically if he tried.

There was actually little reason to think that Truman would be criticized for letting the emperor remain on the throne. Republican leaders had provided Truman all the political cover he needed.

Earlier that month, on July 2, 1945, Senate Minority Leader Wallace White, a Republican from Maine, urged President Truman to clarify what he meant by "unconditional surrender."

In doing so, White hoped to speed Japan's surrender. If Japan ignored or rejected the president's offer to surrender on more favorable terms, White reasoned, "It will not have increased our losses or otherwise have prejudiced our cause. Much might be gained by such a statement. Nothing could be lost."

Republican senator from Indiana Homer Capehart held a press conference to support White's appeal to Truman. Capehart stated that the White House had received an offer by Japan to surrender solely on the grounds that Emperor Hirohito not be deposed.

"It isn't a matter of whether you hate the Japs or not," Capehart told the press. "I certainly hate them. But what's to be gained by continuing a war when it can be settled now on the same terms as two years from now?"

In a June editorial, *The Washington Post* had condemned the use of the term "unconditional surrender"—a "fatal phrase" that conjured up such fears among the Japanese people that it was proving an impediment to ending the fighting.

Changing the surrender terms was not the only way to obtain Japan's surrender without using atomic bombs. The Japanese dreaded the Soviet Union's entry into the war. They had seen what the powerful Red Army did to the Germans.

The Americans knew this.

On July 6, the Combined Intelligence Committee issued a top secret "Estimate of the Enemy Situation" for the Combined Chiefs of Staff, who would be meeting in Potsdam, Germany, on July 17.

The report contained a section that assessed the "Possibility of Surrender." It described the effect Soviet entry would have on the already-hopeless Japanese: "An entry of the Soviet Union into the war would finally convince the Japanese of the inevitability of complete defeat."

The Japanese had another plan to attain more lenient surrender terms: Hold on until the Americans invaded and then resist so fiercely that the war-weary Americans would be willing to compromise.

Japanese leaders had correctly identified Kyushu, the southernmost Japanese island, as the intended Allied landing site and had beefed up their forces there. Civilians armed with sharpened bamboo spears were instructed to fight to the death along with the soldiers.

US leaders knew that either changing the surrender terms or waiting for the Soviet invasion would likely end the war.

Then would the United States use two atomic bombs against an almost helpless population, when it had other means to secure victory?

31

No Foe So Detested

To make sense of the decision to bomb Japan, one has to understand the moral climate within which that decision was made. In the United States, the wartime propaganda took pains to differentiate between evil Nazi leaders and "good Germans." But no such efforts were made to distinguish evil Japanese leaders from good Japanese civilians.

Americans felt a profound hatred toward the Japanese, military and civilians alike. "Probably in all our history, no foe has been so detested as were the Japanese," wrote Allan Nevins, a Pulitzer Prize–winning historian.

As *Newsweek* reported in January 1945, "Never before has the nation fought a war in which our troops so hate the enemy and want to kill him."

Admiral William "Bull" Halsey, commander of the South Pacific Force, was notorious in this regard. He often urged his men forward to kill the "yellow monkeys" and to "get some more monkey meat."

People questioned whether the Japanese were really human.

Time magazine wrote, "The ordinary, unreasoning Jap is ignorant. Perhaps he is human. Nothing . . . indicates it."

The British embassy in Washington, DC, reported back to London that the Americans viewed the Japanese as a "nameless mass of vermin." The British ambassador described Americans' "universal 'exterminationist' anti-Japanese feeling."

Many Americans viewed the Japanese as cockroaches, rattlesnakes, and rats—species to be exterminated. When popular war correspondent Ernie Pyle was transferred from Europe to the Pacific in February 1945, he observed, "In Europe we felt that our enemies, horrible and deadly as they were, were still people. But out here I soon gathered that the Japanese were looked upon as something subhuman and repulsive; the way some people feel about cockroaches or mice."

Some of this sentiment can be attributed to racism. But other powerful forces were also at work in producing this hatred of the Japanese. Even before the United States entered the war, Americans had heard stories about Japan's brutality toward the Chinese—bombings, rapes—especially in Nanjing.

America's hatred of Japan soared with the "sneak attack" at Pearl Harbor. Then, in early 1944, the government released information about the sadistic treatment of US and Filipino prisoners during the Bataan Death March two years earlier in the Philippines.

Soon reports about unspeakable Japanese cruelty—war crimes that included torture, crucifixion, castration, dismembering, beheading, burning and burying alive, vivisection, nailing prisoners to trees and using them for bayonet practice—flooded the media.

Some of Japan's behavior during the war was indeed unconscionable. However, they weren't alone. American soldiers were also sometimes guilty of wretched behavior.

According to US Pacific War correspondent Edgar Jones, atrocities

Many Americans felt a profound hatred toward the Japanese.
Some propaganda even portrayed the Japanese as vermin.

were a matter of fact during war, and civilians who thought otherwise were deluding themselves. "What kind of war do civilians suppose we fought, anyway?" he asked in a February 1946 *Atlantic Monthly* magazine article. "We shot prisoners in cold blood, wiped out hospitals, strafed lifeboats, killed or mistreated enemy civilians, finished off the enemy wounded, tossed the dying into a hole with the dead, and in the Pacific boiled the flesh off enemy skulls to make table ornaments for sweethearts, or carved their bones into letter openers."

Racism also reared its ugly head in the treatment of people of Japanese descent living in the United States before war broke out. For decades, Japanese Americans had faced discrimination in voting, jobs, and education. The Immigration Act of 1924 denied Japanese who had settled in the United States after 1907 the right to become naturalized citizens and prohibited further immigration from Japan and other parts of Asia.

Even before Pearl Harbor, some people on the West Coast began conjuring up fanciful scenarios of Japanese-American sabotage in the event of war. One journalist wrote, "When the Pacific zero hour strikes, Japanese Americans will get busy at once. Their fishing boats will sow mines across the entrances of our ports. Mysterious blasts will destroy navy shipyards and flying fields and part of our fleet. . . . Japanese farmers, having a virtual monopoly of vegetable production in California, will send their peas and potatoes and squash full of arsenic to the markets."

Following Pearl Harbor, rumors and ugliness proliferated. One California barbershop offered "free shaves for Japs," but added, "not responsible for accidents." A funeral parlor announced, "I'd rather do business with a Jap than an American."

Fearful of sabotage from Japanese Americans, the United States developed plans to remove them from the western states and to incarcerate them.

Executive Order 9066

Two days after Pearl Harbor, on December 9, 1941, Lieutenant Colonel John L. DeWitt, commander of the Fourth Army and head of the Western Defense Command, addressed members of the Civil Defense Council. He told them that Japanese warplanes had flown over San Francisco the previous night. The city, DeWitt said, was in imminent danger of Japanese attack.

Rear Admiral John Greenslade informed attendees that they had been "saved from a terrible catastrophe" by "the grace of God."

"Why bombs were not dropped," said DeWitt, "I do not know."

One reason why the Japanese planes did not drop bombs is that the flyover never happened. That would explain why US forces never shot down any of the planes and why the army's and navy's searches for the Japanese aircraft carriers came up empty.

But DeWitt nevertheless ordered a blackout. He was furious with San Francisco residents who didn't turn out their lights and pull down their window shades. He denounced them as "inane, idiotic, and foolish." He threatened, "If I can't knock these facts into your heads with words, I will have to turn you over to the police to let them knock them into you with clubs."

In late January 1942, the Supreme Court released a report on the bombing of Pearl Harbor. It charged that spies had aided the attack. The report reinforced doubts about the loyalty of Japanese Americans.

At first, DeWitt dismissed the proposed evacuation of Japanese Americans as "damned nonsense." But as public pressure mounted, DeWitt changed his mind.

Now he argued that the fact that the Japanese, citizens and noncitizens alike, had not engaged in sabotage proved that they were plotting a future attack.

Others, including Secretary of War Stimson and Assistant Secretary McCloy, echoed DeWitt's reasoning. They pressured Roosevelt to take action before it was too late.

FBI Director J. Edgar Hoover did not agree. He told Attorney General Francis Biddle that mass evacuations were not necessary. All known security risks had already been rounded up. The attorney general assured Roosevelt that "there were no reasons for mass evacuations."

Roosevelt ignored Hoover's and Biddle's advice. Despite the fact that there was no evidence of Japanese-American sabotage, Roosevelt signed Executive Order 9066 on February 19, 1942, ten weeks after Pearl Harbor.

This order laid the groundwork for the evacuation and incarceration of Japanese and Japanese Americans from California, Oregon, and Washington. Two thirds of those affected were US citizens by birth.

In California, the Japanese represented about 2 percent of the population. In total, Executive Order 9066 forced perhaps as many as 120,000 people to evacuate their homes and settle outside the prohibited defense states.

Other states did not want the Japanese. The governor of Idaho, Chase Clark, spewed, "The Japs live like rats, breed like rats, and act like rats. We don't want them."

The attorney general of Wyoming warned that if the Japanese moved to his state, "There would be Japs hanging from every pine tree."

In this photograph taken by Dorothea Lange in Oakland, California, newspaper headlines proclaim the government's plan to expel the Japanese.

Idaho's attorney general said, "We want to keep this a white man's country."

Concentration Camps in America

Over the next eight months, between March and October 1942, the Wartime Civil Control Administration opened temporary camps, known as "assembly centers." At these centers, Japanese inmates were held, registered, and assigned numbers. In Santa Anita and Tanforan, California, some families were housed in horse stables, a single stall accommodating five or six people. They were later moved to more permanent centers, referred to at the time as "concentration camps."

Evacuees were permitted to take only what they could carry. Their former neighbors eagerly bought their property at a fraction of its real value or seized what was left behind, including crops. The Japanese lost an estimated $400 million in personal property—worth about $5.4 billion today.

A leader of the Grower-Shipper Vegetable Association of Central California admitted the prejudice of his own organization. "We're charged with wanting to get rid of the Japs for selfish reasons. We might as well be honest. We do. It's a question of whether the white man lives on the Pacific Coast or the brown man."

Sometimes greed and selfishness went the other way. When US authorities announced plans to round up Hawaii's large Japanese population, wealthy white sugarcane and pineapple plantation owners complained that they would lose their labor force. The government responded by allowing plantation workers to continue working in the fields, but it suspended basic civil rights and locked up some 2,000 *kibei*, people of Japanese descent who had visited Japan.

Starting in March 1942, the War Relocation Authority moved prisoners to ten hastily constructed relocation centers in Arizona, Arkansas, California, Colorado, Idaho, Utah, and Wyoming.

The camps were enclosed in barbed-wired fences. They had machine-gun installations and guard towers. Conditions in the camps were deplorable, often lacking running water, bathroom facilities, decent schools, insulated cabins, and proper roofs.

Inside the camps, Japanese toiled under scorching desert sun in Arizona and California, amid swamplike conditions in Arkansas, and in bitter cold in Wyoming, Idaho, and Utah. They were paid a paltry $12 per month for unskilled labor and $19 for skilled. Japanese doctors earned $228 per year, whereas a white senior medical officer earned $4,600. White nurses earned $150 per month at the Heart Mountain camp in Wyoming—eight to ten times as much as their Japanese counterparts.

Federal authorities sent photographers Ansel Adams and Dorothea Lange to capture images of daily camp life. They were instructed to take no photos showing barbed wire, watchtowers, or armed soldiers. Still, Adams, Lange, and a Japanese inmate, Toyo Miyatake, captured a few of the banned images.

In February 1943, the US government pulled a shameless about-face. Needing more manpower to fight the war, Roosevelt called upon the Nisei—American-born Japanese—to join the segregated 442nd Regimental Combat Team, in conjunction with the Hawaiian 100th Infantry Battalion already stationed in Camp Shelby, Mississippi. The "One Puka Puka," as the Hawaiian members called their unit, had volunteered early in the war. The unit struggled long and hard to be recognized as worthy to serve.

The 442nd Regiment became one of the most decorated units in US military history. They fought bravely in Italy and France, suffering 1,072 casualties, including 216 deaths in October 1944.

That Japanese Americans were capable of such sacrifice for their country was beyond the comprehension of Lieutenant Colonel DeWitt, head of the Western Defense Command. In April 1943, DeWitt told the Naval Affairs subcommittee that he wasn't worried about the Germans or Italians. "[B]ut the Japs we will be worried about all the time until they are wiped off the face of the map. A Jap's a Jap," he observed, whether a US citizen or not.

DeWitt's racist comments rankled *The Washington Post*, which shot back, "The general should be told that American democracy and the Constitution of the United States are too vital to be ignored and flouted by any military zealot. . . . Whatever excuse there once was for evacuating and holding them indiscriminately no longer exists."

Some Americans drew parallels with Nazi policies, although the differences, admittedly, were much greater than the similarities. In June 1942, *Christian Century* wrote, "The whole policy of resort to concentration camps is headed . . . toward the destruction of constitutional rights . . . and toward the establishment of racial discrimination as a principle of American government. It is moving in the same direction Germany moved."

But in June 1942, the Supreme Court ruled unanimously in the government's favor in the first two cases to come before it.

A young evacuee of Japanese ancestry waits with the family baggage before leaving by bus for an assembly center in the spring of 1942.

Inside relocation centers, Japanese toiled under a scorching desert sun in Arizona and California; in swamplike conditions in Arkansas; and in the bitter cold in Wyoming, Idaho, and Utah. They were paid minuscule wages for their labor.

Photographer Ansel Adams stood on a guard tower and took this picture of the Manzanar Relocation Center. It does not show the barbed-wire fences and machine-gun installations to keep interned Japanese from escaping.

On January 2, 1945, the War Relocation Authority "ended" forced incarceration but provided little assistance as prisoners tried to rebuild their shattered lives. Once released, some decided to move as far away from the West Coast as possible. According to the National Park Service, the Japanese received only "$25 per person, a train ticket, and meals en route for those with less than $500 in cash."

It was not until the passage of the Immigration and Naturalization Act of 1952 that many older Issei—Japanese immigrants—were deemed "fit to be citizens." Moreover, it took more than forty years to produce a national apology and payment of $1.5 billion for survivors of the incarceration centers.

A Moral Crisis

What happened to the moral standards of the United States? When did America grow indifferent to human suffering and inflicting civilian casualties on a massive scale?

It didn't change all at once. The moral threshold had been dramatically lowered by years of bombing civilian populations, particularly in the war against Japan. Urban bombing had begun during the First World War. The Germans, British, French, Italians, and Austrians had all bombed one another's cities, and some of this continued in brutal fashion during the interwar period.

To its credit, the United States strongly condemned the Japanese bombing

Members of the 442nd Regiment. Japanese Americans salute the American flag in a brief review held the day of their arrival at Camp Shelby, Mississippi.

During the last week of July 1943, one of the most devastating bombing campaigns took place in Hamburg, Germany. The blasts created firestorms that swept through the city.

of Chinese cities in 1937. When war began in Europe, Roosevelt begged the warring nations to refrain from the "inhuman barbarism" involved in bombing defenseless civilians.

But as the war continued, Americans' ethical standards began to weaken. Unlike Germany and Britain—which had bombed each other's cities, killing vast numbers of civilians—the United States concentrated almost entirely on precision bombing of key industries and transportation networks. The policy began to change in October 1943, with the area-bombing attack on Münster, Germany. It reached its low point in Europe in February 1945, when the United States participated in the Allied bombing of Dresden.

The United States adopted a far more ruthless bombing policy in Japan. When Brigadier General Haywood Hansell, head of the Twenty-First Bomber Command, resisted orders to use incendiaries against large urban areas, he was replaced by General Curtis LeMay, who was more than willing to do so.

LeMay was nicknamed "Iron Ass" by his men because he was so relentless and demanding. He had made his reputation in the air war in Europe. In Japan, he revolutionized bombing tactics and took what was already being referred to as "terror bombing" to an entirely different level.

On the night of March 9–10, 1945, LeMay sent 334 planes to attack Tokyo with incendiary bombs consisting of napalm, thermite, white phosphorus, and other flammable materials. Napalm is a jellylike substance that sticks to anything it touches—such as skin—and burns from 1,600 to 2,400 degrees Fahrenheit for up to fifteen minutes.

The bombs destroyed sixteen square miles, killing as many as 100,000 and injuring far more. The scalding inferno caused canals to boil, metal to melt, and people to burst into flames spontaneously. The victims, LeMay reported, were "scorched and boiled and baked to death."

By May, 75 percent of bombs dropped were incendiaries designed to burn down Japan's "paper cities," buildings made largely of paper and wood. According to Japanese scholar Yuki Tanaka, the United States firebombed more than 100 cities. On the night of August 1–2, 1945, American bombers dropped incendiary bombs on Toyama, destroying 99.5 percent of the city.

Realizing this, Secretary of War Stimson told President Truman that he "did not want to have the US get the reputation of outdoing Hitler in atrocities."

But Stimson did almost nothing to halt the slaughter that was yet to come. He had managed to delude himself into believing General Henry H. Arnold's promise that "damage to civilians" would be limited.

US bombs rain down on Hokodate, Japan.

Hatred toward the Japanese ran so deep that almost no one objected to the mass slaughter of civilians. Oppenheimer recalled Stimson's disappointment over Americans' indifference. "I remember Mr. Stimson saying to me that he thought it appalling that there should be no protest over the air raids which we were conducting against Japan, which in the case of Tokyo led to such extraordinarily heavy loss of life. He didn't say the air strikes shouldn't be carried on, but he did think there was something wrong with a country where no one questioned that."

Brigadier General Bonner Fellers called it "one of the most ruthless and barbaric killings of noncombatants in all history." General Arnold, the Chief Commander of the Army Air Forces, felt that "90% of Americans would have killed every Japanese."

The Atomic Decision

Back at the Los Alamos site of the Manhattan Project, General Leslie Groves's Target Committee decided that the atomic bombs would be dropped on military facilities surrounded by workers' homes in previously unbombed cities of Japan. The explosion would be so spectacular that people everywhere would appreciate the weapons' significance.

But members of Stimson's Interim Committee examined a number of issues surrounding the use of the atomic bombs. They raised alternatives. Truman sent James Byrnes to represent him on the committee. Byrnes overrode all alternatives, including a demonstration in an uninhabited area.

At its May 31 meeting, the Interim Committee also addressed the future of nuclear weapons. Scientists understood that the bombs under production were the most rudimentary, primitive prototypes of what was to follow. The prospect terrified the committee.

Oppenheimer informed the nation's top military and civilian officials that within three years, the United States could have weapons with between 10 and a 100 megatons of destructive force. Such bombs would be 7,000 times as powerful as the bomb that would soon drop on Hiroshima.

Also in late May, three scientists—Leo Szilard, Nobel Prize–winning chemist Harold Urey, and astronomer Walter Bartky—attempted to caution Truman against using the bomb. Unable to meet with Truman, the three men were instead rerouted to Spartanburg, South Carolina, to speak with James Byrnes.

Byrnes's response appalled Szilard. "Mr. Byrnes did not argue that it was necessary to use the bomb against the cities of Japan in order to win the war. He knew at that time, as the rest of the government knew, that Japan was essentially defeated. . . . At that time, Mr. Byrnes was much concerned about the spreading Russian influence in Europe; [insisting] that our possessing and demonstrating the bomb would make Russia more manageable in Europe."

Groves, too, admitted that the Soviet Union had always been the enemy. "There was never from about two weeks from the time I took charge of this Project any illusion on my part that Russia was our enemy," said Groves. "The Project was conducted on that basis."

In March 1944, the general had shocked scientist Joseph Rotblat when he told him the same thing over dinner. "You realize of course that the main purpose of this project is to subdue the Russians," said Groves. And as Byrnes had said to Truman on April 13, the atomic bomb "might well put us in a position to dictate our own terms at the end of the war." He didn't specify to whom, but the answer was becoming clearer.

The fact that the Japanese were holding out for better surrender terms played into the hands of General Groves and the others. If the bomb hastened the end of the war and saved American lives, that would be a bonus. But its primary purpose had now become the projection of American power.

The Russians were the real target. The Japanese were collateral damage.

32

Doubts on Destruction

While the scientists at Los Alamos worked feverishly to complete the bomb, others began to have doubts about the wisdom of actually using what they had helped create.

In June 1945, Chicago Met Lab scientists set up a series of committees to explore various aspects of atomic energy. The Committee on Social and Political Implications was chaired by Nobel laureate James Franck.

The committee issued a report—known as the Franck Report—that questioned whether atomic bombs should be used in the current war. In its preamble, the report acknowledged that nuclear power had to be treated differently "from all the other developments in the field of physics" due to the "possibility of its use as a means of political pressure in peace and sudden destruction in war."

It also warned that an atomic attack could instigate a nuclear arms race with the Soviet Union and noted that "the fundamental facts of nuclear power are a subject of common knowledge." Because there was no secret to the scientific principles behind the bomb, the

Soviet Union would soon catch up and develop its own. This could create the prospect of "total mutual destruction."

And the report warned that a surprise attack on Japan would destroy the United States' moral position. Committee members recommended that Japan be given a "demonstration" instead.

Leo Szilard understood the dangers better than anyone else. He desperately attempted to prevent the use of the atomic bomb. He circulated the report to other scientists at the laboratories. But security officers labeled it top secret and banned its circulation.

Szilard drew up a petition and appealed directly to Truman. The petition stated:

> The atomic bombs at our disposal represent only the first step in this direction, and there is almost no limit to the destructive power which will become available in the course of their future development. Thus a nation which sets the precedent of using these newly liberated forces of nature for the purposes of destruction may have to bear the responsibility of opening the door to an era of devastation on an unimaginable scale.

At Chicago's Met Lab and at the uranium plant in Oak Ridge, Tennessee, 155 scientists signed the petition.

In Los Alamos, New Mexico, however, Oppenheimer banned the petition's circulation. He alerted General Groves, who made sure the petition didn't reach Stimson and Truman until it was too late to stop the bomb.

Groves didn't want anybody to rock the boat. After Szilard circulated the petition, Groves worried that scientists were thinking twice about their work engineering the bomb. He had been concerned about Szilard from the beginning and had written a letter to the attorney general labeling Szilard an "enemy alien." He also requested that Szilard be confined for the rest of the war. Fortunately, Dr. Compton persuaded Groves not to send the letter.

A truck continues through the security checkpoint at Los Alamos, New Mexico.

Groves ordered his own poll among scientists. To his chagrin, he found that 83 percent favored demonstrating the bomb before using it against Japan. He hushed up the results.

Others tried to prevent use of the bomb, but they also failed. On June 27, Undersecretary of the Navy Ralph Bard, the navy representative to the Interim Committee, wrote a memo to Stimson, saying, "During recent weeks I have also had the feeling very definitely that the Japanese Government may be searching for some opportunity which they could use as a medium of surrender."

Bard recommended that the United States, "as a great humanitarian nation," warn Japan about the Soviet entry into the war and the development of the atomic bomb. Perhaps, he suggested, the United States should clarify the surrender terms.

Some historians believe that Bard met with Truman to press these points, but the record is ambiguous. It is clear that on June 18, Assistant Secretary of War John McCloy suggested to Truman that he tell the Japanese "that they would be permitted to retain the Emperor and a form of government of their own choosing."

McCloy also suggested that Truman should say "that we had another and terrifyingly destructive weapon which we would have to use if they did not surrender."

One More Card to Play

On July 17, 1945, Truman arrived in Germany for the Potsdam Conference. As he nervously anticipated his first meeting with Churchill and Stalin, reports began to pour in confirming the Japanese desire to quit the war if allowed to surrender conditionally.

There is a lot of evidence to support this. Navy Secretary Forrestal wrote about "evidence of a Japanese desire to get out of the war." Stimson wrote about "Japanese maneuverings for peace." Byrnes wrote about "Japanese peace feelers."

In his 1966 book *The Secret Surrender*, Office of Strategic Services (OSS) official and later Central Intelligence Agency (CIA) head Allen Dulles recalled, "I went to the Potsdam Conference and reported there to Secretary Stimson on what I had learned from Tokyo—they desired to surrender if they could retain the Emperor and the constitution as a basis for maintaining discipline and order in Japan after the devastating news of surrender became known to the Japanese people."

The Pacific Strategic Intelligence Summary published a report titled "Russo-Japanese Relations (13–20 July 1945)" for the week of the Potsdam Conference. It stated, "It may be said that Japan now, officially, if not publicly, recognizes her defeat. Abandoning as unobtainable the long-cherished goal of victory, she has turned to the twin aims of (a) reconciling national pride

Stalin (*left*) and Truman (*front, second from left*), with
Secretary of State James F. Byrnes (*second from right*)
and Soviet Foreign Minister Vyacheslav Molotov (*right*),
participated in the Potsdam Conference in July 1945.

with defeat, and (b) finding the best means of salvaging the wreckage of her ambitions."

Later, the head of the War Department's Operations Division Policy Section, Colonel Charles "Tick" Bonesteel, recalled, "the poor damn Japanese were putting feelers out by the ton."

And President Truman knew that the Japanese wanted to surrender. Truman referred to an intercepted July 19 cable as "the telegram from the Jap emperor asking for peace."

Truman's principal reason for going to Potsdam, he claimed, was to ensure the Soviets entered the war as they had promised. Truman knew that their entry would deliver the final crushing blow to the Japanese.

He rejoiced when Stalin reassured him. "He'll be in the Jap War on August 15," Truman wrote in his diary. "Fini Japs when that comes about."

The next day, Truman wrote home to his wife, Bess, "We'll end the war a year sooner now, and think of the kids who won't be killed."

But Truman had one more card to play, and his timing had to be precise.

He had hoped the bomb would have been tested before negotiations with Stalin began. Oppenheimer confessed, "We were under incredible pressure to get it done before the Potsdam meeting."

From Truman's perspective, it turned out to be worth the wait.

"Now I Am Become Death"

On July 16, 1945, while Truman was touring Berlin and preparing for the next day's meeting with Stalin, a twenty-minute countdown began in the early-morning hours in the desert outside Alamogordo, New Mexico.

Top-level scientists and military officers had gathered at base camp ten miles away to observe the "Trinity Test"—the detonation of the first atomic bomb.

Trinity exceeded expectations. Given the enormous power of the blast and the brightness of the sky, some scientists feared they had indeed set the atmosphere on fire.

"We knew the world would not be the same," said Oppenheimer about the demonstration. "A few people laughed. A few people cried. Most people were silent. I remembered the line from the Hindu scripture the Bhagavad Gita . . . 'Now I am become death, the destroyer of worlds.' I suppose we all thought that, one way or another."

Test director Kenneth Bainbridge put it more simply, "Now we're all sons-of-bitches."

General Groves telegraphed the preliminary test results to Stimson, who rushed to brief Truman and Byrnes. The two men were elated.

This photograph shows the mushroom cloud from six miles away following the detonation of the first atomic bomb on July 16, 1945, in the New Mexico desert.

Five days later, on July 21, Groves sent a fuller report. "The test was successful beyond the most optimistic expectations of anyone," wrote Groves. He went on to describe the blast results:

> There was a lighting effect within a radius of twenty miles, equal to several suns in midday; a huge ball of fire was formed

which lasted for several seconds. This ball mushroomed and rose to a height of over ten thousand feet before it dimmed. . . . A massive cloud was formed which surged and billowed upward with tremendous power, reaching the sub-stratosphere at an elevation of 41,000 feet, 36,000 feet above the ground in about five minutes. . . . Huge concentrations of highly radioactive materials resulted from the fission and were contained in this cloud.

To General Thomas Farrell, there was a "strong sustained awesome roar which warned of doomsday."

Truman, Byrnes, and Groves believed they now had a way to speed Japanese surrender on US terms without Soviet help. This meant they could deny the Soviet Union the promised territorial and economic concessions.

"The president was tremendously pepped up by [the report] and spoke to me of it again and again when I saw him," said Stimson. "He said it gave him an entirely new feeling of confidence."

So far, Churchill and Stalin had been dominating the Potsdam meetings. Now Truman rode roughshod over the proceedings.

"I couldn't understand it," wrote Churchill later. "When he got to the meeting after having read this report he was a changed man. He told the Russians just where they got on and off and generally bossed the whole meeting."

But Truman's public bravado masked a deeper understanding of the world he was about to usher in with the use of the atomic bomb. "We have discovered the most terrible bomb in the history of the world," he wrote in his Potsdam diary. "It may be the fire destruction prophesied in the Euphrates Valley Era, after Noah and his fabulous Ark."

Unfortunately, Truman's understanding of the horrors he was about to unleash did not impel him to seek alternatives as the day of reckoning approached.

Misgivings?

The historical record shows that President Truman, Secretary of State Byrnes, and General Groves had no serious reservations about using the atomic bomb.

But Secretary of War Henry Stimson did.

Stimson referred to the atomic bomb as "the dreadful," "the terrible," "the dire," "the awful," and "the diabolical." The atomic bomb was not merely a new weapon, he mused, but "a revolutionary change in the relations of man to the universe . . . that might even mean the doom of civilization . . . it might be a Frankenstein which would eat us up."

At the Potsdam Conference, Stimson tried repeatedly to convince Truman and Byrnes to assure the Japanese about their emperor. But it was an exercise in futility. Later, when Stimson complained to Truman about being ignored at Potsdam, Truman told the frail, elderly secretary of war that if he didn't like it, he could pack his bags and go home.

At Potsdam, Stimson informed General Dwight D. Eisenhower, the supreme commander of Allied forces in Europe, that the bomb's use was imminent.

In a *Newsweek* interview, Eisenhower described his reaction to Stimson's news: "[Stimson] asked for my opinion, so I told him I was against it on two counts. First, the Japanese were ready to surrender and it wasn't necessary to hit them with that awful thing. Second, I hated to see our country be the first to use such a weapon."

No Need for the Russians

With the bomb's successful testing complete, Truman decided to inform Stalin. Before the Potsdam Conference was over, Truman walked up to Stalin and casually mentioned that the United States had developed a "new weapon of unusual destructive force."

Stalin seemed uninterested in Truman's news. This gave Truman pause. The president wondered if Stalin understood the magnitude of what he had just heard. What Truman didn't know was that Soviet intelligence had already told Stalin about the atomic bomb. Stalin also knew a test would take place, but he didn't know when.

Now Stalin understood that the test had taken place and it was a success— and he was furious. He immediately berated the chief of the secret police for not having known that the test had been completed.

When Stalin returned to his villa, he remarked that the Americans would use their atomic monopoly to dictate terms in Europe. But he would refuse to give in to their blackmail. To beat Truman at his own game, Stalin ordered Soviet military forces to speed up the country's entry into the war. He also ordered Soviet scientists to pick up the pace of their own atomic research.

At Potsdam, on July 25, Truman initialed a directive signed by Stimson and Marshall ordering that the atomic bombs be used as soon after August 3 as weather permitted.

He knew there was little chance that the final Potsdam Declaration, which contained neither a significant modification of surrender terms nor a warning about the bomb nor notice of Soviet entry into the war, would be accepted by Japan.

Truman did not invite Stalin to sign the declaration, even though Stalin came intending to do so and even brought a draft of his own. Stalin's signature would have notified the Japanese that the Soviet Union was about to come into the war.

The absence of the Soviet leader's signature encouraged the Japanese to continue their futile effort to gain Soviet assistance in securing better surrender terms. Meanwhile, the hours ticked away until the bomb was ready to use.

Truman's behavior at Potsdam reinforced Stalin's belief that the United States intended to end the war quickly and renege on its promised concessions.

During the conference, Stalin told Truman that Soviet troops would be ready to attack by the middle of August.

Truman left Potsdam on August 2. He wanted peace. But first he wanted to use the atomic bomb.

General Douglas MacArthur was the supreme commander of Allied forces in the Pacific and the second-highest-ranking active-duty officer in the US Army. He considered the bomb "completely unnecessary from a military point of view" and became both angry and depressed when he learned that the United States was about to use it.

MacArthur held a press conference on August 6, before the bomb drop was announced. He told reporters that the Japanese were "already beaten" and that he was thinking about "the possibilities of a next war with its horrors magnified 10,000 times."

"A Peep into Hell"

On August 6, 1945, at 2:45 in the morning, three B-29s took off for Japan from the island of Tinian in the Marianas. They were 1,500 miles away from their target, the city of Hiroshima.

The lead plane, the *Enola Gay*, carried the uranium bomb, called "Little Boy." The 5-ton bomb had a yield that measured to be the equivalent of 16,000 tons of TNT.

The bombers' target was the T-shaped Aioi Bridge, near the center of the city. Hiroshima, despite its port and its headquarters for the Second General Army, had not been considered a priority military target for earlier bombing.

It was a cool, clear, quiet morning in Hiroshima, not a cloud in the sky.

At 7:09, the air raid siren sounded, warning Hiroshima residents about approaching planes. Then the all-clear signal was given at 7:31. The Japanese radio told residents that the planes had turned back.

Pilot Paul Tibbets (*center with pipe*) stands with his crew and the *Enola Gay*.

At 8:00 a.m., Hiroshima's approximately 300,000 civilians, 43,000 soldiers, 45,000 Korean slave laborers, and several thousand Japanese Americans, mostly children whose parents were interned in the United States, were just beginning their day.

At 8:15 a.m., the *Enola Gay* flew over its target and released the bomb. Suzuko Numata, survivor of the blast, recalls what happened:

> I was facing [my] yard, in the direction of the hypocenter. I remember a bright mixture of colors: red, yellow, blue, green and orange. I didn't know it then, of course, but later learned that I had seen the flash released at the moment the atomic bomb exploded.

I don't know how long it was, but the next thing I remember was being in the dark, trapped under something extremely heavy. Then I lost consciousness again. Although I had been standing in the hallway, I had been blown by the blast into a room. Everything in the room had collapsed, and my left foot had been almost severed from my leg at the ankle. While I was unconscious, a strange-smelling smoke was spreading through the room. I was found by someone who had escaped to the yard outside, noticed this smoke and came back into the building to help. . . . Later, my father told me that flames were blowing out of the windows like shimmering red curtains. If my rescue had come even a second later, I would not have survived. I would have remained trapped and would have died screaming in agony crying tears of hatred.

The bomb had vaporized buildings and totally destroyed an area extending almost two miles in all directions. Watching the city of Hiroshima disappear horrified the crew members of the *Enola Gay*. Abe Spitzer, radioman on one of the other two B-29s over Hiroshima, the *Great Artiste*, described what he saw:

Below us, spread out almost as far as I could see, was a great fire, but it was like no ordinary fire. It contained a dozen colors, all of them blindingly bright, more colors than I imagined existed, and in the center and brightest of all, a gigantic red ball of flame that seemed larger than the sun. Indeed, it seemed that, somehow, the sun had been knocked out of the sky and was on the ground below us and beginning to rise again, only coming straight up toward us—and fast.

At the same time, the ball itself spread outward, too, until it seemed to cover the entire city, and on every side the flame was shrouded, half-hidden by a thick, impenetrable column of grey-white smoke, extending into the foothills beyond the city, and bursting outward and rising toward us with unbelievable speed.

Then the ship rocked again, and it sounded as if a giant gun—some large artillery or cannons—were firing at us and hitting us from every direction.

The purple light was changing to a green-blue now, with just a tinge of yellow at the edges, and from below the ball of fire, the upside-down sun, seemed to be following the smoke upward, racing to us with immeasurably fast speed—although we at the same time, though not so quickly—were speeding away from what was left of the city.

Suddenly, we were to the left of the pillar of smoke, and it continued rising, to an estimated height, I later learned, of 50,000 feet. It looked like a kind of massive pole that narrowed toward the top and reached for the stratosphere. The scientists later told us they believed the pole was as much as four or five miles wide at its base and a mile and a half or more wide at the top.

As I watched, hypnotized by what I saw, the column of smoke changed its color, from a grey-white to brown, then amber, then all three colors at once, mingled into a bright, boiling rainbow. For a second it looked as though its fury might be ending, but almost immediately a kind of mushroom spurted out of the top and traveled up, up to what some say was a distance of 60,000 or 70,000 feet . . . the whole column seethed and spurted, but the mushroom top shot out in every direction, like giant waves during an ocean storm.

Then, quite suddenly, the top broke off the column, as if it

A mushroom cloud rises over Hiroshima, following the bombing on August 6, 1945.

had been cut away with a sharp blade, and it shot still further up; how far I don't know; nobody did or does; not even the pictures show that, and none of the apparatus could measure it exactly. Some said it was 80,000 feet, some 85,000 feet, some even more. . . . After that, another mushroom, somewhat smaller, boiled up out of the pillar.

According to the *Enola Gay* pilot, Paul Tibbets, who had named the plane after his mother, "The giant purple mushroom . . . boil[ed] upward like something terribly alive. Even more fearsome was the sight on the ground below. Fires were springing up everywhere amid a turbulent mass of smoke that had the appearance of bubbling hot tar."

Later, Tibbets reflected, "If Dante had been with us on the plane, he would have been terrified. The city we had seen so clearly in the sunlight a few minutes before was now an ugly smudge. It had completely disappeared under this awful blanket of smoke and fire."

Tail gunner Bob Caron called it a "peep into hell." Copilot Robert Lewis wrote in his flight log, "My God! What have we done."

The view from the ground was very different and far more harrowing. At the hypocenter, where the temperature reached 5,400 degrees Fahrenheit, the fireball roasted people "to bundles of smoking black char in a fraction of a second as their internal organs boiled away."

Tens of thousands were killed instantly. An estimated 140,000 were dead by the end of the year, and 200,000 by 1950.

The United States officially reported that only 3,243 Japanese troops were killed. Among the casualties were approximately a thousand American citizens, mostly second-generation Japanese Americans, and twenty-three US prisoners of war, some of whom survived the blast only to be beaten to death by bomb survivors.

Injured and burned survivors suffered immensely. *Hibakusha* (bomb-affected persons) described the experience as walking through hell.

The streets were filled with an endless ghostlike procession of horribly burned, often naked people whose skin hung off their bones. They were desperately seeking help for their wounded bodies, searching for family members, and trying to escape from encroaching fires.

Survivors tripped over dead bodies that had been seared into lumps of charcoal. Some were frozen in midstep.

The *B-29* crew members sat silently on the flights back to Tinian. Some took solace in the belief that what they had witnessed was so horrific that it would definitely end the war.

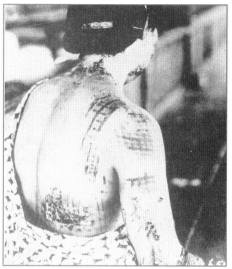

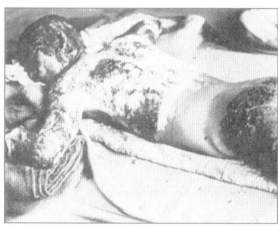

Injured and burned survivors suffered immensely. *Hibakusha* **(bomb-affected persons) described it as walking through hell.**

One of the tail gunners on the mission, Al "Pappy" DeHart, said he wished he hadn't seen what he had just witnessed, adding, "I won't be mentioning it to my grandchildren. Not ever. I don't think it's the kind of thing to be telling kids. Not what we saw."

33

The Race Is Not to the Swift

Truman was dining onboard the USS *Augusta* on his way home from Potsdam when he learned of Hiroshima. He jumped up and exclaimed, "This is the greatest thing in history."

In a radio speech to the American people, Truman announced the news. "The Japanese began the war from the air at Pearl Harbor," he said. "They have been repaid many fold. And the end is not yet. . . . We are now prepared to obliterate more rapidly and completely every productive enterprise the Japanese have above ground in any city. We shall destroy their docks, their factories, and their communications. Let there be no mistake; we shall completely destroy Japan's power to make war."

Shortly thereafter, Truman said that announcing the news of Hiroshima was the "happiest" announcement he had ever made.

Truman's reaction made some people uncomfortable. One member of the Democratic National Committee admonished the president two days later. "No president of the United States could ever be jubilant over any device that could kill innocent human beings," he wrote in a telegram. "Please make it clear that it is not destruction but the end of destruction that is the cause of jubilation."

The Real Target

Soviet leaders were anything but jubilant. They knew that the atomic bomb was not needed to defeat a nation already on life support.

They understood that the Americans were sending them a signal that the United States wouldn't hesitate to use atomic bombs against them, too, if they interfered with US plans for global domination.

A *New York Times* correspondent in Moscow wrote:

> The news [of Hiroshima] had an acutely depressing effect on everybody. It was clearly realized that this was a New Fact in the world's power politics, that the bomb constituted a threat to Russia, and some Russian pessimists I talked to that day dismally remarked that Russia's desperately hard victory over Germany was now "as good as wasted."

The gratuitous nature of the bombings shocked Soviet leaders. It still haunted Marshal Zhukov's memories twenty-six years later: "Without any military need whatsoever, the Americans dropped two atomic bombs on the peaceful and densely populated Japanese cities of Hiroshima and Nagasaki." From this, Zhukov concluded that "the US Government intended to use the atomic weapon for the purpose of achieving its Imperialist goals from a position of strength in 'the cold war.'"

Other military leaders were also appalled. Future Soviet Foreign Minister Andrei Gromyko's son Anatoly remembered his father telling him that Hiroshima "set the heads of the Soviet military spinning. The mood in the Kremlin, in the General Staff was neurotic. Mistrust towards the Allies grew quickly. Opinions floated around to preserve a large land army, to establish controls over extended territories to lessen potential losses from atomic bombings."

A leading Soviet physicist explained that "[t]he whole Soviet government interpreted [Hiroshima] as atomic blackmail against the USSR, as a threat to unleash a new, even more terrible and devastating war."

Stalin summoned nuclear physicists to the Kremlin for daily reports on their progress. Within days, Stalin had launched a crash program to build a Soviet bomb.

The arms race had begun.

Another race began too. Soon after Hiroshima, Japanese leaders asked the Soviets if they would be willing to mediate. The Japanese received a clear answer.

In the early hours of August 9, the powerful Red Army smashed through Japan's forces in Manchuria, Korea, Sakhalin, and the Kuril Islands. The Russians encountered little resistance.

On the morning of August 9, 1945, Japan's four top Foreign Ministry officials went to Prime Minister Suzuki's residence to deliver the bad news about the Soviet invasion. "What we feared has finally come," Suzuki responded.

Also on the morning of August 9, immediately on the heels of the Soviet invasion, another American B-29 bomber, *Bockscar*, carrying an implosive plutonium bomb nicknamed "Fat Man," was headed for Kokura, Japan.

But, visibility was poor, and clouds covered Kokura. The pilot, Charles Sweeney, made three passes over the city, but he could not find a break in the clouds. He then headed for the secondary target—downtown Nagasaki.

Nagasaki was also covered by clouds. Low on fuel, Sweeney nearly turned back. Suddenly, the clouds opened up. The bomb was released. On the ground, air-raid sirens sounded. But the people of Nagasaki had grown accustomed to the raids. Many people didn't heed the sirens.

Eleven-year-old Sachiko Matsuo had been staying in a makeshift shelter outside the city. She saw a flash of light and then heard a thunderous explosion. Then she realized not a blade of grass was anywhere. Her sister lay dead, buried under rubble. "All that was left of her was white ash," said Sachiko. Her brother also died. Her father got radiation poisoning and perished nineteen days later. Forty thousand people died immediately, including 250 soldiers. By year's end, the death toll had reached 70,000. After five years, 140,000 were gone.

Radio operator Spitzer said that he and other crew members could not believe that a second city had been wiped off the face of the earth. "There was no need for more missions, more bombs, more fear and more dying," said Spitzer. "Good God, any fool could see that."

Telford Taylor, the chief prosecutor at the Nuremberg trials, observed, "The rights and wrongs of Hiroshima are debatable, but I have never heard a plausible justification of Nagasaki." He considered Nagasaki a war crime.

The Decisive Factor

Japanese officials were despondent over the Soviet attack. During an emergency cabinet meeting, they received the news about Nagasaki.

Though the amount of damage to Hiroshima and Nagasaki was unfathomable, the atomic bombings did not move the officials closer to surrendering unconditionally. Neither did the army minister's false report that the United States had a hundred more atomic bombs and that Tokyo was the next target. Japanese officials saw little difference between the United States wiping out entire cities with hundreds of planes and thousands of bombs and doing so with one plane and one bomb.

But the Soviet invasion was another matter. It demoralized the Japanese leaders, who just days earlier had sought Soviet help in getting better surrender terms. Japan's diplomatic efforts had come up empty, and its military strategy of inflicting heavy losses on invading Allied troops was also no longer a viable option.

To these officials, the atomic bombs provided an added incentive to surrender, but not the decisive one. The Soviet invasion was the decisive factor, just as Truman had anticipated.

At last, Emperor Hirohito announced his willingness to surrender. He agreed to accept the Potsdam Declaration, but only as long as it "does not comprise any demand which prejudices the prerogatives of His Majesty as a Sovereign ruler."

Prime Minister Suzuki recognized that there was no choice. Japan must surrender immediately, he declared, or "the Soviet Union will take not only Manchuria, Korea, Karafuto, but also Hokkaido. This would destroy the foundation of Japan. We must end the war when we can deal with the United States."

Once the emperor's decision was clear, Japan's top leaders dropped their additional demands that some had insisted on for self-disarmament, no war crimes trials, and no occupation.

As the Red Army rapidly approached the Japanese mainland, the Japanese surrendered to the Americans. They believed the Americans would be more likely to allow them to keep their emperor. They also feared that the advancing Red Army would trigger pro-communist uprisings inside Japan, as it had in parts of Europe.

Truman and his advisers weighed the Japanese offer to surrender. Byrnes again argued that retaining the emperor would cost Truman politically.

Stimson disagreed with Byrnes. He reasoned that "even if the question hadn't been raised by the Japanese we would have to continue the Emperor by ourselves" in order to get Japan's many armies to surrender and to maintain order in postwar Japan.

By now, Stimson had had it with Byrnes. "There has been a good deal of uninformed agitation against the Emperor . . . by people who know no more about Japan than has been given them by Gilbert and Sullivan's 'Mikado,'" he wrote in his diary.

Japanese POWs at Guam, with bowed heads after hearing Emperor Hirohito's August 1945 announcement of Japan's unconditional surrender.

After further debate, the men compromised on a vague statement that promised that "the ultimate form of government shall, in accordance with the Potsdam Declaration, be established by the freely expressed will of the Japanese people."

In what many consider a cruel irony, the United States allowed Japan to keep its emperor, which is exactly what Japan had sought in the months before the bombs were dropped.

Was It Necessary?

After the war, Japanese leaders attributed surrender to both the atom bombs and the Soviet invasion. However, several leaders gave primacy to the Soviet invasion—not the bombs or other US actions.

"It was only in a gradual manner that the horrible wreckage which had been made of Hiroshima became known," explained Deputy Chief of Staff General Torashiro Kawabe. "In comparison, the Soviet entry into the war was a great shock when it actually came. Reports reaching Tokyo described the Russian forces as 'invading in swarms.'"

Navy Chief of Staff Soemu Toyoda agreed: "I believe the Russian participation in the war against Japan rather than the atom bombs did more to hasten the surrender."

The Army Ministry responded similarly, stating, "The Soviet participation in the war had the most direct impact on Japan's decision to surrender."

With the news of the Russian invasion, said Lieutenant General Sumishisa Ikeda, "I felt that our chances were gone."

Why? As General Kawabe explained, "We had been in constant fear of it with a vivid imagination that 'the vast Red Army forces in Europe were now being turned against us.'"

A study conducted by the US War Department in January 1946 came to the same conclusion: "It [is] almost a certainty that the Japanese would have capitulated upon the entry of Russia into the war."

But Americans were convinced that the bombings of Hiroshima and Nagasaki had ended the war. Believing that, almost 85 percent of the American public approved of their use. Nearly 23 percent wished that the Japanese hadn't surrendered so quickly, so that the United States could have dropped more atom bombs on them.

Most Americans did not know that many top US military leaders considered the bombings either militarily unnecessary or morally reprehensible. Truman's own chief of staff, Admiral William Leahy, classified the atom bombs as violations of "every Christian ethic I have ever heard of and all of the known laws of war."

"[The] Japanese were already defeated and ready to surrender," acknowledged Leahy. "The use of this barbarous weapon at Hiroshima and Nagasaki was of no material assistance in our war against Japan. In being the

On August 14, 1945, President Truman announces Japan's surrender.

first to use it we adopted an ethical standard common to the barbarians of the dark ages. I was not taught to make war in that fashion and wars can not be won by destroying women and children."

In 1949, Leahy angrily told a journalist, "Truman told me it was agreed that they would use it . . . only to hit military objectives. Of course, then they went ahead and killed as many women and children as they could which was just what they wanted all the time."

After the war, General Douglas MacArthur always maintained that the war would have ended months sooner if the United States had modified its surrender terms. Other top military leaders agreed with Leahy and MacArthur that Japan was on the verge of surrender and that the bombs weren't necessary, including General Dwight Eisenhower, General Henry

"Hap" Arnold, General Curtis LeMay, General Carl "Tooey" Spaatz, Admiral Ernest King, Admiral Chester Nimitz, and Admiral William Halsey.

Brigadier General Carter Clarke summed up the situation with the Japanese: "We brought them down to an abject surrender through accelerated sinking of their merchant marine and hunger alone, and when we didn't need to do it, and we knew we didn't need to do it, and they knew we knew we didn't need to do it, we used them as an experiment for two atomic bombs."

Six of the United States' seven five-star officers who received their final star in World War II—Generals MacArthur, Eisenhower, and Arnold; and Admirals Leahy, King, and Nimitz—rejected the idea that the atomic bombs were needed to end the war.

Sadly, there is little evidence that they pressed their case with Truman before the fact, though Eisenhower claimed he did, and Leahy's misgivings were well known.

But General Groves, who had worked closely with Dr. Oppenheimer and the Los Alamos team, knew the views of these officers. Before the bomb was dropped on Hiroshima, Groves ordered US commanders in the field to first clear all statements on the bombings with the War Department. The reason for the censorship was simple: "We didn't want MacArthur and others saying the war could have been won without the bomb," confessed Groves.

Truman's closest adviser Jimmy Byrnes admitted the same. *The New York Times* reported that Byrnes had "cited what he called Russian proof that the Japanese knew they were beaten before the first atomic bomb was dropped on Hiroshima."

The Vatican quickly condemned the bombing. *Catholic World* described the bombs' use as "atrocious and abominable . . . the most powerful blow ever delivered against Christian civilization and the moral law."

The leader of the Federal Council of Churches worried for the future. "If we, a professedly Christian nation, feel morally free to use atomic energy in that way, men elsewhere will accept that verdict," warned John Foster Dulles. "Atomic weapons will be looked upon as a normal part of the arsenal of war and the stage will be set for the sudden and final destruction of mankind." Dulles would later become President Eisenhower's secretary of state.

A "Cry-Baby Scientist"

Brave young Americans like Paul Fussell and their Soviet and British counterparts defeated Japan in World War II. Many lost their lives in the process.

Many historians agree with the five-star generals and admirals who believed that the incineration of Hiroshima and Nagasaki wasn't necessary.

Truman, Stimson, and others spread the myth that the atomic bomb was responsible for ending the war without a US invasion. In 1991, former President George Herbert Walker Bush defended Truman's "tough, calculating decision, [which] spared millions of American lives."

The facts show otherwise. Although the atomic bombs certainly contributed to the Japanese surrender, they were ancillary to US island-hopping, bombings, and blockades.

It was the dramatic Soviet invasion that convinced the Japanese leaders that holding out for the last decisive battle on the Japanese mainland was not a viable option.

Nor was an invasion an option for the Americans. "I was unable to see any justification, from a national-defense point of view, for an invasion of an already thoroughly defeated Japan," confessed Admiral Leahy.

Nor did dropping atomic bombs make the Soviet Union more pliable. It merely convinced Stalin that the United States would stop at nothing to impose its will and that the Soviets must speed the development of their own atomic bomb as a deterrent.

Contrary to Byrnes's warning, no one crucified Truman for that decision. He suffered no political repercussions.

Truman always claimed that he felt no remorse, even bragging that he "never lost any sleep over [it]." When a television interviewer asked him, "Any regrets?" Truman responded, "Not the slightest—not the slightest in the world."

When another interviewer asked if the decision had been morally difficult to make, Truman said, "Hell no, I made it like that," snapping his fingers.

On October 25, 1945, nearly three months after the bombing, Truman met Oppenheimer for the first time. Truman asked the scientist to guess when the Soviets would develop an atomic bomb. Oppenheimer admitted that he didn't know. Truman declared that he did: "Never."

This display of ignorance unnerved Oppenheimer. The nuclear arms race was already under way. The science and math that went into the making of the bomb were known to all. It would be just a matter of time before Soviet scientists developed their own atomic weapons.

At one point, Oppenheimer said, "Mr. President, I feel I have blood on my hands."

To this, Truman responded angrily. "I told him the blood was on my hands—to let me worry about that."

Afterward, Truman informed Dean Acheson, who would later become his secretary of state, "I don't want to see that son-of-a-bitch in this office ever again." He later called Oppenheimer a "cry-baby scientist."

A Different Outcome

The horrors and bloodshed of World War II hardened many people to the suffering of others, but not all. Many of the scientists involved in the bomb project became lifelong anti-nuclear activists. Leo Szilard switched from physics to biology and founded the Council for a Livable World. Joseph Rotblat campaigned tirelessly for nuclear abolition until his death at the age of ninety-six. He won the Nobel Peace Prize in 1995.

Even British prime minister Winston Churchill recognized the difficulty of defending the atomic bombings. Toward the end of Truman's presidency, Truman threw a small dinner party. His daughter, Margaret, recalled that everyone was in an ebullient mood, including her father. Suddenly, Churchill turned to Truman and said, "Mr. President, I hope you have your answer ready for that hour when you and I stand before Saint Peter and he says, 'I understand you two are responsible for putting off those atomic bombs. What do you have to say for yourselves?'"

The man who fell five feet away and eighty-two days short of becoming president—former vice president Henry A. Wallace—has been largely lost to history. Few people remember how close Wallace came to getting the vice presidential nomination on that steamy Chicago night in July 1944.

What might this country have become if Wallace had succeeded Roosevelt in April 1945 instead of Truman? Would atomic bombs still have been used in World War II? Could we have avoided the nuclear arms race and the Cold War? Would civil rights and women's rights have triumphed in the immediate postwar years? Might colonialism have ended decades earlier and the fruits of science and technology been spread more equitably around the globe?

We'll never know.

A Time Line of Events

1863 The US War Department's "Lieber Code" prohibits "the use of poison in any manner, be it to poison wells, or food, or arms."

1866 The Ku Klux Klan (KKK) forms in Tennessee.

1866–1877 The KKK's first wave of violence sweeps through the South.

1870 The Fifteenth Amendment is ratified, granting black men the right to vote.

1872 The federal government succeeds in breaking up the KKK.

1877 Railroad workers in the United States strike to protest reduced wages and reduced hours.

1878 European powers—including Britain, France, and Germany—and their former colonies control 67 percent of the world's surface.

May 1886 In Chicago, Illinois, peaceful protest becomes a battle after a bomb explodes in Haymarket Square, killing seven policemen. The police storm the square and kill three workers. Authorities use this protest to launch a campaign targeting labor organizations.

1889 The United States annexes the harbor of the Pacific island, Pago Pago, to support its expanding navy.

May 5, 1893 A financial panic triggers a depression that lasts five years. Four million workers lose their jobs and unemployment approaches 20 percent.

November 3, 1893 The United States helps engineer Panama's independence from Colombia. This will allow the United States to build the Panama Canal.

1898 The United States annexes Hawaii. President William McKinley proclaims the United States has realized its "Manifest Destiny."

April 25, 1898 The United States declares war on Spain, purportedly to deliver Cuba from Spain's tyranny. Secretary of State John Hay calls this three-month war "a splendid little war."

June 15, 1898 The Anti-Imperialist League forms to oppose the United States annexation of the Philippines. Its members include Andrew Carnegie, Clarence Darrow, Mark Twain, Jane Addams, William James, William Dean Howells, and Samuel Gompers.

December 10, 1898 The Treaty of Paris of 1898 cedes Puerto Rico to the United States, making Cuba an American protectorate and indicating that the United States will pay $20 million to Spain for control of the Philippines.

January 23, 1899 Filipinos draft a constitution and establish a republic. Emilio Aguinaldo is instated as president of the Philippines.

February 4, 1899 The United States opens fire in Manila. American newspapers report this as an unprovoked Filipino attack on unarmed US soldiers. Twenty-two are killed and 125 to 200 are wounded. Filipino losses are estimated in the thousands.

July 1899 The Hague Declaration Concerning Asphyxiating Gases of 1899 outlawed the wartime use of "projectiles" whose "sole object" was "the diffusion of asphyxiating or deleterious gases."

1901 The United Fruit Company buys 1.9 million acres of Cuban land at 20 cents per acre for sugar production.

February 1901 US Congress passes the Platt Amendment, which asserts the US right to intervene in future Cuban affairs. A naval base is established at Guantanamo Bay.

September 6, 1901 President McKinley is shot by anarchist Leon Czolgosz. McKinley dies six days later. Vice President Theodore Roosevelt, a committed imperialist, becomes the twenty-sixth president of the United States.

November 1901 US media begins reporting on American soldiers' atrocities against Filipinos. This included reports of waterboarding, murder, and rape.

July 1902 President Roosevelt declares the Philippines pacified.

1903 The United States sends troops to Honduras.

1903 The United States sends troops to the Dominican Republic.

1905 The Industrial Workers of the World—also known as the Wobblies—forms. The IWW believes that the greatest conflict lay between capitalists and laborers. Members include Eugene Debs, an outspoken socialist, and William "Big Bill" Hayword, the organization's leader.

1905 Japan defeats Russia in the Russo-Japanese War. This signifies the first time in 700 years that an Eastern power has defeated a Western one. This war creates a bitterness between Russia and Japan that lasts decades.

1906 The United States sends troops to Cuba.

1907 The United States sends troops to Honduras.

1907 The United States sends troops to Nicaragua.

1907 President Roosevelt establishes the Central American Court, an entity meant to peacefully adjudicate conflict in Central America. The court's authority is destroyed when American authorities ignore its rulings.

1908 The United States sends troops to Panama.

1910 Norman Angell writes *The Great Illusion*. In this book, the future Nobel Peace Prize winner warns that an arms race will not secure peace but will likely increase insecurity and the threat of war.

1910 The United States, under the command of Smedley Darlington Butler, sends troops to Nicaragua. America helps establish a government friendly to US business interests.

1911 Mexican revolutionaries, led by Francisco Madero, overthrow Porfirio Diaz, the Mexican dictator and great friend to American business interests. The revolutionaries are infuriated that what little land they did own was being taken by wealthy imperialists with Diaz's approval.

1911 The United States sends troops to Honduras.

1912 Woodrow Wilson is elected twenty-eighth president of the United States.

1912 The United States sends troops to Honduras.

1912 The United States sends troops to Cuba.

1912 The United States sends troops to Nicaragua. Troops remain until 1933.

1912 The United States sends troops to Panama.

1913 By this time, American businesses own approximately 43 percent of Mexican property. Mexicans nationals own 33 percent. One American publishing magnate, William Randolph Hearst, owns 17 million acres.

1914 European powers—including Britain, France, and Germany—and their former colonies control 84 percent of the world's surface.

1914 The United States sends troops to the Dominican Republic.

1914 The United States sends troops to Haiti. Troops remain until 1933.

1914 Novelist H. G. Wells writes *The World Set Free*, a prophetic novel that describes an atomic war between Germany and Austria on one side and England, France, and the United States on the other.

April 9, 1914 American sailors enter Tampico, a prosperous—and prohibited—oil town in the Gulf of Mexico. They are arrested for trespassing without a permit in a war zone, but then are immediately released.

June 28, 1914 Archduke Franz Ferdinand of Austria is assassinated by a Serbian fanatic. This triggers a chain of events that, in August, will plunge the world into brutal bloodshed.

August 1914 Austria-Hungary declares was on Serbia. World War I begins.

August 1914 President Wilson issues his "Declaration of Neutrality," imploring Americans to not choose sides in WWI. It is, however, a neutrality in principle more than in practice. Economic interests clearly place the United States in the Allied camp. Between 1914, when the war begins, and 1917, when the United States enters, American banks loan Allied powers more than ninety times the amount they loan the Central powers.

August 1914 Germany becomes the first country to bomb civilians from the air.

1915 President Wilson screens *The Birth of a Nation*, directed by D. W. Griffith, at the White House. The racist film is based on a popular book called *The Clansmen: An Historical Romance of the Ku Klux Klan*, a novel written by a Southern Baptist minister, Thomas Dixon Jr.

March 3, 1915 *The Birth of a Nation* opens in New York's Liberty Theater. The movie inspires a resurgence of violence by the KKK. This year, fifty-six blacks and thirteen whites are lynched.

April 22, 1915 Breaking the spirit of the Hague Peace Convention of 1899, Germany uses poison gas during the second battle of Ypres, killing 600 soldiers.

May 1915 Germany sinks the British ocean liner, *Lusitania*, killing 1,200, of which 128 are Americans. Despite US denial, the ship is, in fact, carrying arms from the United States to Britain.

1916 The United States sends troops to the Dominican Republic. Troops remain until 1924.

1917 The United States sends troops to Cuba. Troops remain until 1922.

1917 The Espionage Act passes Congress. It is one of the most repressive pieces of legislation in US history. Under the act, people faced $10,000 fines and up to twenty years in jail for obstructing military operations in wartime.

1917 Socialist Party candidates see their votes increase in cities throughout the country. Ten socialists win seats in New York State legislature.

March 8, 1917 Rioting and strikes break out in St. Petersburg, Russia. Food shortages across Russia have people protesting and shouting for bread. These protests foment, and eventually protestors revolt against the Russian monarchy.

April 2, 1917 President Wilson asks Congress for a declaration of war. Only fifty-six congressmen vote against it. Six oppose it in the Senate, including Robert La Follette of Wisconsin, and fifty vote against it in the House of Representatives, including Jeannette Rankin of Montana, the first woman elected to Congress. Opponents attacked Wilson as a tool of Wall Street.

April 6, 1917 The United States declares war on Germany and enters World War I.

April 13, 1917 The Committee on Public Information (CPI) forms. It establishes an army of "Four Minute Men," orators who give rousing, patriotic speeches to encourage support of the war.

November 7, 1917 The Bolsheviks, led by Vladimir Lenin and Leon Trotsky, seize power in Russia, dramatically changing the course of world history. They are inspired by Karl Marx, a nineteenth-century German-Jewish intellectual who believed that class struggle would eventually result in an egalitarian socialist society.

1918 The United States sends troops to Panama.

1918 The United Fruit Company owns 14,000 acres of land in Honduras.

1918 Soldiers in WWI wear an early form of a gas mask—a filter respirator that uses charcoal and antidotal chemicals. Casualties still skyrockets, but fatalities drop sharply.

January 8, 1918 Wilson announces his Fourteen Points. This anti-imperialist peace plan endorses self-determination, disarmament, freedom of the seas, free trade, and the League of Nations. It promises no more secret agreements and the evacuation of troops from Russia, Belgium, and France. Few of these points make it into the Treaty of Versailles the next year.

March 3, 1918 Lenin signs a peace treaty with Germany and pulls all Russian troops from the war. The Treaty of Brest-Litovsk calls for relinquishing control of more than 30,000 square miles of territory, including Poland, Finland, and the Baltic states. President Wilson sends 15,000 troops to eastern and northern Russia with the hope of maintaining a limited eastern front against Germany.

May 1918 The Sedition Act passes. This act is another one of the most repressive pieces of legislation in the history of the United States. It curbs free speech and creates a climate of intolerance toward dissent.

June 1918 Eugene Debs, one of the founders of the Wobblies, is arrested on ten violations of the Espionage Act of 1917. His arrest occurs after he delivers an antiwar speech outside a prison that houses three socialists incarcerated for opposing the draft in Canton, Ohio.

June 28, 1918 The United States establishes the Chemical Warfare Service (CWS). This large-scale chemical warfare research program is the combination of several different departments. The CWS centralizes the research and prioritizes speedy over safety. As a result, numerous deaths are recorded, according to electrical engineer George Temple, who had been head of motor maintenance at "Camp American University." Each morning, during roll call, workers are asked to volunteer for burning with experimental gases. Temple volunteers seven times.

July 1918 The Chamberlain-Kahn Act passes, giving authorities the right to detain and examine any woman walking alone near a military base and suspected of having sexually transmitted diseases.

July 1918 Theodore Roosevelt's youngest son, Quentin, is a casualty of World War I. He is killed when his plane is shot down over France. All four of Roosevelt's sons enlisted and saw combat in WWI.

November 11, 1918 World War I ends with Germany's surrender. In all, of the two million US soldiers who reached France, over 116,000 died and 204,000 were wounded. By comparison, European casualty figures were truly staggering—perhaps as many as 8.5 million dead soldiers and 13 million dead civilians, the latter due mostly to disease and starvation.

1919 Benito Mussolini forms the Fascist Party in Italy.

1919 The United States sends troops to Honduras.

1919 More than five million workers go on strike this year to protest poor working conditions and the growing income inequality. These strikes include 365,000 steelworkers, 450,000 miners, and 120,000 textile workers.

January 12, 1919 Twenty-seven nations convene in Versailles, just outside of Paris, to work out terms of peace. The victors—particularly Great Britain, France, and Japan—divide the former German colonies and holdings in Asia and Africa along the lines established by the secret 1915 Treaty of London.

1919 Vietnamese man Ho Chi Minh speaks at the Paris Peace Conference and questions the right of France to control Indochina.

1920 The census reports that for the first time, more Americans live in cities and urban districts than in rural areas.

1920 The Versailles Treaty and the League of Nations go to a vote in the US Senate. Wilson watches as the treaty and the league go down to defeat, finally falling seven votes short of ratification.

1920 Warren G. Harding is elected the twenty-ninth president of the United States.

1921 Henry Ford publishes a collection of anti-Semitic articles that are collected into a four-volume work titled *The International Jew*, which is widely read by future Nazi leaders.

1921 The United States sends troops to Panama.

1921 The United Fruit Company owns 61,000 acres of land in Honduras.

1921 From 1921 until 1953, Russian secret police sentence 800,000 to death for speaking out against the Communist Party.

1922 Venezuelan dictator Juan Vincente Gomez appeals to US oil companies for help in writing parts of Venezuela's petroleum law. Oil companies comply, writing business-friendly laws that allow them to reap massive profits. Oil company workers and the environment fare less well. Spills and accidents occur frequently. One oil well blowout in this year spreads twenty-two miles, releasing nearly a million barrels of oil into Lake Maracaibo.

1923 President Harding dies unexpectedly while on a speaking tour. Calvin Coolidge becomes the thirtieth president of the United States.

1923 A *Chicago Tribune* reporter visits Adolf Hitler and notes that a large portrait of Henry Ford hangs behind Hitler's desk.

1924 The United States sends troops to Honduras.

1924 The United Fruit Company owns 88,000 acres of land in Honduras.

1924 Discriminatory immigration legislation passes, limiting the number of people allowed into the United States.

1924 The Immigration Act of 1924 denies Japanese who have settled in the United States after 1907 the right to become naturalized citizens. It also prohibits further immigration from Japan and other parts of Asia.

1925 The violent, Midwest-based Black Legion organization splits from the KKK. Ten years later, the leader of the group, Virgil Effinger, speaks openly about the need for mass extermination of American Jews.

1925 The United States sends troops to Honduras.

1925 The United States sends troops to Panama.

1925 The League of Nations adopts the Geneva Protocol—a protocol to the earlier Hague Conventions—that again forbids the use of chemical and bacteriological weapons in war. Over the next ten years, more than forty countries ratify the treaty, including every great power except Japan and the United States.

1928 Soviet leaders announce the Five-Year Plan, designed by Joseph Stalin. The plan promises a rational, centralized economy that would create abundance. It relies on the rapid industrialization of the Soviet Union and the collectivization of agriculture.

March 4, 1929 Herbert Hoover is inaugurated as the thirty-first president of the United States. He characterized a future that would be "bright with hope."

September 3, 1929 After a summer of surging, the stock market hits its highest levels.

October 29, 1929 The stock market crashes, a day that is now known as "Black Tuesday." The United States plunges into one of the worst depressions in its history. Many Americans lose their life savings.

1930 From 1930 until 1932, one fifth of US banks fail.

1930 The American Legion invites Mussolini to address its national convention.

1931 *The Christian Science Monitor* reports that not only was the Soviet Union the only country to have escaped the Depression, its industrial production has jumped an astronomical 25 percent from the previous year.

September 1931 Japan's Kwantung Army invades Manchuria, a resource-rich and contested region bordered by the Soviet Union, China, and Korea. This invasion is a precursor to further Japanese expansion across Asia.

1932 Unemployment for urban blacks reaches more than 50 percent.

1932 Eben Byers, a wealthy American, drinks so much Radithor, a popular medicine containing radium, he dies of radioactive poisoning.

October 31, 1932 Nevada's lieutenant governor declares a twelve-day bank holiday. This act shuts down banks around the states. Depositors cannot withdraw money.

1933 William Dudley Pelley, an anti-Semite, founds the Silver Legion, which may have enlisted as many as 25,000 members this year.

1933 Unemployment is at 25 percent. The gross national product falls by 50 percent. Farm income plummets by 60 percent. Industrial productions are down by more than 50 percent. The United States is deep into the Great Depression.

January 30, 1933 Adolf Hitler is appointed chancellor of Germany.

February 1933 Former New York County Assistant District Attorney Ferdinand Pecora exposes fraud and wrongdoing on the part of the nation's top bankers, including obscene salaries, unpaid taxes, hidden bonuses, unethical loans, and more. Magazines begin calling bankers "banksters."

February 14, 1933 Michigan declares an eight-day bank holiday. Maryland, Tennessee, Kentucky, Oklahoma, and Alabama banks soon follow suit. Five hundred and fifty state and national banks close.

March 4, 1933 Franklin Delano Roosevelt is inaugurated as the thirty-second president of the United States. In his speech, in response to the magnitude of problems facing the country, he declared famously, "[T]he only thing we have to fear is fear itself."

March 1933 On Roosevelt's first full day in office, the new president takes a conservative approach to solving the banking problems of the day. He declares a four-day national bank holiday. Congress passes, and Roosevelt signs, the Emergency Banking Act, written largely by the bankers themselves. The banking system is restored without radical change.

March 1933 and onward Roosevelt lays out an ambitious recovery program during his first hundred days in office. This "New Deal" includes the Agricultural Adjustment Administration, to save farming; the Civilian Conservation Corps (CCC), to put young men to work in the forests and parks; the Federal Emergency Relief Administration (FERA), to provide federal assistance to the states; the Public Works Administration (PWA), to coordinate large-scale public works projects; the Glass-Steagall Banking Act, which separated investment and commercial banking and instituted federal insurance of bank deposits; and the National Recovery Administration (NRA), to promote industrial recovery.

March 12, 1933 President Roosevelt speaks to Americans over the radio in the first of many "fireside chats" that the president would deliver throughout his time in office.

July 3, 1933 World leaders attending the World Economic Conference in London are taken aback by Roosevelt's announcement that the United States would suspend the gold standard.

October 1933 Hitler withdraws Germany from the League of Nations.

1934 The mid-term elections demonstrate American's shift to the left. The Democrats win twenty-six of thirty-five Senate races, giving them a 69–25 advantage over Republicans in the upper chamber. Their lead in the House jumps to 322–103. *The New York Times* calls it "the most overwhelming victory in the history of American politics."

1934 Workers hold major strikes in Toledo, Minneapolis, and San Francisco, as well as a national textile strike as workers turn to Musteites, Trotskyists, and communists for leadership.

1934 The Soviet Union joins the League of Nations.

January 1934 Hitler signs a ten-year nonaggression pact with Poland to secure Germany's eastern border.

February 1934 Senator Gerald Nye of North Dakota calls upon the Senate Foreign Relations Committee to investigate individuals and corporations involved in manufacturing and selling arms, munitions, and other implements of war. The hearings, headed by the Nye Committee, eventually reveal the nefarious practices and enormous wartime profits of American munitions companies during World War I.

August 22, 1934 Right-wing businessmen and bankers announce the formation of the American Liberty League and claim that Roosevelt's New Deal violates the US Constitution. The group announces its intention to combat radicalism, defend property rights, and uphold the Constitution.

September 1934 The Nye Committee releases documents that show that President Wilson allowed bankers to float loans to warring countries in 1914.

November 1934 Retired Marine General Butler testifies in Congress that two American Liberty League members tried to recruit him to organize a military coup against the Roosevelt administration.

1935 The Congress of Industrial Organizations forms, allowing the labor movement to begin penetrating heavy industry. Communists played a major role in the organizing.

February 1935 During the Nye Committee hearings, the president of Bethlehem Steel Corporation and the Bethlehem Shipbuilding Corporation admits that his company's profits jumped from $6 million before World War I to $48 million once the war started and that he had received personal bonuses of $1.6 million and $1.4 million.

May 1935 Senator Nye introduces a war profit bill as an amendment to another bill. However, the bill is assigned to a subcommittee headed by one of Nye's biggest critics.

October 1935 Mussolini invades Ethiopia.

1936 President Roosevelt is reelected to a second term. Roosevelt defeats Kansas governor Alf Landon 523–8 in the electoral college, winning every state except Maine and Vermont.

1936 Hitler and Mussolini form the Axis. They begin assisting Francisco Franco's overthrow of the Spanish Republic.

January 1936 The Nye Committee hearings continue, asking banking institutions and Wall Street firms: Had the United States pushed into World War I in order to recoup the enormous sums they had loaned the Allies?

March 1936 German troops occupy the Rhineland.

April 1936 The Nye Committee issues its long-awaited third report. It concludes: "While the evidence before this committee does not show that wars have been started solely because of the activities of munitions makers and their agents, it is also true that wars rarely have one single cause, and the committee finds it to be against the peace of the world for selfishly interested organizations to be left free to goad and frighten nations into military activity."

July 1936 Franco's forces set out to topple the elected Spanish government and establish a fascist regime.

1937 Recession hits the United States. Critics call it the "Roosevelt Recession."

1937 Thomas J. Watson, the American head of IBM, meets Hitler. Later that year, Hitler gives Watson the Grand Cross of the German Eagle, a thank-you for IBM's technology: the punch card and card-sorting machine, which helps Nazis locate and identify Jews.

1937 War erupts in China as the Japanese army captures city after city. In December, Japanese soldiers brutalize the citizens of Nanjing, killing 200,000 to 300,000 civilians. Japan soon controls the east coast of China, with its population of 200 million.

1938 Hitler bestows Henry Ford with the Grand Cross of the German Eagle. He gives one to James D. Mooney, the chief overseas executive of General Motors, as well.

1938 Germany annexes Austria. The Allies capitulate to Hitler and give Germany the Sudetenland, in Czechoslovakia. British prime minister Neville Chamberlain infamously proclaims that the settlement has brought "peace in our time."

1938 Two German scientists stun the scientific world by splitting the uranium atom. This accomplishment means that it might be possible to make an atomic bomb.

1939 A Gallup poll finds that 84 percent of Americans want Great Britain and France to win World War II. Only 2 percent root for Germany. Ninety-four percent want America to stay out of the war.

February 1939 New York senator Robert Wagner submits his administration-backed bill for a national health program. But faced with vehement opposition from the American Medical Association, and seeking to avoid a nasty fight with elections approaching, Roosevelt decides to abandon the effort.

Spring 1939 The Spanish republic falls. Franco rules as dictator until his death in 1975.

March 1939 Hitler invades Czechoslovakia.

July 1939 The United States terminates its 1911 commercial treaty with Japan. This move cuts off the flow of vital materials critical to the Japanese war machine.

August 1939 Hitler and Stalin stun the world by signing a nonaggression pact. This pact contains a secret provision that divides Eastern Europe between them.

September 1, 1939 Hitler invades Poland.

September 17, 1939 Stalin invades Poland. The Soviets soon assert control over the Baltic states of Estonia, Latvia, and Lithuania.

October 1939 Roosevelt authorizes the US atomic bomb project. It moves at a glacial pace until 1941, when new information indicates much less uranium is needed than originally thought.

1940 Roosevelt decides to run for a third term. He chooses Secretary of Agriculture Henry Wallace as his running mate.

April 1940 Hitler unleashes his blitzkrieg, or "lightning war." In rapid succession, Denmark, Norway, Holland, and Belgium fall to the Nazis.

Summer 1940 Germany and England engage in the Battle of Britain.

June 22, 1940 France falls to the Nazis.

July 1940 Roosevelt declines the Democratic Party's presidential nomination when Henry Wallace's vice presidential nomination looks like it will not stand.

September 1940 Germany, Italy, and Japan formally conclude the Tripartite Pact, establishing the "Axis powers" alliance. Hungary, Romania, Slovakia, and Bulgaria join soon thereafter.

September 1940 President Roosevelt signs into law the hotly contested Selective Training and Service Act. It establishes the first peacetime military draft in American history.

1941 At the start of World War II, 250 American firms own more than $450 million worth of German assets, with 58.5 percent being owned by the top ten. Among the companies are familiar names like Standard Oil, Woolworth, IT&T, Singer, International Harvester, Eastman Kodak, Gillette, Coca-Cola, Kraft, Westinghouse, and the United Fruit Company.

March 1941 Congress overwhelmingly passes the Lend-Lease Act (HR 1776). This allows Roosevelt to provide noncombat assistance to the increasingly desperate British.

April 1941 Roosevelt allows US ships to provide vital intelligence to the British about the presence of enemy ships and planes, and soon authorizes transporting supplies to British soldiers in North Africa.

June 22, 1941 Hitler double-crosses the Russians when he launches Operation Barbarossa, the code name for a full-scale invasion of the Soviet Union. A total of 3.2 million German soldiers invade along a 2,000-mile-long front.

July 1941 Japan invades French Indochina (Vietnam), seeking resources and bases needed to fortify its position in the region. The United States responds by embargoing petroleum exports to Japan.

August 1941 Roosevelt meets secretly with British prime minister Winston Churchill in Newfoundland. The two craft the Atlantic Charter, which states the ideal goals of a postwar world. Churchill fears that the proposed wording will threaten Great Britain's colonial possessions.

August 1941 Within days of Roosevelt meeting with Churchill, the American destroyer USS *Greer*, together with a British Royal Air Force plane, detect a German submarine in the North Atlantic. Though the ships fire weapons, no vessels are damaged. Roosevelt uses the incident to drum up support for intervention.

November 7, 1941 Roosevelt extends Lend-Lease to the Soviet Union. The Russians are elated. However, US shipments fall very short of what was promised. The failure to deliver the promised equipment deals a crushing blow to Soviet prospects, with Moscow and Leningrad under siege, Ukraine occupied, and the Red Army suffering debilitating losses, and does little to convince the Soviets of US goodwill.

December 7, 1941 The Japanese navy attacks the US naval base at Pearl Harbor, Hawaii. This attack leaves almost 2,500 dead.

December 8, 1941 The United States and Great Britain declare war on Japan.

December 11, 1941 Germany and Italy declare war against the United States.

February 11, 1942 Roosevelt signs Executive Order 9066. This order lays the groundwork for the evacuation and incarceration of Japanese and Japanese Americans from California, Oregon, and Washington. Two thirds of those affected are US citizens by birth.

March 11, 1942 President Roosevelt orders General MacArthur to secretly depart the Philippines for the safety of Australia. He leaves behind approximately 12,000 American and 64,000 Filipino troops. One month later, the surviving troops surrender to the Japanese. In what becomes known as the Bataan Death March, the Japanese force their prisoners to March sixty miles through scorching heat. The guards deny the prisoners food and water. They shoot, beat to death, or bayonet those who fall along the way. Some are beheaded. An estimated 16,500 Filipinos and 650 Americans die during the march or the internment that follows.

March–October 1942 The Wartime Civil Control Administration opens camps known as "assembly centers." At these centers, Japanese prisoners are held, registered, and assigned numbers before being moved to more permanent centers, referred to at the time as "concentration camps."

Late spring 1942 Japan controls the Dutch East Indies (Indonesia), French Indochina, and the British colonies of Malaya, Burma, Western New Guinea, Hong Kong, and Singapore.

June 1942 US forces defeat the Japanese navy at Midway and begin fighting the Japanese for control of the islands in the Pacific. This strategy is known as "island-hopping."

June 1942 The Japanese hope to lure US aircraft carriers into a trap, but American codebreakers are able to warn the United States. Instead, America sets up its own ambush and defeats the Japanese Imperial Navy.

July 17, 1942 The Battle of Stalingrad begins. Casualties exceed three quarters of a million on each side, and civilian deaths total more than 40,000. This defeat begins Germany's full-scale retreat from the eastern front.

Summer 1942 The team of physicists at the University of Chicago's Metallurgical Laboratory realize a frightening possibility: An atomic detonation might ignite the hydrogen in the ocean or the nitrogen in the atmosphere, setting the planet on fire.

September 24, 1942 Twenty-five thousand Americans demonstrate in New York City, demanding that the United States launch a second front in the war to relieve some of the pressure on Russia in its fight against Germany.

December 2, 1942 The scientists at Met Lab succeed in creating the first sustained nuclear chain reaction.

Late 1942 Germany abandons its atomic bomb research.

January 1943 At Casablanca, Roosevelt calls for the "unconditional surrender" of Germany, Italy, and Japan. The Japanese fear that an unconditional surrender means the destruction of its imperial system. For most Japanese, such a thought is too terrible to contemplate since they have worshipped the emperor as god since 660 BC.

March 11, 1943 Vice President Wallace embarks on a forty-seven-day tour of Latin America. It is an overwhelming success. By the time the tour is over, a dozen Latin American countries declare war on Germany; twenty break off diplomatic relations with Germany.

July 1943 One of the most devastating bombing campaigns takes place in Hamburg and Dresden, Germany. Altogether, nearly 70,000 people are killed and more than 50,000 wounded.

November 1943 Stalin commemorates the anniversary of the Russian Revolution with a speech celebrating the survival and future resurgence of the Soviet state.

November 28, 1943 The "Big Three"—Roosevelt, Churchill, and Stalin—meet for the first time in the Soviet embassy in Tehran, Iran.

June 6, 1944 (D-day) Allied paratroopers drop into German-occupied Normandy, France. The long-awaited second front opens. More than 100,000 Allied troops land on the beach. Four thousand men die during the landing.

July 1944 Roosevelt clinches the Democratic nomination for an unprecedented fourth term. His running mate is Harry S. Truman, not Henry Wallace, this time around.

July 1944 The United States invites friendly governments from forty-four countries to a conference in Bretton Woods, New Hampshire. The conference establishes the World Bank and International Monetary Fund.

July 9, 1944 American forces take Saipan, a tropical island in the Pacific. The loss of life is enormous, including 30,000 Japanese troops and 3,000 American troops.

July 18, 1944 Japanese prime minister Hideki Tojo and his cabinet resign.

Summer 1944 The United States deploys almost a hundred aircraft carriers to the Pacific, compared to Japan's twenty-five, for the entire war.

October 1944 Churchill and Stalin secretly meet. On a scrap of paper, they draft a "naughty document," outlining an agreement for the British and Soviet spheres of influence postwar.

End of 1944 Japan's navy is decimated, having lost 7 out of 12 battleships, 19 out of 25 aircraft carriers, 103 out of 160 submarines, and 118 out of 158 destroyers.

February 1945 The Big Three meet in Yalta to develop a postwar plan. The world leaders overcome serious differences over the future of Poland and the rest of Europe.

March 1, 1945 President Roosevelt addresses Congress. This is the first time he has addressed Congress sitting, not standing. Observers of Roosevelt's speech notice how rapidly the president's health is failing.

April 12, 1945 President Roosevelt suffers a massive stroke and then passes away. His vice president, Harry S. Truman, is sworn in.

April 12, 1945 After Roosevelt's death, Truman learns of the United States' secret bomb project. Later that month, Truman learns that within four months, America could expect to have "completed the most terrible weapon ever known in human history, one bomb of which could destroy a whole city."

April 23, 1945 President Truman meets with Russian official Vyacheslav Molotov. Truman accuses Russia of breaking the Yalta Agreement. After arguing, Truman dismisses Molotov. Stalin is furious.

April 25, 1945 The United Nations Conference on International Organization begins in San Francisco for the purpose of developing a United Nations Charter to maintain peace among nations worldwide. The early sessions are marred by the tensions between the United States and Russia.

April 30, 1945 Hitler and his wife, Eva Braun, commit suicide.

May 7, 1945 Germany surrenders.

May 9–10, 1945 General Curtis LeMay sends 334 planes to attack Tokyo with incendiary bombs. The bombs destroy sixteen square miles of land and kill as many as 100,000 civilians.

Spring 1945 At Okinawa, the location of the biggest battle of the Pacific War, as many as 70,000 Japanese soldiers and more than 100,000 Okinawan civilians die, some taking their own lives.

June 18, 1945 The Joint Staff Planners meet with Truman and estimate that it will cost 193,500 dead and wounded to take Japan. Some estimates were higher; some, lower.

July 16, 1945 The United States successfully tests its first atomic bomb in New Mexico.

July 17–August 21, 1945 Truman, Churchill, and Stalin meet in Germany for the Potsdam Conference. During the conference, Truman tells Stalin that the United States has developed "a new weapon of unusual destructive force."

July 25, 1945 At Potsdam, Truman initials a directive ordering that atomic bombs be used as soon as August 3, weather permitting. Truman never issues a direct order to drop the bomb.

August 1–2, 1945 American bombers drop incendiary bombs on Toyama, Japan, destroying 99.5 percent of the city.

August 6, 1945 The US B-29 bomber *Enola Gay*, piloted by Paul Tibbets, drops an atomic bomb on Hiroshima, Japan. Tens of thousands are killed instantly. An estimated 140,000 are dead by the end of the year, and 200,000 by 1950.

August 9, 1945 The United States drops an atomic bomb on the Japanese city of Nagasaki. Poor visibility over the primary target—Kokura—forced the pilot, Charles Sweeney, to switch to downtown Nagasaki. The bomb lands two miles off target in the Urakami district, exploding over the largest Catholic cathedral in Asia, with a force of 21 kilotons. Forty thousand people die immediately, including about 250 soldiers. Seventy thousand die by the end of 1945, perhaps 140,000 over the course of five years.

Summer 1945 Scientists at Met Lab issue the Franck Report. This report questions the wisdom of using atomic bombs in World War II. The report also warns that an atomic attack could instigate a nuclear arms race with the Soviet Union.

September 1945 World War II ends with Japan's surrender. More than 60 million people die as a result of the war, including 27 million Russians, between 10 to 20 million Chinese, 6 million Jews, 5.5 million Germans, and 3 million non-Jewish Poles. Almost 410,000 Americans are killed.

October 25, 1945 Truman meets physicist Robert Oppenheimer for the first time. Truman tells the physicist that Russia will never develop an atomic bomb.

Photo Credits

Every effort has been made to correctly acknowledge and contact the source and/or copyright holder of each image. Simon & Schuster apologizes for any unintentional errors or omissions, which will be corrected in future printings of this book.

Introduction: Rebirth of a Nation

Chapter 1: Writing History with Lightning

p. 4: Movie poster for . . . *of a Nation. Library of Congress*

p. 5: Two members of . . . in their disguises. *Library of Congress*

Chapter 2: The Rumblings of Revolution

p. 14: In this August . . . Strike are shown. *Library of Congress*

p. 15: Poet Walt Whitman . . . disease and monstrosity." *Library of Congress*

Chapter 3: "Workingmen, to Arms!"

p. 19: Jay Gould, railroad . . . century in 1892. *Library of Congress*

p. 21: Haymarket Riot, May . . . were being targeted. *Library of Congress*

Part One: Roots of an Empire

Chapter 4: All That Glitters

p. 26: In 1890, 91 . . . of their children. *Library of Congress*

p. 27: Mark Twain once . . . *Revised Catechism* (1871). *Library of Congress*

p. 28: Colonel Theodore Roosevelt . . . a war hero. *Library of Congress*

p. 30: In this January . . . can govern themselves." *Public domain*

p. 32 *(top)*: Soldiers riding down . . . in Malolos, Philippines. *Library of Congress*

p. 32 *(bottom)*: The bodies of murdered Filipinos. *Ixtlan*

p. 35 *(both)*: The presidential election . . . by the wealthy. *Library of Congress*

p. 36: In the Philippines . . . now call waterboarding. *New Yorker Magazine*

Chapter 5: I Pledge Allegiance to Big Business

p. 39: Plowing on a . . . for American businessmen. *Library of Congress*

p. 40: At forty-three . . . date in 1901. *Library of Congress*

Chapter 6: Wars South of the Border

p. 44: Having already received . . . the Black Star. *Library of Congress*

p. 45: General Butler, shown . . . gangster for capitalism." *US Marine Corps*

p. 48: William Randolph Hearst . . . acres in Mexico. *Library of Congress*

p. 49: Victoriano Huerta (*center*). *Library of Congress*

p. 50: President Wilson stands . . . April 20, 1912. *Library of Congress*

Chapter 7: The "Great War" Begins

p. 53: President Woodrow Wilson. *Library of Congress*

p. 55: *From left to* . . . Duchess of Hohenberg. *Library of Congress*

p. 56: The RMS *Lusitania* . . . in his sights. *Library of Congress*

p. 57 *(top)*: This 1915 drawing . . . the *London Sphere*. *Library of Congress*

p. 57 *(bottom)*: This German U-20 . . . the Danish coast. *Library of Congress*

p. 59: This powerful war . . . a hostile force. *Library of Congress*

Chapter 8: Preaching to America

p. 63: A CPI poster . . . as town criers. *Library of Congress*

p. 64: The US government . . . a German submarine. *Library of Congress*

p. 66: Robert "Fighting Bob" . . . into the war. *Library of Congress*

Part Three: World War II: Who Really Defeated Germany?

p. 215: Under heavy Nazi . . . the Normandy coast. *National Archives and Records Administration*

p. 216: On June 6, 1944 . . . awaited second front. *Library of Congress*

Chapter 25: The Road to a New World Order

p. 218: An abandoned boy . . . and family members. *Library of Congress*

p. 220: Roosevelt criticized the . . . years of French rule. *Library of Congress*

p. 222: In October 1944 . . . scrap of paper. *Utilizator:Mihai.1954 via Wikimedia Commons*

p. 224: Churchill (*left*), Roosevelt . . . States and abroad. *National Archives and Records Administration*

p. 227: This is the . . . Warm Springs, Georgia. *National Archives and Records Administration*

Chapter 26: A New President

p. 231: This photograph of . . . a quick education. *Library of Congress*

p. 233: Henry Wallace (*right*) . . . from his cabinet. *Harry S. Truman/National Archives and Records Administration*

Chapter 27: The End Is Near

p. 239: A Soviet soldier . . . Reichstag in Berlin. *Library of Congress*

p. 243: An American army . . . guard the bunker. *Library of Congress*

p. 245 (*all*): Led by the . . . struggling Soviet allies. *Library of Congress*

p. 248: A crowd cheers . . . in Prague, Czechoslovakia. *Library of Congress*

Part Four: The Bomb: The Tragedy of a Small Man

Chapter 28: "Thank God for the Atom Bomb"

p. 255: President Franklin D. . . . war against Japan. *National Archives and Records Administration*

p. 258: This is one . . . atomic research program. *Wikimedia Commons/Public domain*

p. 260: This is an . . . of the reactors. *National Archives and Records Administration*

p. 261: General Leslie Groves . . . bomb was detonated. *Courtesy of US Department of Energy*

Chapter 29: The Man Who Would Be President

p. 264 *(top)*: A torpedoed Japanese . . . as it sinks. *National Archives and Records Administration*

p. 264 *(bottom)*: US soldiers use . . . along the road. *National Archives and Records Administration*

p. 265: A Japanese plane . . . near Mariana Islands. *National Archives and Records Administration*

p. 266: Henry Robinson Luce . . . for his prejudices. *Library of Congress*

p. 267: Known as a . . . are American fascists. *Library of Congress*

p. 269: RAF Lieutenant Roald . . . *the Chocolate Factory. Library of Congress*

p. 271: Harry Truman, pictured . . . played the piano. *Harry S. Truman Presidential Library*

p. 273: In 1940, President . . . Truman barely won. *Harry S. Truman Presidential Library*

Chapter 30: An Unconditional Surrender

p. 281: Emperor Hirohito salutes . . . this 1945 photograph. *Library of Congress*

Chapter 31: No Foe So Detested

p. 287 *(all)*: Many Americans felt . . . Japanese as vermin. *Library of Congress, University of Minnesota, National Archives and Records Administration*

p. 290: In this photograph . . . expel the Japanese. *Library of Congress*

p. 293 *(top)*: A young evacuee . . . spring of 1942. *National Archives and Records Administration*

p. 293 *(bottom)*: Inside relocation centers . . . for their labor. *National Archives and Records Administration*

p. 294: Photographer Ansel Adams . . . Japanese from escaping. *Library of Congress*

p. 295: Members of the . . . Camp Shelby, Mississippi. *Library of Congress*

p. 296: During the last . . . through the city. *Library of Congress*

p. 298: US bombs rain down on Hokodate, Japan. *National Archives and Records Administration*

Chapter 32: Doubts on Destruction

p. 303: A truck continues . . . Alamos, New Mexico. *Bettman / Corbis*

p. 305: Stalin *(left)* and . . . in July 1945. *Harry S. Truman Presidential Library / National Archives and Records Administration*

p. 307: This photograph shows . . . New Mexico desert. *Library of Congress*

p. 312: Pilot Paul Tibbets . . . the *Enola Gay*. *Wikimedia Commons/Public Domain*

p. 315: A mushroom cloud . . . August 6, 1945. *Bettman/Corbis*

p. 317 *(all)*: Injured and burned . . . walking through hell. *National Archives and Records Administration*

Chapter 33: The Race Is Not to the Swift

p. 323: Japanese POWs at . . . Japan's unconditional surrender. *National Archives and Records Administration*

p. 325: On August 14 . . . announces Japan's surrender. *National Archives and Records Administration*

Sources

As someone who wrote her first high school research paper using index cards, the card catalog, and *The Readers' Guide to Periodical Literature*, I am still awestruck by the Internet and the relative ease with which information—primary documents and other information—can be found. Below I have listed additional sources that helped me to round out this book for young readers. For other sources, I kindly refer you to the 2,723 footnotes in the adult edition. Any mistakes are my own.

For the comprehensive list of sources referenced in the original edition of *The Untold History of the United States*, please visit: books.simonandschuster.com/Untold -History-of-the-United-States-Volume-1/Oliver-Stone/9781481421737.

—Susan Campbell Bartoletti

Books, Journals, and Periodicals

Bartoletti, Susan Campbell. *Hitler Youth: Growing Up in Hitler's Shadow.* New York: Scholastic Books, 2005.

———. *They Called Themselves the K.K.K.: The Birth of an American Terrorist Group.* Boston: Houghton Mifflin Harcourt, 2010.

Chandler, Alfred D., and Stephen Salsbury. *Pierre S. Du Pont and the Making of the Modern Corporation.* Washington, DC: BeardBooks, 2000.

Cook, Bernard A., ed. *Women and War: A Historical Encyclopedia from Antiquity to the Present*. Santa Barbara, CA: ABC-CLIO, 2006.

Deml, John. "Prussianizing Wisconsin." *The Atlantic* 11, no. 1 (1919): 101–102.

Dixon Jr., Thomas. *The Clansman: A Historical Romance of the Ku Klux Klan*. New York: Grosset & Dunlap Publishers, 1920.

Faughnan, Michael. "You're in the Army Now: The Students' Army Training Corps at Selected Virginia Universities in 1918." PhD Dissertation, Virginia: The College of William and Mary, 2008.

Freedman, Russell. *The War to End All Wars: World War I*. Boston: Clarion Books, 2010.

Katz, William Loren. *Eyewitness: The Negro in American History*. New York: Pitman Pub. Corp., 1967.

Lisandrelli, Elaine Slivinski. *Ida B. Wells-Barnett: Crusader Against Lynching*. Springfield: Enslow Publishers, 1998.

Manning, William. *The Key of Libberty: Shewing the Causes Why a Free Government Has Always Failed, And a Remidy Against It*. Billerica, MA: The Manning Association, 1922.

Navari, Cornelia. "Economic Diplomacy at the Atlantic Conference II: A Reply to Pressnell and Hopkins." *Review of International Studies*, 1989: 341–358.

Norton, Mary Beth, et al. *A People and a Nation: A History of the United States*. 7th edition. Boston: Houghton Mifflin Co., 2005.

Roark, James L., Michael P. Johnson, Patricia Cline Cohen, Sarah Stage, and Susan M. Hartmann. *The American Promise: A History of the United States*. 5th edition. Boston: Bedford/St. Martin's, 2012.

Thomas, Hugh. *Cuba, or, The Pursuit of Freedom*. New York: Da Capo Press, 1998, p. 1,171.

Wilson, Woodrow. *Woodrow Wilson, Essential Writings and Speeches of the Scholar President*. Mario R. DiNunzio, editor. New York: New York University Press, 2006.

Websites

"10 Most Devastating Bombing Campaigns of WWII." *Online Military Education.* February 17, 2012. onlinemilitaryeducation.org/posts/10-most –devastating-bombing-campaigns-of-wwii (accessed September 21, 2014).

"1871: The Paris Commune." *libcom.* libcom.org/history/1871-the-paris-commune (accessed September 2014, 2014).

"1921: Merchants of Death." *United States Senate.* senate.gov/artandhistory/history/ minute/merchants_of_death.htm (accessed September 22, 2014).

"Alexander Kerensky." *Spartacus Educational.* www.spartacus.schoolnet.co.uk/ RUSkerensky.htm (accessed September 21, 2014).

"American President: Woodrow Wilson: Foreign Affairs." *Miller Center, University of Virginia.* millercenter.org/president/wilson/essays/biography/5 (accessed September 2014, 2014).

"America's Great Depression and Roosevelt's New Deal." *Digital Public Library of America.* http://dp.la/exhibitions/exhibits/show/new-deal/relief-programs/ federal-emergency-relief-act (accessed September 22, 2014).

Angell, Sir Norman. "Nobel Lecture: Peace and the Public Mind." *Nobel Prize.* nobelprize.org/nobel_prizes/peace/laureates/1933/angell-lecture.html (accessed September 21, 2014).

"Announcing the Bombing of Hiroshima." *PBS.* pbs.org/wgbh/americanexperience/ features/primary-resources/truman-hiroshima (accessed September 22, 2014).

Butcher, Bernard. "A Doomed Democracy." *Standford Magazine.* alumni.stanford. edu/get/page/magazine/article/?article_id=38883 (accessed September 21, 2014).

"Collectivization and Industrialization." *Library of Congress.* loc.gov/exhibits/ archives/coll.html (accessed September 22, 2014).

Ensor, David, and Reuters. "GM, Ford Deny Collaboration with Nazis During WWII." *CNN.* cnn.com/US/9811/30/autos.holocaust (accessed September 22, 2014).

———. "GM, Ford Deny Collaboration with Nazis During WWII." *CNN.* cnn.com/US/9811/30/autos.holocaust (accessed September 22, 2014).

"Eugene V. Debs Internet Archive." *Marxists Internet Archive.* marxists.org/archive/ debs/#1900 (accessed September 21, 2014).

Fleming, Thomas. "The Historians Who Sold Out." *History News Network*. http://hnn.us/article/1489 (accessed September 30, 2014).

"Four Minute Men: Volunteer Speeches During World War I." *History Matters: The US Survey Course on the Web*. historymatters.gmu.edu/d/4970 (accessed September 21, 2014).

"From Our Cabinet: Women and War." *The Massachussets Historical Society*. 2002. mass hist.org/objects/cabinet/june2002/stamps.htm (accessed September 21, 2014).

"General Leslie Groves (1896–1970)." *Atomic Archives*. http://www.atomicarchive .com/Bios/Groves.shtml (accessed September 22, 2014).

"Germany's Use of Chemical Warefare in World War I." *First World War*. firstworldwar. com/features/chemical_warfare.htm (accessed September 21, 2014).

Goldstein, Jacob, and David Kestenbaum. "Why We Left the Gold Standard." *NPR*. npr.org/blogs/money/2011/04/27/135604828 (accessed September 22, 2014).

Hall, Prentice. "History: Causes, Practices, and Effects of Wars: Chapter 6." *Pearson Global Schools*. http://assets.pearsonglobalschools.com/asset_mgr/current/201214/HistoryCausesPracticesandEffectsofWarsChapter6.pdf (accessed September 22, 2014).

Hansen, Jonathan M. "Give Guantánamo Back to Cuba." *The New York Times*. nytimes.com/2012/01/11/opinion/give-guantanamo-back-to-cuba.html?_r=0 (accessed September 21, 2014).

Hayward, Steven F. "Who's Fascist Now?" *American Enterprise Institute*. aei.org/article/society-and-culture/whos-fascist-now (accessed September 22, 2014).

Higgins, A. Pearce. "The Hague Peace Conferences and Other International Conferences Concerning the Laws and Usages of War (1909)." *Online Library of Liberty*. oll.libertyfund.org/titles/higgins-the-hague-peace-conferences -concerning-the-laws-and-usages-of-war (accessed September 30, 2014).

"Historical Gold Prices: 1833 to Present." *National Mining Association*. nma.org/pdf/gold/his_gold_prices.pdf (accessed September 22, 2014).

"Ho Chi Minh." *History Learning Site*. historylearningsite.co.uk/ho_chi_minh.htm (accessed September 22, 2014).

"Honduras." *Country Studies US*. countrystudies.us/honduras (accessed September 21, 2014).

Jacobsen, Louis. "Fox News' Andrew Napolitiano Says US Is Still Paying Interest on World War I Costs." *PolitiFact.com, Tampa Bay Times*. politifact.com/truth-o-meter/

statements/2013/oct/23/andrew-napolitano/fox-news-andrew-napolitiano
-says-us-still-paying-i (accessed September 21, 2014).

"John L. O'Sullivan on *Manifest Destiny*, 1839." *Mount Holyoke.* mtholyoke.edu/
acad/intrel/osulliva.htm (accessed September 21, 2014).

Kazin, Michael. "The Producers." *New Republic.* newrepublic.com/article/
politics/magazine/100526/producers-middle-class-income-inequality-occupy
(accessed September 21, 2014).

Klein, Ezra. "Why the American Medical Association Opposes the Public Insurance
Plan." *The Washington Post.* voices.washingtonpost.com/ezra-klein/2009/06/
why_the_american_medical_assoc.html (accessed September 22, 2014).

Luce, Henry R. "The American Century." *Information Clearing House.* information
clearinghouse.info/article6139.htm (accessed September 22, 2014).

May, Michele. "Aviators: Quentin Roosevelt—He Died Fighting." *History Net.*
October 29, 2007. historynet.com/aviators-quentin-roosevelt-he-died-fighting
.htm (accessed September 21, 2014).

Metcalf, Stephen. "How Combat Changed Paul Fussell, and How Fussell Changed
American Letters." *Slate.* slate.com/articles/arts/the_dilettante/2012/05/
paul_fussell_remembering_the_author_of_the_great_war_and_modern_
memory.2.html (accessed September 22, 2014).

Moser, John E. "The American Liberty League (1935)." *The American Liberty
League (1935).* personal.ashland.edu/~jmoser1/libertyleague.htm (accessed
September 22, 2014).

"Measuring Worth—Results." *Measuring Worth.* measuringworth.com/uscompare/
relativevalue.php (accessed September 21, 2014).

"Neil Maher: The Civilian Conservation Corps." *American Experience, PBS.* pbs
.org/wgbh/americanexperience/features/interview/ccc-author-neil-maher
(accessed September 22, 2014).

Olga, Sak. "Russian War Relief." *Museum of Books.* February 1, 2012. museum.lib
.kherson.ua/en-slidami-odniei-publikatsii.htm (accessed September 22, 2014).

"Wilson—A Portrait." *American Experience, PBS.* pbs.org/wgbh/amex/wilson/
portrait/wp_african.html (accessed September 21, 2014).

"Protocols of the Elders of Zion." *United States Holocaust Memorial Museum.* June 20,
2014. www.ushmm.org/wlc/en/article.php?ModuleId=10007058 (accessed
September 22, 2014).

"Relations With Japan: 1938–1940." *Mount Holyoke.* mtholyoke.edu/acad/intrel/WorldWar2/japan.htm (accessed September 22, 2014).

Roosevelt, Franklin D. "Fireside Chat 18: On the *Greer* Incident (September 11, 1941)." *Miller Center, University of Virginia.* millercenter.org/president/speeches/speech-3323 (accessed September 22, 2014).

———. "Franklin D. Roosevelt: Fireside Chat on Banking." *The American Presidency Project.* www.presidency.ucsb.edu/ws/index.php?pid=14540 (accessed September 22, 2014).

———. "Franklin D. Roosevelt's Statement on the National Industrial Recovery Act." *The Our Documents.* docs.fdrlibrary.marist.edu/odnirast.html (accessed September 22, 2014).

Rosen, David. "Illegal Arrests During Periods of National Crisis." *CounterPunch.* September 9–11, 2011. counterpunch.org/2011/09/09/illegal-arrests-during-periods-of-national-crisis (accessed September 21, 2014).

Sierra, J. A. "The Bitter Memory of Cuban Sugar." *History of Cuba.* historyofcuba.com/history/havana/Sugar1b.htm (accessed September 21, 2014).

Smith, Matthew. "Twentieth Century Atlas—Death Tolls." *Necrometics.* necrometrics.com/20c5m (accessed September 21, 2014).

"Social Security History." *Social Security Administration.* ssa.gov/history/corningchap2.html (accessed September 22, 2014).

Stalin, Josef V. "Victory Speech." *Marxists Internet Archive.* marxists.org/reference/archive/stalin/works/1945/05/09v.htm (accessed September 22, 2014).

"Sugihara: Conspiracy of Kindness: The Bushido Code, An Overview." *PBS.* 2005. pbs.org/wgbh/sugihara/readings/bushido.html (accessed September 22, 2014).

"The Assassination of Franz Ferdinand—World War I Document Archive." *World War I Document Archive, Brigham Young University Library.* February 10, 2013. wwi.lib.byu.edu/index.php/The_Assassination_of_Archduke_Franz_Ferdinand (accessed September 2014, 2014).

"The Battle of Saipan 1944." *History Learning Site.* 2012. historylearningsite.co.uk/battle_saipan_1944.htm (accessed September 22, 2014).

"The Bolsheviks." *History Learning Site.* 2012. historylearningsite.co.uk/bolsheviks.htm (accessed September 21, 2014).

"The Bombing of Nagasaki." *History Learning Site.* 2011. historylearningsite.co.uk/bombing_of_nagasaki.htm (accessed September 22, 2014).

The Editors of Encyclopaedia Britannica. "Gulag (Labour Camps, Union of Soviet Socialist Republics." *Encyclopaedia Britannica.* May 13, 2013. britannica.com/ EBchecked/topic/249117/Gulag (accessed September 22, 2014).

"The Great Railroad Strike." *Digital History.* www.digitalhistory.uh.edu/disp_ textbook.cfm?smtID=2&psid=3189 (accessed September 2014, 2014).

"The Great War. Resources. WWI Casualty and Death Tables." *PBS.* pbs.org/ greatwar/resources/casdeath_pop.html (accessed September 21, 2014).

"The League of nations 1920—1914–1920—Milestones—Office of the Historian." *Office of the HIstorian.* history.state.gov/milestones/1914-1920/league (accessed September 22, 2014).

The Learning Network. "March 8, 1917, Russia's February Revolution Begins in St. Petersburg." *The Learning Network, The New York Times.* March 8, 2012. learning. blogs.nytimes.com/2012/03/08/march-8-1917-russias-february-revolution -begins-in-st-petersburg/?_php=true&_type=blogs&_r=0 (accessed September 21, 2014).

"The National Archives: Exhibits and Learning Online: First World War— Spotlights on History." *The National Archives.* nationalarchives.gov.uk/pathways/ firstworldwar/spotlights/blockade.htm (accessed September 21, 2014).

"The Richest Man in America: Andrew Carnegie—Gilded Age." *American Experience, PBS.* http://www.pbs.org/wgbh/amex/carnegie/gildedage.html (accessed September 21, 2014).

"The Rise and Fall of Jim Crow. Jim Crow Stories. Great Depression." *PBS.* pbs.org/ wnet/jimcrow/stories_events_depression.html (accessed September 22, 2014).

"The Tampico Affair." *Mount Holyoke.* mtholyoke.edu/acad/intrel/tampico.htm (accessed September 21, 2014).

The US Navy. navy.mil/navydata/nav_legacy.asp?id=142 (accessed September 22, 2014).

"The World of 1898: The Spanish-American War." *Library of Congress.* loc.gov/rr/ hispanic/1898/chronology.html (accessed September 21, 2014).

"Theodore Roosevelt and the Panama Canal." *American Experience, PBS.* pbs .org/wgbh/americanexperience/features/general-article/tr-panama (accessed September 21, 2014).

"Theodore Roosevelt on the Sinking of the *Luisitania*, 1915." *The Gilder Lehrman Institute of American History.* gilderlehrman.org/history-by-era/world-war-i/resources/theodore-roosevelt-sinking-lusitania-1915 (accessed September 21, 2014).

"Treaty of Versailles, 1919." *United States Holocaust Memorial Museum.* ushmm.org/wlc/en/article.php?ModuleId=10005425 (accessed September 22, 2014).

"Truman Library—Pendergast." *Harry S. Truman Library & Museum.* trumanlibrary.org/trivia/penderga.htm (accessed September 22, 2014).

"Why Buy Liberty Bonds? School Children Answer." *Google News.* October 14, 1918. news.google.com/newspapers?nid=110&dat=19181014&id=1X5SAAAAIBAJ&sjid=fEADAAAAIBAJ&pg=6996,3044211 (accessed September 21, 2014).

Wilson, Woodrow. "President Wilson's Declaration of Neutrality." *World War I Document Archive.* May 29, 2009. http://wwi.lib.byu.edu/index.php/President_Wilson%27s_Declaration_of_Neutrality (accessed September 21, 2014).

———. "Woodrow Wilson: The Tampico Affair." *Mount Holyoke.* mtholyoke.edu/acad/intrel/tampico.htm (accessed September 30, 2014).

"Woodrow Wilson, The White House." *The White House.* whitehouse.gov/about/presidents/woodrowwilson (accessed September 22, 2014).

"Woodrow Wilson's Fourteen Points." *History Learning Site.* 2006. historylearningsite.co.uk/woodrow_wilson1.htm (accessed September 21, 2014).

Acknowledgments

In the adult edition of *The Untold History of the United States*, authors Oliver Stone and Peter Kuznick acknowledged the team of researchers, graduate students, archivists, historians, and colleagues who provided support and assistance. I also thank these individuals.

I would also like to thank Peter Kuznick; Eric Singer, the vetter; the amazing copyediting team of Cindy B. Nixon and Jeannie Ng, for their forbearance and gaffe protection; the design team of Sonia Chaghatzbanian and Vikki Sheatsley; and production manager Chava Wolin. I especially thank Wonder Editor Ruta Rimas for her patience, strength, energy, and smarts (you deserve a superhero cape), and Super Agent Ginger Knowlton.

The archivists and librarians at the following institutions deserve special mention and thanks: the Library of Congress, the National Archives and Records Administration, the Dwight D. Eisenhower Presidential Library, the Franklin Delano Roosevelt Presidential Library, the John F. Kennedy Presidential Library, and the United States Holocaust Memorial Museum.

And I thank my husband, Joe, for his immense help and support.

—*Susan Campbell Bartoletti*

Index